Winning EVERY Moment

Soul Conversations with the Baal HaTanya

Yehiel Harari

gefen גפן
publishing house בית הוצאה לאור
JERUSALEM ◆ NEW YORK   Est. 1981

Originally published by Yedioth Ahronoth Books 2015
Published by arrangement with Assia Literary Agency, Israel (asia01@netvision.net.il)

Translation from the Hebrew: Zalman Nelson
Cover Design: Leah Ben Avraham
Cover Photograph: Phillip Goldsberry
Typeset in Arno Pro by Raphaël Freeman MISTD, Renana Typesetting

ISBN: 978-965-7023-37-2

1 3 5 7 9 8 6 4 2

Gefen Publishing House Ltd.   Gefen Books
6 Hatzvi Street   c/o 3PL Center
Jerusalem 94386,   3003 Woodbridge Ave.
Israel   Edison NJ, 07081
+972-2-538-0247   516-593-1234

orders@gefenpublishing.com
www.gefenpublishing.com

Printed in Israel

*   *   *

Names: Harari, Yehiel, 1973- author.
Title: Winning Every Moment : Soul Conversation with Baal Hatanya / by
Yehiel Harari.
Other titles: Le-natseah kol rega me-hadash. Hebrew
Description: Jerusalem ; Edison NJ : Gefen Publishing House Ltd., [2019]
Identifiers: LCCN 2018048363 | ISBN 978-965-7023-37-2
Subjects: LCSH: Shneur Zalman, of Lyady, 1745–1812. | Shneur Zalman, of
Lyady, 1745–1812. Likute amarim. | Habad. | Habad--Biography. |
Theological anthropology--Judaism.
Classification: LCC BM755.S525 H3713 2019 | DDC 296.8/332092 [B]
--dc23 LC record available at https://lccn.loc.gov/2018048363

Contents

Preface

*I*t was fifteen years ago, while I was exploring the Tel Aviv University library, that a small yet gripping book found its way into my hands: *Body and Soul,* which discusses the core points of the mind-body connection. Its review of the popular and commonly discussed ideas on the relationship between the body and the mind inspired me to do personal research on the subject.

It's true that my university-level research in political science had no specific connection to the interaction of the body and mind or between the spiritual and physical realms. But the book exposed me to the concept, and I was inspired, as a private side project, to try to grasp the link between the social sciences and the science of the soul. I sought out the answers in what Western thinkers had contributed toward understanding this connection. Starting with the ancient Greeks, I moved on to the writings of the Renaissance and to modern periods until reaching the thinkers and researchers of our own time.

The questions I came across were phrased as philosophical inquiries, yet seemed to have practical application and meaning. During the time I was studying this material, I was serving as a government advisor. Close encounters with politicians strengthened the questions I had about personality and the structure of the psyche. For example, how can the people we meet be so full of self-confidence, outgoing and generous one moment, and yet a moment later retreating and disappearing into themselves? What is the source of people's outbursts and anxiety attacks? Why do some people appear to have it all, but have tendencies toward bitterness, unhappiness, and lack of life satisfaction? Why are they struck with the feeling that life has no meaning or purpose? What causes a person to be arrogant or reserved?

My search produced an interest in Jewish teachings about the soul. Many notes and references pointed to the Tanya, the work of Rabbi Shneur Zalman, the Alter Rebbe, as offering a deep and thorough discussion on the world of the soul.

I met a doctoral student in neuroscience more than ten years ago who over time became a good friend. I tried to engage her in a discussion regarding the insights I'd acquired from the Tanya that dealt with the mind-body connection. She shut down the conversation immediately. "Don't you know that the question of the mind-body connection was solved long ago?" she said. "There is no such thing as a soul that is separate from the body."

Her decisive answer shook me. She had expressed a striking trend in the research of the field: in recent years, questions about the body and soul were no longer a part of the study of the humanities but rather an aspect of scientific research. Still, my friend's idea contradicted the fundamental human instinct about the soul's existence. Her words infused me with a huge desire to dive deeply into the Tanya to see what it had to say. It did not fail to deliver, and the more I learned, the more the complete picture came into focus. The Tanya is clearly a fundamental work featuring a comprehensive approach to our understanding of the structure of the soul.

With that said, there's a significant gap between the way the general public, primarily Chassidim, study the Tanya, and the way in which academics approach it. The difference can be summed up in one main point. For researchers, the Tanya is an in-depth study and an important stage in the development of the teachings of Kabbalah and Chassidut. Academics thus look for contradictions, repetitions, and unclear passages that demonstrate elements in the life and teachings of its author. In contrast, those who study the Tanya in a religious context see it as guidance on how to live, a work of practical psychology, an effective prescription for achieving inner stability, overcoming difficulties and insecurities, and for living a lifestyle that leads directly to a connection with the Creator and a revelation of the soul's potential. For the Chassidim who study it, the Tanya is an expression of our current reality and not merely a part of an ancient religious debate. The students grasp its message through its hundreds of discourses which expand upon the Tanya's fundamental principles. Academics may see these discourses as being unclear or poetic, but nothing more.

I came to the book with the eyes of an academic, but like a dedicated student, became enthralled by its magic. Reading the Tanya as a book of guidance to heal the soul was, in my eyes, far more fruitful and thrilling than reading it from an academic view. Through the Tanya, I was looking to learn about the nature of personality, but I discovered instead a series of responses to many difficult challenges in life that were woven into the Tanya's teachings on the soul. Who am I? Who is God? What is the connection between us? What are the core points of Judaism? What is the role of Judaism in the relationship between a person and God?

The Tanya's author does not debate these topics with his readers. In fact, he does not even try to rationalize or justify what he himself identifies as the fundamentals of Jewish thought. For years I have felt that not all of the answers he provides are easy to digest. The Tanya views life as an endless stream of tests and challenges. The vision of life is not one of harmony, security, and magical solutions. Nevertheless, from the start, his system attracted tens of thousands of eastern European Jews who were drawn to its practical approach to human struggle and societal ills.

In this book, readers are invited on a journey through the Tanya. But the journey is not a replacement for a methodical learning of the text. Rather, it outlines its fundamental points and core ideas. *Winning Every Moment* places Rabbi Shneur Zalman's therapeutic teachings in historical and biographical context. It presents the deep philosophical questions regarding which the author offers his approach. In so doing, he invites the reader into a private meeting or *yechidut* – or as one might say nowadays, to come sit on the therapist's couch.

To enter into an intimate meeting with the Tanya's author, which he himself describes as being the reason the book was written, is different from having a modern-day psychotherapy session. The experience is not what we typically view as a conversation. Granted, in both interactions the person is seeking comfort for the soul and reaching out his hand for help in dealing with his failures, depression, anxiety, tension, feelings of guilt, loneliness, lack of purpose, or low self-esteem. The treatment approach in the Tanya, however, is not the same. A Rebbe's relationship with his Chassidim differs from that of a psychologist and patient. As a healer, the author insists on discovering the source of the problem afflicting his patients within his own self. His identification with them isn't merely superficial, but rather creates a calmer environment of attention and non-judgment. If he could not identify with and sense the source of the potential problem, blemish, or lack within his own self, this would cause him to hold back his advice and support on the issue.

At the same time, a *yechidut* meeting demands from the patient effort, concentration, work on the self, and readiness to change. Such work features learning, reviewing, and internalizing the ideas shared. According to Rabbi Shneur Zalman, treatment and self-realization have always been seen as part of a broader system of values, attitudes, and approaches to the world and man's purpose.

Winning Every Moment emphasizes the principles of the Jewish Chassidic system of psychology and outlines the foundation that enables the reader to open up his own soulful session with the author. Indeed, this entire book is infused with the events of Rabbi Shneur Zalman's life, and he states – right from the Tanya's introduction – that a person who learns Tanya joins the select group he calls "those I deeply know and recognize." At the same time, the main goal of a face-to-face conversation is that the student will come to recognize himself clearly. For this reason among others, the wondrous impact of the soulful conversation that grows as one reads the Tanya does not fade over time. Therefore, the author's invitation to his readers to enter into an intimate talk with him by studying his book is open-ended and relevant beyond time.

My own personal conversation with the Tanya's author has been in process for more than ten years. It's a conversation that has its ups and downs. Sometimes, the conversation serves as a source of trust, joy, and strength, while at other times it leads to conflict and self-doubt. This book is therefore in large part the result of my own ongoing soul-to-soul conversation.

Many teachers, friends, and authors have participated in my personal conversation with the Tanya. In the footnotes, I mention the sources that supported my conversation and, naturally, contributed to the formation and structure of this book. I need to mention further mentors not found in the pages of sources whose words impacted my understanding of many of the Tanya's fine points and angles. These are Rabbis Yoel Kahn, Menachem Mendel Vechter, Yair Calev, and Yosef Yitzchak Jacobson.

As impactful as the lecturers and books I was exposed to while studying the Tanya were the Tanya study groups I instructed over the years, as well as personal meetings and practical workshops I guided, which helped me build a context for this insight, clarified many topics, challenged my understandings of the text, and helped me translate its ideas into practical daily language.

I also want to take this opportunity to express special gratitude to those who read through chapters of this book throughout stages of the writing process and gave comments and encouragement. I also wish to express gratitude to the Sternthal family for their support in fond memory of their dear mother Nelli Sternthal, and in honor of the Chabad emissaries worldwide.

Yet, after having the pleasure of thanking everyone to whom I am indebted, I attest that the responsibility for all that is written here, for better or for worse, shall fall upon the writer.

INTRODUCTION

The Tanya – An
Invitation to *Yechidut*

*I*n the second decade of Rabbi Shneur Zalman's leadership, the battle between the Mitnagdim (the opponents of Chassidut) and the Chassidim reached a boiling point. The growth of the Chassidic movement under Rabbi Shneur Zalman's direction outpaced its development in all other regions and drew the most fire. With the death of the Vilna Gaon, an opponent of the Chassidic movement, conflict intensified further between the two camps.

On Tuesday of Chol Hamoed (the intermediate days) of the holiday of Sukkot, in the year 1797, the Vilna Gaon passed away at the age of seventy-seven. While the Gaon's students and all of Vilna were in mourning, a rumor spread that while the Chassidim were joyfully celebrating the Sukkot holiday, they were simultaneously rejoicing at the passing of the Gaon. The Gaon's students soon retaliated by sending a stream of accusatory letters against the Chassidic movement to the czar's procurator (prosecutor) general, the mayor of Vilna, and local police captains. Their accusations led to the first arrest and interrogation of Rabbi Shneur Zalman, who was then fifty-three years old.

Along with the Rebbe, an estimated fifteen Chassidim were also arrested. The civil leader of the governorate of Vilnius (Vilna), Yakov

Ivanovitch Bolgokov, concluded the interrogation of the group of Chassidim by saying the following: "People see him as so important that they come from a hundred miles away and more in order to hear his Torah teachings."[1]

The findings of the investigation were passed on to the procurator general of the Russian Governing Senate, Prince Pyotr Vasilyevich Lopukhin, in a letter dated 15 Cheshvan 5559 (October 25, 1798). The esteem voiced by Bolgokov expressed how moved he was by the large number of followers and the unusually strong dedication the Chassidim had to their Rebbe.

Rabbi Shneur Zalman was born and lived for most of his life in Liozna, a picturesque town in Belarus or White Russia that is close to the Russian border and about three hundred miles (500 km) from Moscow. In response to political pressures, at the age of fifty-six, the Rebbe and many of his Chassidim moved to Liadi, also located in the Vitebsk region of White Russia. The well-known artist Marc Chagall was born near the city of Liozna, some eighty-five years after Rabbi Shneur Zalman was forced to leave. He is quoted as saying that the Rebbe's impact and impression on the city was still felt so many years later. Several of Chagall's paintings depict the life, buildings, and scenes of the famed Jewish village.

In 1769 the residents of Liozna already wanted to appoint the young Rabbi Shneur Zalman as their spiritual mentor.[2] For many years he

---

1. Immanuel Etkes, *Rabbi Shneur Zalman of Liadi: the Origins of Chabad Hasidism,* trans. Jeffrey M. Green (Jerusalem: Merkaz Zalman Shazar, 2012), 272.

2. There is a lack of agreement concerning the year Rabbi Shneur Zalman arrived in Liozna as a speaker and teacher. According to one opinion it was in 1769. See Avraham Henoch Glitzenstein, *Sefer Hatoldot,* vol. 1, *Rabbi Shneur Zalman Mi'Liadi – The Alter Rebbe* [Hebrew] (New York: Kehot Publication Society, 1967), 81. According to another opinion, it was in 1767. See Nissan Mindel, *Rabbi Schneur Zalman of Liadi Rabbi Schneur Zalman of Liadi: A Biography* (New York: Kehot Publication Society, 2002), 19. Rabbi Shalom DovBer Levine, who arranged the new version of *Igrot Kodesh – Alter Rebbe* (New York: Kehot, 2012), writes that Rabbi Shneur Zalman wasn't appointed to the position in Liozna until 1783. In 1767, he was still in Mohilev. He then returned to Vitebsk, the city that Rabbi Menachem Mendel Horodoker had transformed into a center of Chassidut, and in 1781 moved to nearby Horodok. See Rabbi Shalom DovBer Levine, "His Leadership and His Communal Efforts" [Hebrew] in *Harishon: Baal Hatanya; Rabbi Shneur Zalman mi'Liadi* (Jerusalem:

served in this role, tasked with inspiring the community. The majority of his time spent in Liozna saw him sequestered in his room, delving deeply into Torah study and writing. In addition, he opened a yeshiva there for outstanding pupils, which quickly included dozens of students.

Twenty years after the passing of the Baal Shem Tov, in the year 1760, Chassidic centers and strongholds had already spread throughout Europe. In Galicia, Rebbe Elimelech of Lizhensk, author of the book *Noam Elimelech*, had become well known. Rebbe Levi Yitzchak of Berditchev, known as the defender of the Jewish people, was active in Ukraine, along with Rebbe Nachum of Chernobyl, author of *Meor Einayim*. Rebbe Sholom of Karlin and Rebbe Chaim Chaikel of Amdor were operating in Lita. The Chozeh of Lublin's fame spread throughout Poland.[3] And Rabbi Shneur Zalman led the Chassidim in White Russia. Called the Alter Rebbe (the Old Rabbi) by his successors, Rabbi Shneur Zalman was a Chassidic leader with a vast reach and impact from a relatively young age. By 1786, at the age of forty-one, he was already considered the leader of the Chassidic movement in White Russia. He was preceded by two students of the Maggid of Mezeritch, Rebbe Menachem Mendel of Vitebsk and Rebbe Avraham of Kalisk, both of whom immigrated to the northern Galilee region of Israel in 1777 along with a group of close to three hundred.

Rabbi Shneur Zalman's success in cultivating such a huge and growing following in such a relatively short time was completely unprecedented. His new approach to Torah invigorated and inspired people, drawing them from all over eastern Europe to Liozna to receive guidance. He quickly became the Rebbe and leader for thousands of families. In fact, the flow of visitors seeking private audiences for personal guidance grew so much that Rabbi Shneur Zalman and his inner circle of followers were forced to institute policies in order to regulate the traffic.[4] Rabbi Shneur Zalman described the need for regulations for the huge number of people who sought meetings with him:

Maayanotecha, 2014), 70–71. From these sources, collectively, it stands to reason that Rabbi Shneur Zalman spent a significant period of time in Liozna before leaving for other roles and missions.

3. Understandably, this is only a partial listing.

4. For full regulations, see Etkes, *Rabbi Shneur Zalman of Liadi*, 70–79.

Everyone is trying to get in to see me, and it's impossible for me to divide them up; "zeal is as strong as the grave" from those pushing and entering. Given my nature and soft heart, I cannot bear to see the distress of those not granted entrance, returning home disappointed out of jealousy – the jealousy of Torah scholars, each on their level.[5]

Just how strong and significant Rabbi Shneur Zalman's abilities were at that time can be appreciated from a meeting he had with Rebbe Nachman of Breslov. In 1810, several months before Rebbe Nachman passed away at the age of thirty-eight, Rabbi Shneur Zalman, twenty-seven years older than Rebbe Nachman, took a trip through several areas of Russia to help local Jewish villagers who had been displaced by decree of the czar. He stopped to visit Rebbe Nachman along the way. It wasn't the first meeting between the great-grandson of the Baal Shem Tov and the leader of Chassidut in White Russia. Rebbe Nachman was joined by many others in going out to greet the guest. "Give honor to the General," Rebbe Nachman called out to the procession.

During the meeting, Rebbe Nachman asked Rabbi Shneur Zalman if it was true that he already had eighty thousand Chassidim.[6] At that time, there were about two and a half million Jews in the world, two million of whom lived in Europe and one million of whom in eastern Europe.[7] Accordingly, the number Rebbe Nachman mentioned appears exaggerated. The Russian authorities estimated that Rabbi Shneur Zalman's supporters numbered about forty thousand.[8] Even if both of these numbers were inflated, we're still talking about a significant

---

5. *Igrot Kodesh – Alter Rebbe*, letter 52 (New York: Kfar Chabad/Kehot Publication Society, 1979), 112. Note that there are different versions of *Igrot Kodesh – Alter Rebbe*. In 2012, the most updated and corrected version was printed by Kehot Publication Society. The new version only includes letters from Rabbi Shneur Zalman and not from the other Chabad *rebbeim*.
6. For a description of this meeting and Rabbi Shneur Zalman's responses, see Yehoshua Mondshine, "The meeting of the Alter Rebbe and Rabbi Nachman of Breslov" [Hebrew], *Maayanotecha* 39 (December 25, 2013): 11–13.
7. Regarding the number of Jews in eastern Europe, see Shimon Dovnov, *Divrei Yemei Olam*, 7th ed., vol. 8 (Or Yehuda, Israel: Dvir Publishing, 1972), 5. See also Israel Bartal, *Me'Uma l'Leum: Yehudi Mizrach Europa, 1772–1881* (Ra'anana: Misrad HaBitachon/Lior Publishing, 2002), 44.
8. See Etkes, *Rabbi Shneur Zalman of Liadi*, 14 (and ch. 7). It stands to reason that

percentage of Russian Jews at that time who viewed themselves as followers of Rabbi Shneur Zalman.

What characterized the kind of people for whom Rabbi Shneur Zalman's message resonated? What kinds of questions did they grapple with? To what extent was the climate right for absorbing his ideas?

The final decades of the eighteenth century were an extremely turbulent time. Regimes were toppled and new countries born, along with many political changes, wars, and revolutions.[9] Prior to that were times when the autonomy enjoyed by Jews enabled their numbers to quickly climb to the hundreds of thousands, constituting a small, self-determined Jewish world unto its own. The historian Israel Bartal describes it in the following way:

> In the mid-eighteenth century, due to the changes and modernization occurring in eastern Europe, a simple Polish Jew living in cities like Kharkov or Lublin could live his entire life within the bubble of the local Jewish community. He'd have next to no direct contact with the outside world of the government and political system. Contact between communities and the outside world were left up to representatives appointed by each community.[10]

This state of affairs was about to change. During the twenty years (approximately 1776–1796) in which the Tanya, the fundamental work of Rabbi Shneur Zalman, was compiled, Jews experienced unprecedented upheavals. At that time, Poland fell apart, and the empires of Russia, Prussia, and Austria twice divided up the country, in 1772 and 1793. Austria annexed Galicia. Pomerania and Poznan were allocated to Prussia, which encompassed what today is Germany. Russia tore Belarus, the region where Rabbi Shneur Zalman was located, away from Poland.[11] The Russian Empire, which cited religious reasons for refusing to allow

---

there were waves of growth in the numbers of those who were connected to Rabbi Shneur Zalman.

9. See Bartal, *Me'Uma l'Leum*, 23.

10. Bartal, *Me'Uma l'Leum*, 20.

11. For a broader discussion and footnotes regarding the political situation of that era up until the times of the Baal Shem Tov, see Moshe Rosman, *Habaal Shem Tov Mechadesh Hachassidut* (Jerusalem: Merkaz Zalman Shazar, 1996), 102.

Jewish settlements, annexed regions with hundreds of thousands of Jews, deeming them descendants of the "murderers of Christ."[12]

Generally speaking, there were no noticeable differences from one country to the next in what Jews throughout Europe faced. In most places, Jews were subjected to arbitrary legislation that limited their rights in various ways, in some cases even to the point of total loss of rights.[13] Jews were considered as lacking citizenship, and the areas in which they could live were limited. Moreover, permission to settle in areas that had already been permitted to them generally included the obligation to pay a head tax to the treasury, such as "protection money" or payment for "settling rights."

The differences in rights corresponded to differences in the financial state of affairs. Jews were displaced from most of their positions of authority and business associations. They were also limited in the type and scope of professions in which they were permitted to engage, so as to limit competition with the local general population. For the most part, Jews were only allowed to work in trading and money lending. The majority of Jews struggled mightily to earn a living. Nevertheless, it should be noted that this time period witnessed the gradual development of a group of Jewish businessmen, bankers, and craftsmen who succeeded in escaping poverty. In the century to come, with the movement toward emancipation and equal rights inspired by the spread of capitalism, many Jewish businessmen utilized their companies, businesses, and banking connections to successfully achieve significant financial breakthroughs and advancements. However, in the last twenty-five years of the eighteenth century, in which Rabbi Shneur Zalman's approach grew and developed, Jews were relegated to the lowest and most menial of professions and were associated with the lowest levels of society. The jobs they were forced into in eastern Europe – money lending, selling rags, making bootleg liquors, and managing bars for the local landowners – only increased local hatred toward them.[14]

While the overall picture didn't seem to indicate massive changes

---

12. See Bartal, *Me'Uma l'Leum*, 37.
13. Dovnov, *Divrei Yemei Olam*, 5.
14. Rosman, *Habaal Shem Tov*, 102.

in the state of affairs for European Jewry, the trend in eastern Europe was different from that in western Europe. In the one hundred years leading up to the French Revolution, as western Europe was moving toward the Age of Enlightenment and political independence and the Industrial Revolution began to spread from England throughout Europe, eastern Europe was moving in the opposite direction. Life for Jews in the majority of countries was on the decline in terms of their rights as citizens and their financial status. The Polish territories held by Russia, Ukraine, and Cossack settlements underwent a Catholic revival that restored the fear and terror of the Middle Ages and the Crusades. The Jews of Poland, who a few hundred years prior had fled to the country to escape the Crusades and the Black Death, began moving west, primarily to Germany. There they established a Jewish center that rivaled what they had built in Poland. Those remaining in Poland began to dwindle, and many were absorbed into the general Polish public.[15]

With the disintegration of the Jewish community in Poland, the Vaad Arba Aratzot (Council of the Four Lands), the governing body that had overseen all communal affairs throughout Poland for 250 years, ceased to function. They had been entrusted with collecting taxes, ruling on internal issues, and representing the Jewish community before governing authorities.[16] Due to the division of Poland and the new geopolitical situation that was changing the region, the group lost its ability to serve the mission for which it had been formed. Its end was ethical collapse and decay, which only added to the financial hardships of the time.[17] However, the division of Poland and annexation of its eastern regions by the Russian czars marked the end of the purchasing of rabbinical positions from Polish nobles and paved the path for the spread of Chassidut.[18]

---

15. Rosman, *Habaal Shem Tov*, 113n1.

16. For discussion of groups overseeing communal affairs and the Vaad Arba Aratzot, see Bartal, *Me'Uma l'Leum*, 18.

17. According to Rabbi Yosef Yitzchak, closing down the Vaad Arba Aratzot caused concern and distress among the Torah leaders of the time. See Rabbi Yosef Yitzchak, *Reshimot – Divrei Yemei Chayei Admor Hazaken* (New York: Kehot, 2001), 7.

18. See Etkes, *Rabbi Shneur Zalman of Liadi*, 261. See the words of Rabbi Shneur Zalman himself during his investigation. For a translation of a summary report of

The drastic changes unfolding in Europe in the last quarter of the eighteenth century left the Jews searching for answers and guidance. More than intellectual and theoretical approaches to the changing times, they were desperate for practical solutions and methods for handling and improving the situation.

In general, feelings of distress, frustration, and lack of trust increased with the enlarging gap between reality and the hope for freedom, equality, and progress.

In cases where the difference between the ideal and actual becomes unbearable, historians expect to find changes in world outlook, agitation, and a desire for change. Approximately 250 years ago, natural human rights were outlined and clarified by the founders of modern political philosophy – Thomas Hobbes, John Locke, and Jean-Jacques Rousseau – and awareness of them quickly spread throughout Europe. The placement of man as the central focus and the advancement of the fundamentals of freedom and equality led to the French Revolution. But while Europe was stirring, its Jews remained outcasts and underprivileged, as if these ideas had no relevance to them. Even the empress of Russia, Catherine II, who followed an enlightened approach and promised the Jews religious freedom and personal protection, was forced to deal with an internal conflict that arose from her religious role as the head of the Church, a body that generally loathed the Jews and viewed them as a hostile religious group.[19]

On the whole, we can say that the ensuing years of the budding new period – the beginning of the modern age – brought four major developments that shook up and changed the face of Judaism: accelerated numbers of intermarriages; secularization in the face of the spread of the Enlightenment; nationalism, which would emerge at a later stage; and the spread of the Chassidic movement, the most significant spiritual development in the observant Jewish world.

In large part, each of these developments reflected coping methods for dealing with the difficulties of the time. They each offered responses

---

the investigation from Russian into Hebrew, see Yehoshua Mondshine, ed., "Iyun v'Choker b'Mishnat Chabad, Divrei Yemei Hachassidut v'Darchei Hachassidut," *Kerem Chabad* 4, no. 1 (5752): 111–13.

19. Bartal, *Me'Uma l'Leum*, 72.

to the different questions and issues then confronting the Jewish people. What is so unique about the Jewish people? How can the financial, social, cultural, and political situation be improved? What should the relationship be between Jews and Gentiles? And, no less important: Why do the Jewish people continue to suffer so much?

Slowly, these approaches moved people into camps. At the height of Rabbi Shneur Zalman's activities, around the time of the French Revolution and a few years after the American Revolution, when Europe was raging and fluctuating between the fight to protect human and natural rights and the zealous grip of religious and royal forces, these camps stood ready and alert to battle for Jews' minds and hearts.

RABBI SHNEUR ZALMAN AS "HEALER"

What was so inspirational about the message presented by Rabbi Shneur Zalman, causing the masses to push for private audiences with him?

Ordinary Jews, submerged in financial and political uncertainty, deprived of their rights and ostracized by the business community, were drawn to Rabbi Shneur Zalman's path due to his unique personality, as well as his wisdom and the natural charisma he radiated.

Generally speaking, people read or listen to things because they personally find them interesting. Readers and listeners are attracted to messages that offer them something useful to apply to their lives and to the challenges and struggles they face.

The people Rabbi Shneur Zalman met in Liozna or in the villages he toured came with questions, doubts, uncertainties, and worries. Like most of their Jewish neighbors, they lived lives fraught with agony and suffering, financial turmoil, and lack of security. It was with this package of troubles and spiritual quandaries that they sought an audience with Rabbi Shneur Zalman, in order to receive proper guidance.

Simon Sinek, the well-known author and public speaker on behavioral research, claims that good leaders are those who inspire others to believe what they believe.[20] He says that people are not interested in what others do, but rather in why they do it. People are attracted to a vision,

---

20. See his popular TED talk: http://www.ted.com/talks/simon_sinek_how_great _leaders_inspire_action.

not a product. An analysis of the examples he presents is very compelling. For example, tens of millions of people prefer to purchase from Apple, a brand and idea that is as recognized as its products. And it is the idea associated with the brand that continues to fuel the company's innovation and to excite customers. Likewise, more than 250,000 protestors arrived in Washington in August 1963 not to hear Martin Luther King, but rather for themselves. King had succeeded in connecting them to what he believed in. His dream had become their dream.

We can similarly analyze Rabbi Shneur Zalman's contribution. He had a vision – a belief that he could change the world with his approach. With his guidance, he infused meaning and optimism into the lives of those who turned to him. He clearly outlined the fundamentals of Jewish life, presenting them in the most radiant way possible. Based on the fundamental works and concepts of Judaism, Rabbi Shneur Zalman provided answers to crucial questions: Where is God? What is His relationship to creation? What is the purpose of life? What is the purpose of suffering? His guiding principle was that deep contemplation of the world and God's interaction with it would help his Chassidim better handle the darkness generated by the regimes of eastern Europe – and not only handle reality, but also make progress in overcoming it.

However, Rabbi Shneur Zalman's system did more than just provide comprehensive answers to questions about the purpose of creation and man's relationship with the Creator. It offered practical steps for facing the reality of the times and for infusing it with meaning and purpose. Selections of his teachings point out, for example, how to deal with depression, anxiety, and fear; how to overcome emotional and intellectual insensitivity and blockage; and how to develop an appreciation for the value of effort, instead of worrying.

Despite his tendency toward deep intellectual exploration, Rabbi Shneur Zalman quickly became a source of trust and strength in a time of insecurity and crises. His visitors absorbed personal and direct instruction from him. In Chassidic literature, the Baal Shem Tov is referred to as the "Premier Educator," while Rabbi Shneur Zalman is considered the "Premier Guide."[21]

As in the concepts discussed by Sinek, Rabbi Shneur Zalman did not

---

21. See Rabbi Yosef Yitzchak, *Sefer Hasichot 5703/1943*, 187; it has also been said that

limit instruction to matters of spiritual service. He didn't sell a product. His approach was akin to offering a companion product. The vision he put forth concerning the challenges people faced gave people a strong foothold in life, a vision combining both the physical and spiritual worlds, the ideals of Judaism alongside the practical and tangible. As expressed by Sinek, Rabbi Shneur Zalman inspired others to believe what he believed. They connected to his vision, which reflected the way he saw the world, and they naturally wanted to hear and follow his guidance and direction.

THE BOOK OF TANYA

Rabbi Shneur Zalman crystallized the essence of the system he developed in his years of seclusion and in the years in which he offered guidance and direction and collected it all into his primary work, the Tanya. As Rabbi Shneur Zalman himself testifies, the Tanya is a collection of guidance he shared throughout the years and organized into a polished and comprehensive teaching. It is a written summary that underwent twenty years of contemplation, meetings, and discussions[22] in which tremendous attention was invested into every letter and word.[23] The result is a deep intellectual and philosophical synthesis of personal psychological guidance.

Six years before the Tanya appeared in book form, Rabbi Shneur Zalman would regularly share parts of it during his public talks on Shabbat and holidays before the Chassidim.[24] In other words, it was not the printing of the Tanya that made his approach known. His teaching had already been in process during the twenty-two years leading up to the book's printing.

Rabbi Shneur Zalman's technique was to explain and outline his

---

"The Baal Shem Tov taught how one needs to serve God; Rabbi Shneur Zalman taught how one is able to serve God." Rabbi Yosef Yitzchak, *Igrot Kodesh*, vol. 2, 365.

22. See *Hayom Yom – 6 Adar II*, p. 12; also the introduction to Yehoshua Mondshine, *Likkutei Amarim Hu Sefer Hatanya – Mahadurotova, Targumov, v'Biurav* (1982).

23. For an example of this, see the letter from Rabbi Yosef Yitzchak, 28 Tammuz, 5692 (1932), in introduction to *Likkutei Sichot* 4:1212; the Lubavitcher Rebbe, *Igrot Kodesh*, vol. 5, 295; and other sources.

24. Rabbi Yosef Yitzchak, *Sefer Hasichot 5703/1943*, 23.

approach such that its learners could stand on their own two feet and implement it in ways that met their own needs.[25] Writing down the core points, despite how uncommon that was then among Chassidim, was the only way Rabbi Shneur Zalman could respond to the thousands knocking on his door. Furthermore, Rabbi Shneur Zalman pleaded that anyone who struggled to grasp the Tanya's ideas should seek out trusted local guides for help in reading, learning, and applying the points expressed in the text.

The Tanya was printed two years after Rabbi Shneur Zalman's first imprisonment, about 220 years ago, in the year 5557 (1796). As soon as the first edition left the printing press, it was immediately burned in Vilna by the opponents of Chassidut.[26] Nevertheless, it quickly became a popular book that enjoyed tremendous praise.

Proof of the huge demand for Rabbi Shneur Zalman's message at that time is apparent by the volume of copies of the Tanya that were printed beginning with the first edition. According to Chassidic sources, the first edition of the Tanya was printed on 20 Kislev (December 20, 1976), with fifteen thousand copies. Today, when printing is incomparably easier and less expensive, it is hard to think of deep intellectual books which already in their first printing rival the print volume of the Tanya. A year later, the second edition was printed, with five thousand copies. Three years after the first printing, an additional twenty thousand copies were produced. From that point onward, editions were printed in accordance with the demand of readers.[27]

While it's obvious that Chabad Chassidim were the source of energy driving the spread of the book, the two hundred years since its first printing have seen it transformed into a widely desired book outside the Chabad camp as well. Early on, the Tanya won over most of the leaders and followers of the other Chassidic groups whose intense push to study it was beyond comprehension. For example, Rabbi Zusha of Anipoli, a student of the Maggid of Mezeritch, wrote a full approbation

---

25. This approach is the cornerstone of Chassidic thinking. See also the "Compiler's Foreword" to the Tanya.

26. Haim Meir Heilman, *Beit Rebbe*, 1st ed. (Berdichev, 1902), 49.

27. Description of the printings of the Tanya can be found in several sources. For example, see Mindel, *Rabbi Schneur Zalman of Liadi*, 122–23.

in praise of the book. The Koznitzer Rebbe, Yisrael Hopstein, among the great Chassidic leaders of Poland, learned a chapter of Tanya daily while wearing Rabbeinu Tam tefillin. It is told that the Chozeh of Lublin, who was the same age as Rabbi Shneur Zalman, said: "Mashiach will only come once the teachings of Reb Zalman are widely spread."[28]

Rabbi Mendel Vechter is a good example in our times of the extent to which the Tanya penetrated groups outside of Chabad. Earlier in his life, Rabbi Vechter served as the *rosh kollel* for outstanding students in the Satmar community of Williamsburg, New York. Despite the tremendous tension at the time between Chabad and Satmar, Rabbi Vechter was committed to teaching Tanya to his students. For two years, he secretly met with Rabbi Yoel Kahn, the Lubavitcher Rebbe's lead scribe, learning Chassidut and receiving guidance in navigating the Tanya's concepts. The learning was with one condition from Rabbi Vechter: only Tanya and nothing from the latter Rebbes of Chabad. This condition shows the extent to which he didn't see Rabbi Shneur Zalman as having been part of any disagreement with Satmar. Rabbi Kahn, however, failed to uphold the deal. When it became known to members of Rabbi Vechter's community that his Tanya studies with Rabbi Kahn also included commentary from the then Lubavitcher Rebbe, they banned Rabbi Vechter from the community.[29]

CAUSES OF THE TANYA'S POPULARITY

What was it about Rebbe Shneur Zalman's message that attracted such a following during his lifetime? What is it about the Tanya that enabled it to be so well received among such a diverse readership until today? An examination of the components of the Tanya's success demands

---

28. Avraham Shmuel Bukiet compiles in his book, *Hatanya Nachalat Ha'am* (Kfar Chabad: Yad Hachamishah, 5768/2008), a list of Torah giants and how they related to the Tanya. The statement of the Maggid of Koznitz is quoted in the book by Rabbi Shimon Zelichover, *Naharei Eish*, 213. For the Chozeh of Lublin's statement, see *Olam Hachassidut* 63, p. 38.

29. Rabbi Vechter has shared his story on many occasions. See the article "Rabbi Vechter: My Lynching: They Asked for Forgiveness from Jail" [Hebrew], *B'Chadrei Charedim*, February 14, 2012, https://www.bhol.co.il/forums/topic.asp?cat_id=4& topic_id=2943600&forum_id=771.

separate, thorough treatment. In order to understand how the Tanya became so widespread and successful, we first need to understand what makes any book popular. Marketing and distribution are essential for the success of any book. Without an army of Chabad emissaries who drew nourishment from the book and actively sought to expose it to others, it's quite likely that the Tanya would have been relegated to an ignored corner. In light of this, it is customarily said that unlike many other authors, Rabbi Shneur Zalman not only left his books to the world, but also to trustworthy people who spread those books.[30]

Promotion and distribution are important conditions for the success of any product, but they aren't the only ones. The Tanya's clarity and orderly structure are important factors in its popularity. It wasn't crafted according to the weekly Torah portion, holidays, or topics in Jewish law. The Tanya is unique among works of Chassidic thought in that it presents a complete and crystallized subject which invites the learner to go through an internal, personal process. It creates a journey that begins at one point and ends at another, and along the way the reader undergoes a significant experience of self-awareness, one that deeply alters a person's perspective.

For a Jewish reader today, the Tanya may seem like a difficult text to navigate. In most cases, the main reason for this is a lack of sufficient familiarity with the world of Kabbalistic and Chassidic concepts that provide the infrastructure of the book's ideas. However, to a person knowledgeable in Rabbi Shneur Zalman's other writings, it is clear just how much effort the author invested in an attempt to make the Tanya as clear and accessible as possible.

First of all, the Tanya is written in relatively clear Hebrew, in the style that Rabbi Shneur Zalman was insistent on using in his writings and letters. Even when responding to the Russian authorities' investigation in the year 1798, he chose to write in Hebrew, which was then translated into Russian. The first books in Hebrew script were printed in Italy in 1475,

---

30. "The Vilna Gaon left us books. The Baal Shem Tov, the founder of Chassidut, left us people. However, Rabbi Shneur Zalman left us books as well as people who distributed and spread those books." From Rabbi Shlomo Yosef Zevin's article "Rabbi Shneur Zalman Mi'Liadi" in *Machanayim* 46 (5720/1960).

with the aid of a printing press. Since that time, it had become customary to print commentaries and works of musar with the Rashi version of the Hebrew alphabet. Rabbi Shneur Zalman departed from this approach and used block versions of the Hebrew alphabet with a large font that was easy to read. In this way, readers who were already comfortable with the concepts and principles discussed by Rabbi Shneur Zalman found the Tanya flowing and easy to follow, certainly in comparison to works written in Kabbalistic Aramaic, and even in comparison to other talks and discourses from Rabbi Shneur Zalman himself.

Still, distribution and promotion along with a clear, structured style are not enough to transform a book into a success. What was said previously concerning the teachings in Rabbi Shneur Zalman's intimate one-on-one meetings also applies to those of the Tanya itself. One of the fundamental conditions for the success of any book is that it addresses questions that are relevant to the reader. In general, a reader takes interest in a given book because it speaks to him on some level. The book can enrich his knowledge, his speech and language, provide a source of entertainment, or serve as a practical guide to living a life of meaning. In the introduction to the Tanya, Rabbi Shneur Zalman testifies that one's interaction with a book is mostly subjective and personal. Everyone reads from an individual vantage point, and thus each person understands the material differently. How we read is not solely a function of our intellectual ability. Being stressed, anxious, confused, or unsure can lead a person to understand written material differently than in times of calm and security.

Moreover, all people are different in their intellectual abilities and the ways in which they connect to occurrences and ideas. Some people are enthralled with a book and others with other books. For example, some people study physics and astronomy and are excited by the universe. The scientific knowledge they seek out comes together to produce an intellectual pleasure with each new bit they uncover. Others, however, become quickly bored when studying science. The best books are the ones that successfully provide answers to the questions readers ask themselves in a broad range of situations. The Tanya meets this requirement. Its declared mission, according to Rabbi Shneur Zalman, is to serve as a replacement for a personal conversation and face-to-face meeting. It's a conversation between the reader who seeks to grow and develop and the writer who understands the challenges of the soul and directs his theories and discussions toward the challenges faced by the reader.

For this reason, we see today that study of the Tanya's approach and treatment according to the Tanya has spread far beyond the world of Chassidut. The collapse of ideologies, including socialism and nationalism, brought on by the spread of the culture of capitalism, led to an increased interest in approaches that feature a central focus on the person. Along with this, the system presented by Rabbi Shneur Zalman to his Chassidim approximately two hundred years ago has also gained momentum. In a world in which people seek meaning in life and, thus, seek out methods for addressing the alleviation of the soul's distress, the Tanya stands out as a highly sought-after book of guidance. It's a book in which readers encounter Rabbi Shneur Zalman's perspective on the purpose of life and his structured approach to spiritual efforts.

PATHWAY OF THIS BOOK

A Journey in Time: The First Two Chapters

From where did Rabbi Shneur Zalman derive his approach? What were the fundamental topics in Judaism that he was trying to tackle?

Many people recognize the fundamental topics addressed in Rabbi Shneur Zalman's writings: first and foremost in the Tanya, and, second, in his discourses on the weekly Torah portion in *Torah Ohr* and *Likkutei Torah*, which were organized and printed by his grandson, the Tzemach Tzedek. In recent years, many collections have been printed of the discourses Rabbi Shneur Zalman delivered publicly to his students over the years. Some of these emerge from the years prior to the Tanya's printing, including before he became an official Chassidic leader. These books contain the core ideas that appear later in the Tanya; they attest to the spreading of Rabbi Shneur Zalman's approach long before the Tanya was printed. The volume of discourses and the subject matter they touch upon highlight the strong bond he had with his audience and the tremendous efforts he invested in them. But they also show us that Rabbi Shneur Zalman was engaged in an ongoing conversation not only with his audience but also with his teachers, as well as the works of Kabbalah upon which he based his approach.

Winning Every Moment focuses on the psychological aspects of Rabbi Shneur Zalman's teachings. At the same time, it should be noted that in the eyes of Rabbi Shneur Zalman, topics connected to the structure of the soul were not detached from the fundamental questions handled by the previous generations of Torah leaders. For this reason, before we can examine Rabbi Shneur Zalman's approach, chapter 1 will take a step backward to the Safed of 450 years ago, the time of the Arizal (Rabbi Yitzchak Luria, a tremendously influential teacher of Kabbalah). The purpose of this journey in time is to clarify the primary questions, theories, and activities in which the Jewish world was engaged before the modern age, and which concepts persisted until the times of Rabbi Shneur Zalman, demanding attention and exploration.

Chapter 2 presents a biography of Rabbi Shneur Zalman's character. The chapter highlights the crucial points in the life of Rabbi Shneur Zalman in order to identify the factors that led him to write the Tanya and to clarify fundamental issues in the teachings of the Arizal and the Baal Shem Tov.

Assessment and Treatment: Chapters 3 to 9

What did Rabbi Shneur Zalman say to his audience which touched their hearts? What approach did he seek to design for them to help them face their struggles? Out of these concepts, which remain relevant today?

This book seeks to answer those questions. As mentioned in the introduction, *Winning Every Moment* invites the reader into an intimate conversation with the Tanya's author, in an attempt to create a meeting that might feel similar to *yechidut*, as the core points of Rabbi Shneur Zalman's theory and approach to treatment are outlined. A *yechidut* is a private meeting between a Rebbe and Chassid, in which the Rebbe provides the Chassid with personal guidance. During the *yechidut*, the Rebbe focuses on the Chassid, his challenges, and his needs. Chassidim would prepare for the *yechidut* in personal, private ways. The questions weighing on them would be put in writing prior to the meeting, and then handed to the Rebbe either before the *yechidut* or right at the beginning.

In today's language, *yechidut* might be described as a form of spiritual treatment and guidance that Chassidim merited to receive from their Rebbe. It typically featured three fundamental components.

1. The Rebbe objectively assesses the current state of affairs – that is, the distress, dilemmas, and challenges the person before him is facing, including the psychological distress produced by deficiencies in spiritual nourishment.
2. The second phase centers on describing the optimal state of affairs toward which the person should strive. This by necessity includes the solution to the presenting problem and the spiritual sustenance.
3. Finally, the Rebbe lays out the pathway: guidance tailored to the case, in order for the Chassid to overcome the current situation and reach the ideal.

Due to its many details and dimensions, those who learn the Tanya struggle to grasp the full process outlined by Rabbi Shneur Zalman. This book discusses the three aspects provided by Rabbi Shneur Zalman during a *yechidut* meeting: assessment, description of the ideal state, and a suggested path for treatment and change. The next chapters, therefore, are built upon these steps.

Chapter 3, "The Inner Battle," presents a general picture of what the soul experiences. That very struggle produces the first insights into the awareness that Rabbi Shneur Zalman wants his readers to obtain. The next chapters, 4 and 5, offer a dissection of the soul: its faculties, how they are expressed, how they interrelate, what produces states of spiritual depletion, and how to characterize different personality types. Together, these three chapters produce a picture of the soul's structure, which helps a person assess his or her personal state. From the comprehensive framework of concepts described by Rabbi Shneur Zalman, the reader receives tools to identify the self, to understand the makeup of the soul, and to identify potential causes of the emotional and intellectual processes he experiences.

Chapter 6 presents the ideal state to aim for and the preferred way of life. People may be categorized into three groups: *tzaddikim* (the perfectly righteous), *beinonim* (the average, comprising most of humanity), and *reshai'im* (the perfectly wicked). The Tanya is often called the Sifran shel Beinonim, the book of the average, in which the figure of the *beinoni* takes center stage. The *beinoni* is the hero of the Tanya, who battles for victory in every moment of his life.

After dissecting the structure of the soul and presenting the ideal vision, the next three chapters outline Rabbi Shneur Zalman's approach to treatment. Chapter 7 looks at the technical aspects of contemplation. Chapter 8 presents a collection of practical advice offered by Rabbi Shneur Zalman to readers of the Tanya in order to help them handle spiritual issues. By reviewing them, we encounter the common factor they all share. Chapter 9 highlights our connections with others and compares the value of giving versus working on ourselves.

THE FUNDAMENTALS OF JEWISH THOUGHT

Based on our discussion up to this point, it can be understood that the Tanya is a book of deep contemplation, filled with guidance the author shared with his followers to enable them to apply his philosophy in their daily lives.[31] However, further review of the Tanya reveals an additional challenge Rabbi Shneur Zalman faced, which in particular stands out against the backdrop of its historical context.

As Rabbi Shneur Zalman earned more admiration, opposition to him increased. New ideas began to move throughout the Jewish world, and changes were imminent. Against his will, Rabbi Shneur Zalman was forced to counter the opposition. Frequent battles appeared against him, on four different battlegrounds.

One front was the Mitnagdim, the opponents of Chassidut. Their war against Chassidim inspired deep discussion and explanation which can be found throughout many books and discourses. The lingering memory of the false messiah Shabbtai Tzvi (who did devastating damage to the Jewish community's faith) remained a deeply felt pain to many rabbinic and community leaders. Such memories led to concerns over anything seemingly new or different. Besides fears over changes, those in opposition also played on people's political and financial concerns. Rabbi Shneur Zalman was often compelled to dampen the excitement and passion of Chassidut and prove that not only did it change nothing of the Torah, but it actually enlightened it and appropriately encapsulated its spirit.

The second front was Gentile ruling authorities and the Russian rulership in particular. Rabbi Shneur Zalman was involved in improving Jewish life in practical terms, including dealings with Gentile authorities.

---

31. See "Compiler's Foreword" to the Tanya: "...to derive spiritual guidance."

Slander from the opponents of Chassidism led to Rabbi Shneur Zalman's arrest on two occasions for his seeming efforts to undermine the czar. During each incarceration, he was called upon to demonstrate his dedication (and that of his Chassidim) to the Russian rulership, which had conquered territories that previously belonged to Poland. These arrests impacted Rabbi Shneur Zalman's approach to how he constructed and advanced Chassidut.[32]

A third front concerned the Haskalah, the Enlightenment movement. The plan to blend into German culture, as seen clearly for example in the behavior of such notable figures as Moshe Mendelssohn and Naftali Tzvi Hirsh, led to quickly decreasing levels of Jewish observance and increased secularization. Rabbi Shneur Zalman aligned himself with those who fought against the spread of the movement, while offering an alternative to the idea that blending into German culture was the path to a better Jewish future.

Finally, the fourth front was internal opposition and conflict. Rabbi Shneur Zalman's success not only aroused arguments based on principle, but also generated instances of jealousy, lack of consensus, and internal splits. Confrontations flared on many occasions.

However, the Tanya was not written as a response to these four fronts. Its composition long preceded the battles that Rabbi Shneur Zalman had faced and, rather, was based on his understanding of the world of Jewish thought. With that said, the formulation of the Tanya was not only as a book of guidance for Chassidim, but also as powerful ammunition for future conflict regarding the shape of Judaism. In a certain sense, Rabbi Shneur Zalman perceived the future sequences of events that would hit the Torah- and mitzvah-observant world, and, in response, sought to delineate and describe Judaism: What is unique about a Jew, what is his purpose in the world, and what are the core principles of Judaism?

For twenty years, Rabbi Shneur Zalman toiled over his book, taking great care with every word and letter. Not only did he employ great precision in order to craft a book of psychological, spiritual, and faith-related guidance, but also to bring order to the world of Jewish thought.[33]

---

32. See Adin Even Yisrael (Steinsaltz), "Maamarei Admor Hazaken," *Maayanotecha*, November 15, 2011, http://www.toratchabad.com/contents.asp?aid=79519.
33. "...Not only does in-depth study of Tanya show a person the approach of

Rabbi Shneur Zalman wrote a letter comparing the ideas held by the opposition to his approach and Chassidism with the opposition experienced by the Rambam. He ends this letter by expressing his faith that his approach will enjoy success (as did the Rambam's) and make its mark on Jewish thought. In his words:

> Remember days gone by, for who is greater than the Moses of the generation – the Rambam. And throughout Spain his reputation greatly grew and spread. However, in regions far from where his name had yet to become known and his greatness was not yet seen, he was viewed as an apostate and a denier of *techiyat hameitim* [the revival of the dead that is prophesied to be accomplished by the messiah]. His books were burned.... But with the passage of time... truth will sprout from the earth, and the entire Jewish people knew that Moses was true and his Torah was true, etc. May it be so for us soon. Amen.[34]

In addition to the faith that there would be victory and that the opposition would be vanquished, a historical perspective indicates several criteria that support a comparison of Rabbi Shneur Zalman's activities with those of the Rambam.[35] Both of them wrote their fundamental works themselves – not via their students. Both of them feared the pressure of the times, and that the descent of the generation would lead to the loss of parts of the Torah. This pushed them to write. Until the times of the Rambam, Jewish law was a collection of details and was complete with sources, but it lacked a transcribed order and structure. The Rambam was the first to succeed at putting Judaism into a structured

---

Chassidut to serving God, but even much more than that – among its lines one can clearly and deeply discern the novelty of the Baal Shem Tov's path to grasping the fundamentals of Judaism." Rabbi Yoel Kahn, *Sugiyot b'Chassidut* (Jerusalem: Maayanotecha, 2013), 21.

34. *Igrot Kodesh – Alter Rebbe*, letter 52 (5557), 187.

35. See the comparison presented by the Lubavitcher Rebbe between the Rambam's *Mishneh Torah* and Rabbi Shneur Zalman's *Shulchan Aruch Harav*, and between the Rambam's *Moreh Nevuchim* (Guide for the Perplexed) and the Tanya: *Likkutei Sichot* 26:30. A comparison between Rabbi Shneur Zalman and the Rambam was also constructed by Rabbi Yitzchak of Amshinov. See *Yemot Olam*, 116, and in Bukiet, *Hatanya Nachalat Ha'am*, 95.

system. His largest and greatest effort, the *Mishneh Torah*, was written when he was in his thirties, but he continued to refine it throughout his life. It was a project of mammoth proportions. This awesome structured system, which was the totality of all existent Jewish texts, he successfully fit into fourteen books. Just how extreme was his grandiose vision for the work can be gleaned from the Rambam's own words: "Read the Torah, read my book – the *Mishneh Torah* – and that's it; you won't need to read any other book in between."[36]

From a certain vantage point, the Tanya is also a work of similar grandiose goals, but in the realm of the inner dimension of Torah. In the Tanya, Rabbi Shneur Zalman collected all of the concepts in the Torah's inner dimension which had been revealed up to that point in time, arranging them with an orderly system and approach, and boldly connected them to the structure of the Torah's commandments. Along the way, he answered fundamental questions in Jewish thought, such as what is a person, who is the Creator, what is the connection between the Creator and man, what is the value of the physical commandments, and what is the purpose of creation. From the Chassidic standpoint, Jewish thought is directly linked to the works of Kabbalah and Chassidut just as it is to the world of halachah (Jewish law). Throughout his life, Rabbi Shneur Zalman was involved in both realms, of *halachah* and Kabbalah, as if the two bodies of knowledge were enmeshed with each other.

In light of this, *Winning Every Moment* explores the characteristics of Judaism through a focus on psychology and the workings of the soul, as outlined by Rabbi Shneur Zalman.

Before describing the structure of the soul, outlining the guidance for living, and describing the characteristics of Judaism, we first need to go back in time. The purpose of doing so is to determine the central questions about the psychology of the soul that the great Kabbalists and Jewish thinkers grappled with, since these are questions that Rabbi Shneur Zalman also sought to address in the Tanya.

---

36. "For a person will first read the Written Torah, and then read this work and know the entire Oral Torah, and have no need for other books in between." Rambam, Introduction, *Mishneh Torah*.

CHAPTER 1

The Arizal's Question

It was the Hebrew month of Tammuz, 5330 (1570). Many of the thousands of Safed locals escorted the funeral procession of the deceased Rabbi Moshe Cordovero. Nearly all the local scholarly leaders attended. Each wanted to accompany the esteemed rabbi, covered in shrouds and a tallit, on his final journey to the Jewish cemetery. Rabbi Yosef Karo, the city's senior Torah authority, delivered a heartfelt eulogy. His advanced age of eighty-two, the steep slopes, and the Galilee Mountains didn't prevent him from walking with the large group.

Despite the glorious mountaintop scenery, one can still picture the oppressive summer weather and the heavy sense of loss felt by everyone. Facing the Kinneret (the Sea of Galilee), Rabbi Karo roused the crowd with his emphasis that "here the ark of the Torah will be buried."[1] He was not the only one to eulogize the rabbi. As customary in such processions, when a Torah giant leaves the world, the eulogizers seek to awaken the attendees, deliver a practical message, and encourage Torah study and fulfillment of the deceased's final directives. In this case, the deceased's wishes included a request that people increase their involvement with

---

1. See Naftali Yaakov Hakohen's *Otzar Hagedolim Alufei Yaakov* (Amsterdam, 1908), 173.

the Torah's wisdom, the revealed dimension and, all the more so, the concealed.[2]

It was a period of rejuvenation for Safed. The Ottoman ruling authority had pushed out the Mamluks, freeing the city to develop security and to thrive financially. Business flourished and, along with it, in-depth Torah study did too. Only a few years prior, the wealthy Portuguese businesswoman Dona Gracia Mendes-Nasi (Chanah Nasi, as she was called in Hebrew) had leased nearby Tiberias from the Turkish sultan and begun to advance the development of an autonomous Jewish state.[3] Although these plans never reached fruition, her actions surely impacted the region and the state of security for Jews throughout the area. After the Jews were expelled from Spain in 1492, destroying the largest center of Jewish life, Safed became a magnet for Torah scholars around the world. They flocked to it, seeking to continue their development and advance their proficiencies. They would settle there or take up temporary residence before continuing their travels elsewhere.

Safed's name spread far, promoted by the brilliance of its Kabbalah scholars. Rabbi Karo, known as the Beit Yosef for his work by the same name, was acclaimed for his works of Jewish law, primarily the *Shulchan Aruch*. This book of practical Jewish law, arranged in a terse and clear style, is a codex used until today as the basis for halachic rulings. Despite not mentioning Kabbalistic ideas in his legal writings, he was deeply involved in learning the Torah's inner dimension. In *Maggid Meisharim*, a form of autobiography that he wrote and which only became known after his death, he provides in-depth descriptions of experiences and spiritual concepts using Kabbalistic terminology.[4] It reads like a diary, granting insight into the prophetic knowledge of one of the great Torah giants and codifiers of Jewish law.[5]

---

2. For example, see the work he composed at the end of his life, *Ohr Nehratz* (Venice, 5346/1586), which was specifically to inspire people to learn the teachings of the Torah's inner dimension.

3. See Yakov Haruzan, *Dona Gracia and the Jewish State in Tiberias in the Galil* (Jerusalem: Tzur-Ot, 1980).

4. See the discussion from the Lubavitcher Rebbe, "Menachem Av, 5713," *Torat Menachem*, vol. 9, 1953, part 3, 104.

5. See Mor Altshuler, "Prophecy and Maggidism in the Life and Writings of R. Joseph Karo," *Frankfurt Jewish Studies Bulletin* 33 (2006): 110–81.

Rabbi Karo wasn't the first to integrate Kabbalah and Jewish law. Also joining in the procession was a sage who was older than the deceased, Rabbi Shlomo Alkabetz, a noted author of important works of Kabbalah whose fame spread due to the poetic Lecha Dodi prayer he composed. His poem penetrated the Jewish prayer book and was a focal point in the order of welcoming in Shabbat in most Jewish congregations. Rabbi Alkabetz was approximately seventeen years the senior of the deceased Rabbi Moshe Cordovero and was about sixty-five when he escorted his brother-in-law to his final rest. Walking next to Rabbi Alkabetz were students in Kabbalah. This group of learners of the Torah's inner dimension comprised scholars from Saloniki as well as those who were banned from Spain and Portugal, all of whom had beaten a path to Safed specifically to learn the secrets of the Torah.[6] Most of them held the belief that from their perch in the Galilee Mountains they could influence the entire world. Their intense involvement in Kabbalah was due to far more than intellectual interest and pursuit. It stemmed from faith that learning the Torah's secrets could speed up the coming of the end, of the final redemption, and bring understanding to the suffering of the past.[7]

If Rabbi Karo was considered the senior rabbinical authority, Rabbi Moshe Cordovero (or the Ramak, as he became known based on his initials) was viewed as the highest authority in teachings of Kabbalah.[8] At a young age he was one of four to receive rabbinic ordination from the head of the sages of Safed, Rabbi Yaakov Beirav,[9] an ordination

---

6. In addition to Rabbi Shlomo Alkabetz, Rabbi Yosef Karo, and Rabbi Moshe Cordovero, the distinguished students of Kabbalah included Rabbi Elazar Azkari (author of Sefer Chareidim), Rabbi Avraham Galanti (author of Yere'ach Yakar), Rabbi Shmuel Galiko (author of Asis Rimonim – a commentary on Pardes Rimonim), Rabbi Eliyahu De Vidas (author of Reishit Chochmah), and Rabbi Chaim Vital, who arrived in Safed before the highly influential Kabbalistic master the Arizal.

7. Much has been written on the subject of the connection between messianism and Kabbalah. See Moshe Idel, Messianic Mystics (New Haven, CT: Yale University Press, 1998).

8. He directed a yeshiva, gave public lectures, and was even installed as one of the city's rabbinic judges. In the responsa of Rabbi Karo, Avkat Rachel, he shares two responsa from Rabbi Cordovero.

9. Regarding Yaakov Beirav and the renewal of rabbinic ordination, see, for example,

that attests to the high level the Ramak had achieved. He advanced in his studies at a dizzying pace. By the age of twenty-six, he had already completed his first book, *Pardes Rimonim*, an encyclopedic collection of approaches – the first of its kind – which summarized all writings on Kabbalah up to that point. The Ramak's activities had a broad scope. Rabbi Cordovero sought to arrange, organize, and catalog the entire library of the Torah's inner dimension. By the age of forty-eight, he had managed to produce at least nine massive collections dealing primarily with in-depth discussion and learning of the teachings of Kabbalah, the most important of which, I would suggest, was his commentary on the *Zohar*, the fundamental Kabbalistic work.

One of the eulogizers for Rabbi Cordovero was a sharp and brilliant Torah scholar in his mid-thirties named Rabbi Yitzchak Luria, known as the Ari (and later as the Arizal, or the Ari of blessed memory). Only a few months prior he had reached Safed coming from Egypt, accompanied by his wife, mother, and two daughters. While in Egypt, which had been in a period of financial growth at the time, he had been supported by his uncle and was able to delve deeply into Torah study. Later on, he tried his hand in the business of spices, wheat, wine, and likely leather and textiles. He resumed these businesses even after he relocated to Safed.[10] It seems that he wanted to avoid relying on others and chose to preserve a quality of life that he and his family preferred.

The Ari studied the writings of Rabbi Cordovero while he was still in Egypt. Upon arriving in Safed, he immediately joined his study hall. Although he was young, others quickly came to appreciate and praise his level, discussing his legendary grasp of the Torah's secret wisdom. The stories surrounding him, even during his lifetime, were incredible, and included his knowledge of the language of the trees, animals, and birds, and his ability to tell the future.[11] According to legend, on the day of Moshe Cordovero's passing, a pillar of fire descended from the sky and

Natan Shor, *Toldot Safed* (Ra'anana: Am Oved Kinneret Zmora Bitan-Dvir, 1983), 71.

10. Eliav Shochtman, "Mekorot Chadashim min Hageniza l'Peluto Hamishcharit shel Ha'Ari b'Mitzrayim," *Pe'amim* 16 (1983): 56–64.

11. For a source of stories about the Ari, see Tamar Alexander, "Demuto shel Ha'Ari b'Sippur Hasefardi-Yehudi – Sippur Ha'anos v'Halechem' b'toch Me'am Loez," *Pamayim* 26 (1986): 87–107.

radiated during the funeral procession. Only the Ari merited to see the light that emanated from the pillar.[12]

During the funeral of Moshe Cordovero, the Ari delivered a eulogy in the customary style of public Torah speakers: with a question on the weekly Torah portion, Ki Tetzei, which is the sixth portion in the book of Devarim (Deuteronomy). However, his question was not ordinary, nor was it expressed in simple language. It was a question intended to stir those listening. It's no wonder many Torah giants quoted his eulogy in their books throughout the generations.[13]

The question that introduced the Ari's eulogy was seemingly a simple one: a request. It was the kind of question that was designed to settle into one's mind. Still, it wasn't a question that brought relief. It was the type of question you sense in the background but, for the most part, cannot be openly discussed. The Ari had asked: Why did Rabbi Cordovero pass away? In other words, it seemed the Ari was asking why Rabbi Cordovero passed away at such a young age. Why was he taken from the world when he was only forty-eight years old? It's as if the Ari was saying that had he lived longer like Rabbi Karo, he would have been able to give so much more to those who study Torah. At the very least, he had yet to reach the pinnacle of his level, both in learning and in the guidance he offered. When looking at the big picture, it's impossible to ignore potential questions regarding the passing of the most senior Kabbalist.

The Ari then sharpened his question. People die due to their sins, but the residents of Safed were well aware that Rabbi Cordovero was completely righteous according to all measures and free from all sin.

If he didn't sin, why did he pass away?

Though legitimate, the Ari's question was not the kind one asks in front of a large audience at a ceremony eulogizing the deceased. What

---

12. See Mordechai Margoliot Orech, *Encyclopedia L'Toldot Gedolei Yisrael* (Tel Aviv, 1946), s.v. "Moshe Cordovero," 1149–57.

13. See Rabbi Yonatan Eibeshutz, *Ye'arot Devash*, vol. 2, derashah 2 at the end (Warsaw printing, 126, 20); Rabbi Chaim Yosef David Azoulai, *Nachal Kadmonim*, Parashat Ki Tetzei and in derashah 20 (107, section 74) and other places; Rabbi Yeshayahu Halevi Horowitz writes a similar explanation on the same verse with which the Ari opened his talk in Parashat Ki Tetzei ("V'Ehyeh b'Ish…"), quoting *Tikkunei Zohar*. See *Shnei Luchot Habrit, Drush l'Hesped*, 209b quoting the *Tikkunim*.

was the sin or lack of it that caused Rabbi Cordovero to pass away? What inappropriate thing did he do in his lifetime? And if he didn't sin, why did God allow for him to pass away at such a young age? Why was death able to reach a righteous man who merited long life?

From a historical perspective, there's a layer of irony regarding the eulogy. Two years after escorting the esteemed master's funeral procession, the Ari passed away from tuberculosis. This was a two-year period in which he successfully transmitted to his students a new and comprehensive conceptualization that enabled a better understanding of creation and its purpose. This was two years of presenting a new paradigm that quickly developed free of opposition from the majority of Jewish communities.

This new world of ideas, the paradigm delivered by the Ari, did not contradict or replace anything that preceded it, as is customarily believed.[14] Rather, it added further understanding and comprehension. Instead of the traditional form of overturning predecessors, the Ari's revolution offered continuity, revelation, and logical advance. However, his awesome grasp transmitted in such a short period of time leads one to ask the same question the Ari had asked regarding his own teacher. Again, why did the Ari pass away when he was only thirty-eight years old? Since he did not sin, why did he die? Why did a righteous person who contributed so massively to our understanding of the relationship between Creator and creation leave this world, putting an end to the knowledge he imparted?

The Ari was a Torah genius with a natural inclination for deeply abstract, analytical contemplation. It's not possible to think he asked that kind of a question at a somber event attended by a large audience featuring Safed's Kabbalists and the Jewish community without intending to explain it.

Therefore, what did the Ari want to explain? Why did he choose to begin his eulogy with such a question? Based on his answer, it's clear he had no intention of challenging what had happened or of doubting

---

14. See Yehuda Libes, *Kivunim Chadashim b'Cheker Hakabbalah*, the talk he delivered at Machon Ben Tzvi, 28 Nissan, 1991 (with additional materials and notes): https://liebes.huji.ac.il/files/kivunim.pdf.

people's faith. Undoubtedly, he wasn't looking to scrutinize the life of one of the generation's great Torah leaders and hunt for his sins.

It had been only eighty years prior to that funeral procession that the golden age of Jewry in Spain had come to an end. Tens of thousands of Jews were banished from Spain and Portugal or were forced to convert. The country's rulership and its church leaders lost patience in the face of low numbers of conversions. Despite the choice they had presented to Jews to either convert or leave, they engaged in many aggressive and especially violent efforts of force. Jews who still refused to convert faced bitter consequences. Many were raped, murdered, or sold into slavery.

The destruction of Spain's thriving Jewish communities was not only shocking to the Jewish populace, but it also aroused questions. What future is there for the Jewish people? What is the point of suffering? Why does it occur? What relationship is there between man and God? How is God involved in a person's life?

Generally speaking, questions like these do not come under much popular scrutiny during peaceful, unchallenging times. History has shown that times of crisis, challenge, and personal or communal pressures lead to growth and advancement in the realms of Jewish thought and faith beyond what is seen in times of bounty. Such was the case in the time of tremendous Talmudic and intellectual growth that occurred in the wake of the Second Temple's destruction. Likewise it was in the days of the major commentator Rashi (Rabbi Shlomo Yitzchaki of France) and the Baalei Tosafot who followed him; they all achieved tremendous things in the times of the Crusades and during Jewish persecution. The same was true following the banishment from Spain: those expelled in 1492 sought answers and understanding in Jewish paths, including, and some say primarily, in the Torah's inner dimension.

Therefore, the Ari's question was challenging but consistent with the spirit of the times. The thirst for the teachings of Kabbalah was born, in a certain sense, of the need to provide the public with answers to such questions. Of course, involvement in the study of the Torah's inner dimension did not develop as a series of questions and answers. However, when seen in retrospect, it is noteworthy that the concepts seemed to emerge in parallel to the questioning.

The mounting pressure would not provide catharsis – instead, such feelings created future waves of pressure, provoked further by interpretations of the Ari's answer. The Ari's question had been crystal clear: For what spiritual reason did Rabbi Cordovero pass away? If we can understand why a *tzaddik* passed away, perhaps we could also understand the role of the soul in our physical life, the application of reward and punishment, free choice, and a person's mission in life. Despite the clarity of the question, however, on a practical level, the question was less straightforward. The Ari answered the question in his eulogy, but it was still met with debate and interpretation.

While the Ari's answer encouraged broad speculation, it failed to satisfy. It did not seem to get to the heart of the important philosophical debate. The Ari's answer was this: Rabbi Cordovero had not passed away due to any sin. He was completely righteous, a *tzaddik*. However, he had descended into an impure world full of spiritual filth and sin. In such a world, even for a *tzaddik* it's impossible to avoid contact with sin.[15]

Based on the commonly accepted understanding, the Ari did not completely resolve the inquiry. The questions about the connection between reward and punishment, between divine providence and free choice, remained open. However, an additional perspective was added: Even the righteous can be negatively affected in this world. Even they cannot fully protect their righteousness, and thus, they pay the price for interacting with this lowly, impure place.

Seen in a different and deeper perspective, the Ari's response presents an alternative way to understand life, death, and the relationship between them, as well as the meaning of the early passing of Rabbi Cordovero. The Ari's response implies significant parts of his teachings, which would later be revealed by his students. In order to understand the Ari's response, we need to look further into what death is, according to the ideas of Kabbalah and Chassidut, and in general.

DEATH ACCORDING TO JOBS

In general, Jewish thought views death as an important and significant topic, the study of which can provide insight into the meaning of

---

15. See the sources presented in the talk of the Lubavitcher Rebbe concerning the eulogy: *Likkutei Sichot* 24:132n5.

existence and the soul.[16] The circumstances of the end of a person's life reveal something of what his or her overall situation and purpose might have been.[17] In the field of psychology, research views the stages of birth and death as far more than mere beginnings and endings. Increasingly, theorists are pointing to the huge importance of one's own perspective of death. Many feel the impact one's view of death has, and their fear of it can explain a person's conduct and emotions throughout the course of his or her life.[18]

An interesting example of the impact of contemplating the significance between life and death comes from Steve Jobs, who was the famed CEO of Apple who passed away in 2011. Jobs, who was one of the richest men in the world, discussed the meaning of death in context of his business success. In June 2005, about a year after he was diagnosed with pancreatic cancer, Jobs gave a talk to the students of Stanford University entitled "How to Live before You Die." It quickly grew in popularity and went viral, earning the title of the most inspirational speech in history. Death, argued Jobs, is an ingenious way for life to push people to change. According to Jobs, by contemplating death, a person discovers meaning in life. The prospect of death is a motivator to take action.

In Jobs's view, death is a tool for treatment, a source of inspiration. Contemplating mortality can help a person learn a lot about life and can serve as a vehicle for success.

In the third part of his speech, where he addressed death's imprint on his entire life and revealed the disease he was fighting, Jobs shared a quotation that emphasized the powerful impact death had on every day of his life even before he became sick: "If you live each day as if it were your last, someday you'll most certainly be right."

Jobs emphasized that the amount of life we have is limited. And this

---

16. For example, see Rav Joseph B. Soloveitchik, *Out of the Whirlwind: Essays on Mourning, Suffering and the Human Condition* (Jersey City, NJ: Ktav, 2003). For discussion of the topic in greater depth, see Dov Schwartz, "Sofiot v'Sevel 'Min Hase'arah,'" ch. 9 in *Haguto Haphilosophit shel Harav Soloveitchik* (Alon Shvut: Tevunot, 2004), 228.

17. See Talmud, *Eruvin* 13b.

18. For example, see Robert Kastenbaum, *The Psychology of Death* (New York: Springer, 2000).

is our task in life: to fully utilize the time we are granted. The way to get the most out of life is to live each day as if it's your last. Living this way does not mean running after pleasures. Rather, we extract all life has to offer by being involved in the things we love. From his words, we understand that a person who lives life without loving what he or she does is destined to experience frustration, go through inner struggle, and suffer from a lack of joy.

Jobs acknowledges that we can't live in stubborn denial. Death comes to everyone. The old is replaced by the new. And with an awareness of life's brief and temporary nature, understanding that we can build something new today that will be old by tomorrow, he asks Stanford University's graduating class to squeeze out all they can from their allotment of time, and to be "new."

AN ALTERNATE VIEW OF MORTALITY

Jobs's view, which spoke to so many people, was related here in order to emphasize a viewpoint that's similar yet also different: the view presented by Rabbi Shneur Zalman. On the one hand, according to Rabbi Shneur Zalman, contemplation of "the soul exiting the body" can arouse and inspire a person to appreciate things of true value and recognize inner strengths:

> After the soul leaves the body, a person sees his entire existence and being…past, present, and future, without any change…and understands that it was a totally mistaken perspective to see the world as having independent existence. At that point, the shame and embarrassment is tremendous – that all of his thoughts and involvements were with the vanities of the world. That he'd taken action in the world under the delusion of being an independent being – how brazen and disrespectful…[19]

In a different sense, however, Rabbi Shneur Zalman's perspective on life and death provides us an alternative understanding of the Ari's eulogy. According to Rabbi Shneur Zalman, a person needs to live every day as if tomorrow he will be living eternally – not as if tomorrow he will

---

19. *Likkutei Torah*, Emor 33c.

die. According to Rabbi Shneur Zalman, awareness of eternal life – not mortality alone – is what urges a person to seek out life's transcendent and timeless spiritual dimension, instead of the tangible, physical, and temporary, which is ultimately disappointing. A person is not motivated by the thought that he has nothing to lose and therefore should take chances in life that enhance his sense of self. Rather, the proper perspective, according to Rabbi Shneur Zalman, is that a person already has everything: we are alive, complete beings, unafraid and not lacking, bearing an expression of unlimited potential. It is for this reason that we have nothing to fear, worry over, or feel tormented by. Our challenge is to come to this recognition and to act on it.

According to Rabbi Shneur Zalman, a person is faced with a choice in every moment. But it's not a choice to recognize death as being close and therefore a motivator to utilize our time. It's a choice between life and death. A person has to choose between a true life of depth and meaning, which is also eternal life, or to latch onto a life that is shallow and fading, the physicality of life that reveals the temporariness. In the second choice, a person is actually dead in every moment, even while appearing to be alive, like a corpse that moves as if it's living. Choosing to focus on all that physicality has to offer is choosing death. On the other hand, deciding to cling to the spiritual dimension and to inner, deeper meaning is to live forever. Such awareness connects a person to eternal life, granting a full and meaningful life that transcends sin and lack.

Rabbi Shneur Zalman has a source for his approach. In Devarim, the fifth book of the Chumash (Pentateuch), we find a request made of everyone: "See that I have placed before you today life and good, and death and evil…choose life."[20] Rabbi Shneur Zalman asks the following question regarding this verse: "Is there someone who would not choose life?"

> We need to understand: Who wouldn't choose life? Doesn't everyone love life? In fact, a person who loves life naturally despises the opposite – i.e., the pleasures of this world…. However, we need to understand what is meant here by "life."[21]

20. Devarim 30:15–19.
21. *Likkutei Torah*, Va'etchanan 11b.

And the answer, as mentioned, is that there are two types of life: the life of the body, including the natural soul (which animates the body), and the life of the godly soul. The life force of the body is not true life force; rather, it is death "because it fades and disappears..."[22] The life force of the godly soul, however, is true and real and eternal. It is expressed via the attachment found in a person's essence to its godly source. One who makes this his life mission is elevated above the daily grind and social pressures. He doesn't worry about what others might say about him, and he doesn't seek out honor and glory. Instead, he lives a life of freedom and focuses on that which truly matters.[23] In Rabbi Shneur Zalman's own words:

> For, everything in the world comprises physicality and spirituality. Its spirituality and godly life force is life and good. Physicality is death and evil, since it's fleeting and temporary. Therefore, a person sees that every physical thing is nullified and subservient to the spirituality that animates it, and thus, so is it in every person: the body is nullified and subservient to the spiritual and animating force inside.[24]

Rabbi Shneur Zalman's approach to life and death offers a critique of Jobs's approach. While Jobs presents a view that is worthy of praise, it typically fails to hold up in reality. However, his words do give a starting point: do what you love! But this is not a message appropriate for all. Most people are chained to their jobs, their mortgages, the challenges of their life, raising children, or health issues. In each and every moment, they aren't able to create an entirely new life. In these cases, contemplating death might only bring on fear, not openness and empowerment. It threatens to push a person further into worry, into tangible, temporary physicality, and not into growth and elevation.

Let's use an analogy of a mother. She does physically demanding work without monetary compensation, and at the end of the day she asks herself if she feels satisfaction. You'd think her answers would be in the negative. However, it's also most likely that she couldn't possibly imagine allowing herself to quit the job. According to Rabbi Shneur

---

22. *Likkutei Torah*, Tzav 12d.
23. See the Lubavitcher Rebbe, "Eve of Simchat Torah, 1968," *Likkutei Sichot*.
24. *Torah Ohr*, Ki Tisa 85c.

Zalman, even if she can't switch jobs, she still needs to teach herself to love what she does. This is not an instruction to avoid changing jobs when it's possible and necessary to do so. Rather, it's a call to each and every person to connect to the experience of what they're doing and not get lost longing for things they don't have.

An additional issue with Jobs's perspective is that most people do not truly know what would bring them happiness and fulfillment. Currently, their happiness is based on social and popular measures. Seemingly, success determines happiness. Often, happiness is an elusive notion that's tied to pursuing things we don't have. In the eyes of Rabbi Shneur Zalman, a person has to pour meaning and purpose into everything he does, seeking his timeless mission in them. True inner joy, happiness, and everlastingness can only come from overcoming one's ego and sense of independent existence. As long as a person is happy *because of something*, his joy will always be limited and bound. He will always be held back by his thirst to obtain new things, and if he assesses himself accordingly, very few will be the days in which he feels satisfaction.

Rabbi Shneur Zalman's approach is not limited to Stanford graduates. Rather, it also applies to those working for modest wages, people who never change jobs, and those in their fifties, sixties, seventies, and eighties. That which is "old" for each of them can become "new" in each and every moment. The "old" is never old if you discover meaning and content that can be unlimited in how it's utilized, whether through the potential of time, or by dependence on social or financial success.[25]

Now it's possible to understand the Ari's eulogy in a different light. He presented a different way to understand life. Why did Rabbi Moshe Cordovero pass away? Seen superficially, in a physical way, he died because that's how God made the world. Death is part of the structure God uses to remain concealed in His world. Death is a natural part of life. The Angel of Death was created, in the words of the Midrash, already on the first day of creation. However, part of the Creator's plan was that the decree of death would come about in response to man.[26] Therefore,

---

25. See also the Lubavitcher Rebbe, "Sichah of 19 Kislev," *Torat Menachem*, vol. 2, 1951, part 1, 118.
26. See *Midrash Tanchuma*, Vayeishev 4. See the Lubavitcher Rebbe, *Likkutei Sichot* 24:133.

the intellectual explanation for death, from a Jewish perspective, is the sin of the Tree of Knowledge. Adam, the first man, sinned when he was seduced into eating the tree's fruit. It was decreed that his punishment be meted out over everyone: they would die and not be immortal.

However, according to Chassidic explanations of the Ari's words, the death that was decreed upon Rabbi Cordovero was only superficial.[27] On a deeper, more inward level, dealing with the essence of the soul, Rabbi Cordovero had lived a true life, which was wholesome, complete, and blemish free. It was life without sin or lack, because it put to use a connection with the essential depths of the soul.

The Ari wanted to convey the message that a person can live a flawed, lacking existence, one that's akin to death, or, on the other hand, he can reveal his inner wholesomeness and perfection. Clearly, Rabbi Cordovero had chosen the second path, and sharing this revelation can rouse a person from his lowly state to seek growth and elevation. But this response is not a direct answer. It doesn't answer why Rabbi Cordovero died at a young age. Rather, it sets aside the question and instead unearths the higher perspective on life that hides beneath it, which is partly the issue of free choice.

TZIMTZUM AND THE STRUCTURE OF THE SOUL

What is the path to choosing the deeply meaningful timelessness of the soul?[28] How is a person free to shape his life and his relationship to it? The answers to these questions and more are presented in depth throughout the Tanya and are a fundamental part of Rabbi Shneur Zalman's psychological teachings. But before getting to that, there are important questions that still remain unaddressed, which require a deep theoretical approach to answer. To reveal our eternal, non-egocentric dimension, we need to know that there is a transcendent source and that we have the freedom of choice to connect ourselves to this inner, timeless spiritual aspect. From Rabbi Shneur Zalman's vantage point, to prove that overcoming ego and choosing life leads to a revelation of one's

27. The sin of the Tree of Knowledge caused death to be experienced even by the righteous, because they also possess a sense of self and independent existence.
28. On this point see *Maamarim Melukatim*, vol. 3 (1927), 403.

wholesome inner transcendent dimension requires yet another visit back into the past, to the Ari and the concepts with which the Kabbalists and Torah scholars were engaged until his time.

In the two years between Rabbi Cordovero's funeral and the Ari's passing, the Ari's wide-reaching work generally focused on one fundamental question, which is perhaps the most important one in all of Judaism: How can there be a connection between that which is infinite and unlimited and that which is finite and limited, between Creator and creation? How does the connection occur?

The resolution offered by the Ari is mostly technical. One of its main concepts is that of *tzimtzum*, an idea that demands broad, deep discussion. This idea is first and foremost relevant when answering the question of how there can be a connection between man and God. *Tzimtzum* is a core component to consider when examining the logical progression that answers said question.

To describe it in simple terms, *tzimtzum* is a creative process in which the Creator appears to remove Himself from the world, making Himself compressed and compacted, in order to leave space for the world to exist in such a way that it appears to be operating independently. In other words, *tzimtzum* creates the illusion that God is not present. In the beginning, the Creator was found everywhere. However, in order for the world to exist, God needed to contract Himself.

The Ari's theory of *tzimtzum* constitutes a threat to Rabbi Shneur Zalman's view of free choice in life because it could wind up not leading to anyone having choices. *Tzimtzum* could be explained, and in fact is explained, as a kind of disconnect between Creator and the world. To express it simply, if God contracts Himself – meaning, He is no longer present in certain parts of the creation – then we have to conclude that things are conducted, at least to a certain extent, according to the system of laws that God established in His world. In other words, God is responsible for the process of creation. Yet when He left the world, the moment He contracted Himself and left, He became no longer present in it. Instead, He watches over it and controls it.

The Ari's teachings weren't spread by his students until ten years after his passing. In light of the challenging and complex nature of the Ari's work, it stands to reason that the public at large would have a hard time with its concepts.[29] His influence on the masses did not derive directly from his writings, but his crucial contribution to all areas of Kabbalistic teachings indirectly came to influence people and transform certain ideas into household notions.

The Ari's teachings began to have a significant influence over one hundred years after his passing. Developments in the seventeenth century, headlined by the scientific revolution and, in the Jewish world, the pogroms of 1648–1649 in which thousands of eastern European Jews were slaughtered and had suffered, provided fertile ground for discussion. At that point, Jewish communities were ready to absorb the teachings of the Ari.

Many of the Torah scholars in that time were searching for ways to explain how it can be that the Creator contracted Himself, yet one can still continue having passionate Jewish faith. For example, Rabbi Emmanuel Chai Riki, an Italian Torah scholar and Kabbalist, went to Safed and delved deeply into the teachings of the Ari approximately 150 years after his passing. In the introduction to his book *Yosher Levav*, he mentions the time he spent in Syria and the struggles he had with a particular topic that he would be addressing in the book. The first question that engaged him was the relationship between free choice and God's omnipotence regarding what will occur in the world. If He is found in every detail of creation, how is it possible for a person to have free choice? According to Riki's words, after he read the unsatisfying answer of the Rambam and the objections to it, he decided to further explore the topic. He knew that the path to solving it required dealing with the issue of *tzimtzum* – what it is and how it occurs. Riki says that he grappled with the issue of *tzimtzum* his entire life. Finally, he came to a resolution and decided to present it in his book, which relied on Kabbalistic teachings.

Rabbi Emmanuel Chai Riki's book offers a full exploration of the concept of the Creator's unique connection with His creations. Riki sees it as possible for the Creator to both be in the world and contract

---

29. See the discussion and sources in Moshe Eidel, "Echad Meir v'Shnayim mi'Mishpacha – Iyun Mechudash b'Bayat Tefutzata shel Kabbalat Ha'ari v'Hashbata'ot," *Pe'Amim* 44 (summer 1990): 5–30.

from it at times, in certain places, and as He chooses: it's impossible to say that the "lofty and exalted" Creator is found within physical things and lowly, forbidden actions. Riki's commentary on the Ari's concept of *tzimtzum* was born of his passionate faith. His core objective was "to avoid blemishing His honor by thinking His essence is present even in lowly physicality."[30]

Rabbi Yonatan Eibeshutz was born into a celebrated rabbinic family and served as rabbi for several German communities. He lived at the same time as the Baal Shem Tov and was well known for his Torah brilliance and ability for deep analysis. It's apparent that he was also taken with questions akin to those weighing on Emmanuel Chai Riki. In the introduction to *Shem Olam*, we see the author express his surprise at Rabbi Eibeshutz's approach to *tzimtzum*. How could such a tremendous Torah mind accept the notion that the Creator contracted His tremendous light after creating the world? While Rabbi Eibeshutz did broaden the discussion, he was, nevertheless, admitting that after *tzimtzum* the world was like an independent entity. The Creator is no longer dwelling in it.[31]

Not everyone accepted such a straightforward view of *tzimtzum*. Many Torah greats who lived after the Ari objected that such was the Ari's opinion in the first place. In order to broaden the possible interpretations of the Ari's teachings, the teachings of *tzimtzum* enjoyed commentary from widely diverse perspectives and numerous authors, while also serving as a source of disagreement for a long period of time.[32]

In the middle of the eighteenth century, the concept of *tzimtzum* went from being a plausible number of technical details in the process of creation to a significant topic in its own right. The simple approach to *tzimtzum* was free from apparent contradiction with Jewish life, but it put distance between Creator and created. The primary opposing approach held that *tzimtzum* is not literal. According to this view, the

30. Emmanuel Chai Riki, *Yosher Levav* (Cracow, 1890), 30.

31. Primarily, the discussion is whether *tzimtzum* occurred in the Creator's essence, or in the source of light that he emanated, or only in the light. See Rabbi Yonatan Eibeshutz, *Shem Olam* (Pressburg, 1891).

32. For more on the various sides in the argument, see a detailed treatment from the Lubavitcher Rebbe in *Igrot Kodesh* vol. 1, letter 11.

Creator contracted Himself, but only seemingly so. *Tzimtzum* means concealment. The Creator is still in the world, but He's undetected. He moved Himself aside in order to make room for free will by concealing Himself within the world and nature.

THE BAAL SHEM TOV'S CONTRIBUTION

The one who sought to explain the Ari's words and present an opposi-tional view to *tzimtzum* being literal was the founder of the Chassidic movement, the Baal Shem Tov. To a certain extent, the idea that the Baal Shem Tov wanted to promote concerning the relationship between Creator and created was linked to the very establishment of Chassidut.

The Baal Shem Tov was primarily known as a miracle worker and a charismatic righteous man with the ability to heal. However, one of his greatest contributions to Judaism, upon which he based Chassidut, was his explanation and addition of two essential logical layers to the Ari's teachings. His novel fundamental points led to a revolution in under-standing creation, and thus also in understanding life for Torah believers. The Baal Shem Tov recognized the threat created by misunderstandings regarding *tzimtzum*, a threat generated by turning the Creator into something far away.

The first component he emphasized was that the world, in all its details, is being created anew every moment. It's constantly dependent on the Creator for existence.[33] In other words, creation is not an event that occurs at one random point in time or in space. Rather, it's a constant, ongoing process.[34]

Now, if the world is constantly being created, then what a person sees and the existence in which he lives are not static. Everything surrounding a person is part of the dynamic existence that's constantly being recre-ated. Practically speaking, the fact that the Creator continuously brings the world into existence, creating it anew in each and every moment, has

---

33. Concerning the fundamental teaching that there is no other existence in the world besides the Creator, see the commentary of the Baal Shem Tov on the verse in Tehillim (Psalms) 119:89: "Forever, God, your words stands in the heavens." Quoted in Tanya, *Sha'ar Hayichud v'Ha'emunah*, ch. 1.

34. For example, see the Lubavitcher Rebbe's *Torat Menachem*, vol. 15, 1956, part 1, 194.

far-reaching implications for us and generates changes in how we see the world. If the world is in a constant state of creation, then man and his surroundings are also constantly being renewed via ongoing creation. Therefore, everything one does, thinks, or feels is new and original, even if it had already been expressed many times before.[35] Every week, every day, and every moment is unique and unprecedented, even though, seemingly, they are continually repeating.

The second component emphasized by the Baal Shem Tov is that the power of the Creator serves as the inner life force of every creation. The Baal Shem Tov did not accept the view that the Creator created the world yet remains separate from it or only partially connected. He did not believe that the world was formed out of preexisting material, or that it is like a building constructed by a contractor, after which the structure has practically no need for the contractor. The Creator, according to the Baal Shem Tov, is the One Who brings into existence all of the material from which all of the building materials are crafted in the first place.

The new, deep idea suggested by the Baal Shem Tov is not only that creation depends on the Creator in order to exist. It's also that the Creator's power is invested directly into the creations. Creation is sustained by the "speech" of the Creator.[36] Each and every creation has its own word from the Creator Himself which serves as its inner vitality. The perspective of the Creator's presence in everything strengthens the viewpoint that there is nothing random or without meaning. Purposelessness is only an inability to identify an entity's truly existent inner dimension.[37]

The Baal Shem Tov helped develop the understanding that the Ari's concept of *tzimtzum* is not that of an event that occurred at one

---

35. On the subtle difference between completely new versus renewing, according to which creation is renewed but in many aspects not completely new, see the Lubavitcher Rebbe, Shabbat Parashat Naso, 12 Sivan, *Torat Menachem – Hitvaaduyot 5751*, vol. 3, 313ff.

36. See Tanya, *Sha'ar Hayichud v'Ha'emunah*, ch. 1.

37. "*Tzimtzum* not being literal" and the idea of continual ongoing creation are not two separate, interdependent concepts. "*Tzimtzum* not being literal" does not force there to be continual ongoing creation. However, the other approach of "*tzimtzum* is literal" negates there being continual ongoing creation. See *Likkutei Sichot* 8:283.

particular point in time at a particular place. Rather, *tzimtzum* describes a process by which the Creator moved everything toward the universe and enabled it to exist in a form that's seemingly independent. The Baal Shem Tov was successfully able to explain that in order for the Creator to be one, unique, and wholesome, free from any change or addition due to having created the world, there is no choice but to accept that in fact, He's present in every facet of everything.

TZIMTZUM IN RABBI SHNEUR ZALMAN'S TEACHINGS

The Baal Shem Tov's message was refreshing, but not accessible enough for a larger audience to be able to grasp. No book was written by him or in his name that summarized, clarified, and explained the ideas. The challenging work of explaining and refining the idea of the connection between Creator and created was passed on to his student.

Karl Popper, one of the celebrated philosophers of the last century, would customarily turn to his students and ask them to pick up a paper and pencil, feel anticipation and expectation, and then write their immediate observations. The first question asked by the students was what they should expect. With this activity, Popper wanted to demonstrate to them that there is no observation that isn't intentional and directed Observation, study, research, and investigation always require a defined task – an interest, a point of view, a problem, or a theory.

The Ari, and later the Baal Shem Tov, guided, directed, and sharpened the topic of *tzimtzum* and the relationship between the Creator and His creations. Now, the framework was in place and more or less clarified. Into this situation entered Rabbi Shneur Zalman. As did the students of the Ari and the Baal Shem Tov, Rabbi Shneur Zalman chose to invest tremendous energy in the subject and to produce a systematic response to the question at hand: What is the relationship between man and Creator, between the finite and the infinite?

Just how central the concept of *tzimtzum* is in the teachings of Rabbi Shneur Zalman can be discerned from his own testimony. Rabbi Shneur Zalman was pained at not meriting to have learned directly from the Baal Shem Tov, who had passed away before Rabbi Shneur Zalman had turned twenty. Over the years, he expressed that he was consoled over not having merited learning directly from the Baal Shem Tov by hearing the teachings from the Maggid of Mezeritch on the subject of *tzimtzum*:

> Encountering the concept of *tzimtzum* and its commentary, I discovered a reply and solace over having been prevented from seeing and receiving directly from the Baal Shem Tov.[38]

Rabbi Shneur Zalman sought to understand how *tzimtzum*, if not taken literally, was the sole way for there to be choice between the true and the superficial, and how it would create the choice of life. According to his investigation, the infinite light of the Creator is present within His creations, but if a person lacks a sense of the eternal – if the Creator is distant from him – Rabbi Shneur Zalman's approach would not be possible. According to his thinking, a person who overcomes his superficial and egocentric dimension and chooses true life has the power to attain closeness with the Creator and get to know his own sublime potential. One who works on himself can reveal his inner essence, which transcends *tzimtzum* and is beyond the concealment that covers the godly soul.

What Rabbi Shneur Zalman chose to clarify in his debate regarding the Ari's teachings served as the foundation of his personal guidance and of the structure of the soul presented in the Tanya. This is so noticeable, in fact, that extraordinary testimony offered by his son revealed that everything issuing from his father's mouth throughout his life, including general talks and individual guidance, was part of the same drive, issuing from the thinking that *tzimtzum* is not to be taken literally. The result of adopting this view is accepting the Creator's oneness.

> Being that it's well known ... that he clearly said ... my master, father, teacher, and Rebbe of blessed memory, in all of his regular Shabbat talks throughout his life – both in public and in private – [that everything] was all for the purpose of establishing the Creator's simple Oneness ... in everyone's hearts and minds on their level ... well explained and clarified to all those listening and receiving.[39]

---

38. Cited in Glitzenstein, *Sefer Hatoldot*, vol. 1, 101.
39. Introduction of the Mitteler Rebbe to the book *Imrei Binah*. See also *Maamarei Admor Hazaken* (5571/1810), 44.

What in his life experiences pushed him to take on such a fundamental question in Jewish thought? The next chapter highlights the milestones in Rabbi Shneur Zalman's life, and additional details from his life are scattered throughout the book's chapters. Two trends stick out in the description of his life. The first focuses on the sources of inspiration that drove Rabbi Shneur Zalman to clarify fundamental questions in the teachings of the Ari and the Baal Shem Tov. The second looks at his ability to attract a large following, connect them to his teachings, and instill in them a desire to be close to him and his path. In nearly every place he visited and each podium from which he spoke, the outcome was that more and more young people became connected to his message and sought out his guidance and direction.

CHAPTER 2

Milestones

While Rabbi Shneur Zalman's background differed from what might be expected of a Chassidic leader, he certainly presented as a person engaged in deep thought and Jewish contemplation. The fact that he was born on the very same day as the Baal Shem Tov, 18 Elul, forty-seven years later, was seen by his Chassidim as a sign of their direct connection. Rabbi Shneur Zalman even called the founder of Chassidism his grandfather, for he felt like his spiritual grandson.[1] Nonetheless it was only later on in his life that he was seen as a successor to the Baal Shem Tov, for Rabbi Shneur Zalman lacked what is called a celebrated lineage. Already in his youth, however, he was deemed as destined for greatness, and early on, his fame as a tremendous scholar of incredible ability and dedication had spread.

At the age of nine, his parents sent him to Lubavitch to acquire Torah knowledge. Lubavitch, located not far from his birthplace of Liozna, was a small, isolated town surrounded by forest. Its setting attracted students who sought a place to delve deeply into their studies, free from the noise common to larger villages. Rabbi Shneur Zalman's son, DovBer Shneuri, known as the Mitteler Rebbe, returned to that very setting of the center

---

1. *Likkutei Sichot* 4:1136–39.

of the Chassidim in 1813, shortly after his father had passed away.[2] In the two years Rabbi Shneur Zalman spent in Lubavitch, he became a common topic of discussion due to his dedication and commitment to learning and his ability to quickly absorb material, as well as his insistence on strict adherence to a learning schedule and precise times for eating and resting. As often found by professionals in training, his daily schedule earned the young boy tremendous results in his studies and efforts at self-perfection.[3]

By the age of thirteen, he was already attracting recognition that indicated his tremendous learning abilities. He was made a member of the local organization empowered in each community to oversee and direct daily Jewish life. His fame as a scholar of tremendous stature led to his marriage to Shterna, the daughter of Yehuda Leib Segal, at the age of fifteen, which was then customary. Segal was one of the dignitaries of Vitebsk, a neighboring city of Liozna. In an unusual move that speaks volumes of a personality already emerging at a young age, Rabbi Shneur Zalman insisted on investing their wedding gift of five thousand Polish gold coins into a fund to help Jewish families engage in farming. True to the values he absorbed from his father, early on, he appreciated the gains in getting Jews out of the business world and into a life of agricultural work. He urged farmers supported by the fund to make set times for Torah study.[4]

As a youth, his conduct and dedication to Torah study was so dogged and rigid that his father-in-law thought he had lost his mind and pushed his daughter to divorce the young man.[5] Rebbetzin Shterna refused and clung to her husband throughout his life's work.[6]

The young Shneur Zalman built up a reputation for his unique abilities, having recognized early on the scholarly mission he'd been given

2. Shalom DovBer Levine, ed., "Lubavitch in the Second Generation of Chabad," in *Lubavitch: Toldot Ha'ayarah b'Meshech Dorot* (New York: Agudat Chassidei Chabad b'Medinot Chever Ha'amim, 2001), 7.

3. See Glitzenstein, *Sefer Hatoldot*, vol. 1, 73; from Rabbi Yosef Yitzchak, *Sefer Hasichot 5705/1945*, 53

4. See Mindel, *Rabbi Schneur Zalman of Liadi*, 10.

5. Heilman, *Beit Rebbe*, ch. 1.

6. Glitzenstein, *Sefer Hatoldot*, vol. 1, 87.

in life. As he himself attested, from the moment he realized his talents, even before reaching the age of eighteen, he gathered a group of learned students around him, and together, they had regular learning sessions in the Torah's revealed and mystical dimensions.[7] This continued even in later years: preparing exceptional students in both dimensions of Torah was a central tool by which he spread the ideas of Chassidut.

Rabbi Shneur Zalman's self-awareness rendered him fit to guide and direct himself along the proper path. In *Likkutei Dibburim*, a collection gathered by the sixth Rebbe of Chabad, Rabbi Yosef Yitzchak Schneerson, this testament from Rabbi Shneur Zalman is quoted:

> At the age of thirteen, I began spending most of my eighteen hours a day of learning on my own. For a period of three years straight, I spent two-thirds of the week learning Talmud and the Rishonim [early legal codifiers], and one-third on Chumash, *aggadah*, *Zohar*, Midrash, Kabbalah, and *chakirah* [Jewish philosophy]. On Shabbat, one-third on Talmud and codifiers; one-third on Chumash, *aggadah*, and *chakirah*; and one-third on Midrash, *Zohar*, and Kabbalah. One day, a heavy thought came to me: *Will I remain without a teacher and mentor? What will be with me?* I decided that the time had come to travel to a place of Torah, where I might find a mentor.[8]

As he describes, the age of nineteen found him at a crossroads in life. Having gained mastery of Talmudic knowledge and the writings of the early and late codifiers (Rishonim and Achronim), as well as the teachings of musar and Kabbalah, he felt he'd gained all the development he could from the opportunities available in his hometown and resolved to travel elsewhere and develop expertise in something else.

He grappled with two options. The first was to go to Vilna, a center of Torah study under the leadership of Torah master and genius Rabbi Eliyahu, known as the Vilna Gaon. The other center was in Mezeritch, home of the Maggid, Rabbi DovBer, successor of the Baal Shem Tov and leader of the fledgling Chassidic movement. Until this period, young Shneur Zalman didn't identify as a member of the Chassidic movement.

---

7. Rabbi Yosef Yitzchak, *Sefer Hasichot 5705/1945*, 131.
8. From *Likkutei Dibburim*, vol. 4 (1902); in Glitzenstein, *Sefer Hatoldot*, vol. 1, 104.

His father, Rabbi Baruch, a descendant of the Maharal of Prague, didn't identify publicly as a Chassid, but he did visit the Baal Shem Tov several times. As a young groom, he had visited the Baal Shem Tov to ask for blessings to have children. After Shneur Zalman was born, he returned to him a few more times. One of those times was for the purpose of receiving instructions in how to raise the child. A second was to fulfill the young boy's celebratory first haircut at age three. Chassidic lore talks of the Baal Shem Tov's knowing of the boy's incredible qualities via prophetic vision.[9]

Not only was Rabbi Shneur Zalman not outwardly affiliated with the Chassidic movement, but Vilna was closer to his hometown than Mezeritch. The distance from the Liozna-Vitebsk region to Vilna was approximately 250 miles (400 km), while Mezeritch was 435 miles (700 km) away. Moreover, in the 1760s Vilna was a major Jewish city and business hub. It hadn't yet been conquered from the Polish by the Russians, and the tremendous influence it enjoyed from the Vilna Gaon earned it the title of the Jerusalem of Lithuania.

It was widely known that Vilna was a place where you learn how to learn, while in Mezeritch you learn how to pray. For Shneur Zalman, Mezeritch was further both geographically and intellectually, and Vilna, known for its outstanding ability to cultivate scholarship, was more on par with his intellectually inquisitive style. Nevertheless, he chose to make his way to Mezeritch on the grounds that he already knew how to learn, and now wanted to develop expertise in the secrets of prayer.[10] He planned to later make his way from Mezeritch to Vilna and continue his studies there.

> My deep desire for Torah knowledge compelled me to go to Vilna, and for many days I traveled to Vilna in deference to that drive. Along the way, however, I thought about it further: I know how to learn a little, but how to serve God I don't know. So, I decided to first travel to Mezeritch and learn of their path, and from there make my way to Vilna.[11]

---

9. See Glitzenstein, *Sefer Hatoldot*, vol. 1, ch. 3, "Chinucho v'Gidulo."
10. Rabbi Yosef Yitzchak, *Sefer Hasichot 5705/1945*, 132.
11. *Likkutei Dibburim.*

Choosing Mezeritch became a turning point in his life. He traveled there with his brother and joined the younger students. His first impression of the place, however, was disappointing. He discovered that Chassidim invested tremendous amounts of time – too much time, in his view – in prayer and in preparing for prayer. Such a practice took significant time away from Torah study. He quickly decided that Mezeritch wasn't for him. According to one version of the story, he left the city, and the Maggid, DovBer, did not attempt to persuade him to change his mind.

However, soon after leaving, young Shneur Zalman remembered that he had left something in the study hall and resolved to return for it. Upon opening the door, he found the Maggid responding to a legal question. The answer he heard left a deep impression. Apparently, the impact was not just from the broad knowledge of the Maggid, but also the discovery of a complete system of thought heretofore unknown to him in understanding Judaism and arriving at legal rulings. This unexpected encounter with the Maggid brought him to change his mind and give Mezeritch another chance.[12]

Rabbi Shneur Zalman's wife had given him a year and a half for the experience, after which he was to return home. He fully utilized the allotted time. For eighteen months, he sat rooted to the benches of the Maggid's study hall, and then he returned home.[13] He wrote and journaled about his experiences in great depth during that time. In so doing he collected things for himself, primarily recorded customs and stories, as well as notes written by others. For forty years he held onto the journal. Unfortunately, the book, along with his later writings and works on Jewish law, was burned in a large fire that broke out in his home in Liadi in 1810. At the time of the fire, the Rebbe was not present in the city.[14] According to his son's description, the fire was so strong and spread so rapidly that they were unable to save anything from the house.[15]

---

12. According to one version of the story, the Maggid turned to Shneur Zalman at this point and revealed to him that he knew that his successor would one day appear, then leave, and then return. He then told Shneur Zalman all about his life's mission. See *Sefer Hamaamarim* 5708 (1948), 176.

13. Glitzenstein, *Sefer Hatoldot*, 2nd ed. (undistributed), 21.

14. *Hatamim* 2 (1936): 46.

15. *Igrot Kodesh – Alter Rebbe*, addendum 38, 512.

THE ERA FOLLOWING THE MAGGID'S PASSING

Even after returning from Mezeritch, Rabbi Shneur Zalman continued to visit his teacher, the Maggid. Rabbi Shneur Zalman quickly became known as the sharpest among the students, particularly excelling at the intellectual aspect of Chassidut. Considering his young age, his ability to absorb the Maggid's teachings earned him the nickname "the young old man."[16] He had also earned an additional name upon his arrival in Mezeritch, "the Lita'i" or "the Litvak."[17]

From the moment he returned home, Rabbi Shneur Zalman worked at spreading the teachings of the Maggid, which invited arguments from the opponents of Chassidut. However, Rabbi Shneur Zalman followed the approach of revealing the secrets of the Torah without limits, as he had inherited from the Maggid. To a large extent, one of the greatest obstacles was bringing into daily life and living the deep intellectual concepts presented by the teachings of Kabbalah and Chassidut.

In the first place, Shneur Zalman's trip to Mezeritch had met with the opposition of his father-in-law. Many were under the impression that the Chassidic movement was dangerous, a distortion of the accepted Lithuanian approach to learning and likely to cause breaches in Judaism. Rabbi Shneur Zalman's decision to venture to Mezeritch led his father-in-law to cease the couple's financial support and leave them on their own. The young couple remained in Vitebsk for another few years.[18]

In his twenties, Rabbi Shneur Zalman accepted the job of being Liozna's spiritual mentor and teacher, and the couple moved to the city. On 19 Kislev in 1772/5553, the Maggid of Mezeritch passed away after twelve years of leading the Chassidic movement. Leadership was expected to pass on to his son, Rebbe Avraham, who was known as "the Malach," meaning the angel. But the Malach's leadership was to be short-lived, as he soon after passed away at the age of thirty-six. While the Malach had earned tremendous praise and honor, he maintained a preference for a spiritual path of separation and isolation. Leadership of

---

16. Rabbi Yosef Yitzchak, *Sefer Hasichot 5700/1940*, 171.

17. For example, see: Mindel, *Rabbi Schneur Zalman of Liadi*, 52.

18. See the personal notes of Rabbi Yosef Yitzchak that appear in *Sefer Hatoldot*, vol. 1, 81.

the Chassidic movement at such a critical time, however, demanded a different leadership style. The students of the Maggid understood that the increasing strength of the opposition to Chassidut necessitated strong leadership that was capable of standing up to the bans and proc-lamations against the Chassidim. Accordingly, they resolved to set up a leadership group composed of the Maggid's senior students. The group was tasked with helping the Maggid's son lead the Chassidic movement. Rabbi Shneur Zalman, then twenty-seven years old, was selected as the group's general secretary.[19]

During the three years of doing this job, Rabbi Shneur Zalman's time was primarily spent traveling among different cities. He would visit the Maggid's students and review their learning schedules while inspiring and encouraging local community members to join the path of Chassidut. His level of knowledge fascinated a great many people, especially the outstanding scholars he met.

As part of his efforts in Liozna, Rabbi Shneur Zalman established a flourishing educational system in the city. Despite the growing worldly issues at that time, Liozna continued to be considered a city free of financial pressure and lack. Its residents, still under Polish rulership, did brisk trade with communities in the Russian mountains. The following is a description from Rabbi Shneur Zalman about the state of the city at the time of his arrest.

> Liozna is a small city, and things there are less expensive, with plenty of animals and milk. That's why I live there and not in a larger city. And also regarding garments, I have no natural interest in fancy, dis-tinguished garments. This is readily clear from the types of garments that I wear here.[20]

The financial stability of the town enabled Rabbi Shneur Zalman to provide support to its residents by establishing the aforementioned education system. He invited outstanding students to his yeshiva for several months of learning and training. The locals supported the stu-dents during their studies. This system implemented by Rabbi Shneur

---

19. See Glitzenstein, *Sefer Hatoldot*, vol. 2, 302.
20. From the introduction to *Igrot Kodesh – Alter Rebbe*, letter 58, 225.

Zalman brought him publicity as dozens of students quickly flocked to the town for the financial support and then worked on adjusting to his rigorous and deep learning schedule.[21]

Over the years, Rabbi Shneur Zalman's yeshiva grew and expanded. His three brothers helped with its administration, giving regular classes and selecting students. They compiled a detailed weekly report about the state of each student.[22] His brother Rabbi Yehuda Leib was an expert in writing down Rabbi Shneur Zalman's talks and in editing the writings of Chassidut that were in the hands of many Chassidim. The students would show him the writings of Chassidut they had noted down and he would check them to verify they were free of mistakes or copy errors which perverted understanding of the texts.[23]

Students of the yeshiva who had completed their studies, training, and development of expertise would then return home. In their hometowns, the students would spearhead efforts to advance and spread the teachings of Chassidut, serving as Rabbi Shneur Zalman's trusted emissaries. They each created a base for the speedy dissemination of Chabad Chassidut.

IMMIGRATION TO THE LAND OF ISRAEL

In the early years following the Maggid's passing, from 1773 to 1777, Rabbi Menachem Mendel of Vitebsk served as the senior member among the disciples and the leader of the Chassidic movement in Russia and Lithuania. In 1776, in advance of the anniversary of the Maggid's passing on 19 Kislev, Rabbi Shneur Zalman traveled to Rabbi Menachem Mendel, and a gathering of the Chassidic leadership took place. A famous decision was made regarding the transition of Rabbi Menachem Mendel, Rabbi Avraham of Kalisk, and other Chassidim to move to the Holy Land. Rabbi Shneur Zalman asked them to push off the trip for a year. Ultimately, it was decided that the move would occur in the month of Adar of 1776. It was no simple matter to choose to leave behind the

---

21. Glitzenstein, *Sefer Hatoldot*, vol. 2, 303.
22. Regarding the yeshiva's learning schedule, see *Hatamim* 2 (1936): 52. See also Glitzenstein, *Sefer Hatoldot*, vol. 2, 310.
23. See *Igrot Kodesh – Alter Rebbe*, 26, 40; letter 67.

Chassidic communities and community life in Poland in favor of Israel.[24] It also wasn't the first large wave of immigration to the Holy Land. Many individuals and groups had already taken this step. Most of them acted out of ideology, making the move despite knowing the difficulties they would face in making a living in the Holy Land. They did it out of an appreciation for the holiness of the land, and with the faith that their actions could help speed up the coming of the redemption.[25]

In Adar 1777, the Chassidim gathered for the journey and prepared to go. Along the way, approximately three hundred people joined up with the caravan. When it came time for them to depart for good, Rabbi Shneur Zalman was gripped by a strong desire to join them. After a campaign full of deliberation and persuasion, he accepted upon himself to remain in Russia, to provide the leadership the country required. "I fully resolved to not travel to the Holy Land, and for several reasons. The main one: who else would be there for the remaining members of the Chassidic brotherhood, our fellow Jews . . . ," he wrote.[26]

Despite his decision to stay behind, he found himself once again with a strong desire to join and go to the Holy Land many months after the caravan departed. In general, the Holy Land is uniquely featured in his letters. His relationship to the Land of Israel, as can be seen in his writings and discourses, is full of longing and holy trepidation.[27] In the

---

24. Glitzenstein, *Sefer Hatoldot*, vol. 2, 334.

25. Mordechai Wilansky quotes the following in his discussion of Rabbi Menachem Mendel of Vitebsk's 1781 letter: "I, in the Holy Land, am like an emissary from all other countries to the King's palace." See Mordechai Wilansky, *Hayishuv Hachassidi b'Teveria* (Jerusalem, Mosad Bialik, 1988), 19.

26. See *Igrot Kodesh – Alter Rebbe*, letters 116, 118, and 119.

27. As stated, there are many letters that deal with raising monies to help the congregation of Chassidim who moved to the Holy Land. Rabbi Shneur Zalman emphasized giving charity to the Land of Israel, the place through which all prayers travel. "My heart is there always." Tanya, *Iggeret Hakodesh*, siman 4. In one of his discourses, Rabbi Shneur Zalman highlights "the primary purpose and ultimate goal of creation" – moving to the Holy Land, based on the story of Moses: "Moses, who was part of the 'Generation of Knowledge' and on an extremely high and lofty personal level of spirituality, was unable to enter into the Land of Israel. Still, he offered up 515 prayers (the numerical equivalent of the word 'Va'etchanan') to be allowed to go to Israel, because that is the primary purpose and ultimate goal of creation; as mentioned previously . . ." *Likkutei Torah*, Parashat Shelach, 37a.

beginning of Iyar, about three months after the Chassidim left, Rabbi Shneur Zalman went with his family, his brothers, and several students from Liozna in an effort to catch up to the travelers and journey with them. Many of his students, upon hearing of his intentions to go to Israel, dropped what they were doing and went to escort him, while also mourning his departure. Rabbi Shneur Zalman and his family caught up to the large caravan of Rabbi Menachem Mendel of Vitebsk and Rabbi Aharon of Kalisk in the city of Mohilev. But there, the previous instance repeated itself. The caravan's leaders insisted that Rabbi Shneur Zalman remain in Russia so as not to abandon the Chassidim. For a second time, Rabbi Shneur Zalman agreed to turn back. Having left Liozna with the intention of never returning there, he seemingly hesitated about where to go, but the residents of Liozna who were escorting him offered a surprising suggestion. The community offered not only to support those who returned to the town, but also, to support the needs of fifty new students who would come learn in the Liozna yeshiva.

Rabbi Shneur Zalman accepted the offer to return to Liozna, which would transform into a center for the teachings of Chabad Chassidut. Over the next eight years, Rabbi Shneur Zalman increased the number of his students and followers at a dizzying pace. It was also then that he perfected his approach, which would enjoy tremendous publicity.

ACCEPTING CHASSIDIC LEADERSHIP

In the year 1786, Rabbi Shneur Zalman officially accepted the mantle of leadership for the Chassidim in White Russia.[28] Until that time, he had been known as "the Maggid from Liozna," meaning the teacher or mentor of Liozna, while leading a quickly growing congregation of Chassidim. Rabbi Shneur Zalman was practically forced to transform into a leader, accepting it only after it was thrust upon him by the Chassidic leaders departing for Israel, Rabbi Menachem Mendel of Vitebsk and Rabbi Avraham Kalisk.[29]

"Now, even I have no delight from those who travel to me," he wrote about twelve years after being appointed, expressing his preference for

28. See Etkes, *Rabbi Shneur Zalman of Liadi*, 24. *Sefer Hatoldot* mentions that he accepted leadership in the year 1788. See also Glitzenstein, *Sefer Hatoldot*, vol. 2, 456.
29. For example, see *Igrot Kodesh – Alter Rebbe*, addendum 6, 488.

living a life dedicated to deep, contemplative study. "But what can I do? Such are we obligated by Judaism: whoever knows is obligated to teach it to those who don't. Therefore, I am appointing teacher guides in every city; and I, myself, was already appointed teacher of the entire congregation..."[30]

His appointment generated a substantial buzz. Rabbi Shneur Zalman advanced his young, outstanding students in a very noticeable way. As a result, elder Chassidim of Rabbi Menachem Mendel of Vitebsk expressed a preference for bringing a rabbi from Poland to serve as an alternative leader of the Chassidic movement. However, Rabbi Menachem Mendel intervened from his new location in the Holy Land and pressed them to accept Rabbi Shneur Zalman. He wrote the following to them in two letters:

> I am not in favor of those members of the Chassidic brotherhood who seek an alternative rabbinical leader from another place.... Listen, my dear beloved brothers:
> My beloved brothers, what is it that we ask of you other than your love of our beloved, the honorable, cherished, true friend, whose soul is forever bound with mine... and it is him that has been anointed as the righteous leader and guide in your region, so that God's congregation should not be bereft of a shepherd...[31]

THE REGULATIONS

The success of the Chassidim and everything going on in Rabbi Shneur Zalman's court in Liozna can be gleaned from the "Liozna Regulations." This set of rules was implemented in order to reduce the volume of visitors seeking private *yechidut* audience with Rabbi Shneur Zalman for personal guidance and advice. The logic behind the rules was as follows: make a separation between new Chassidim and veterans, and enable the new ones to get their first set of instructions.[32] The first rules to appear

30. *Igrot Kodesh – Alter Rebbe*, letter 58, 219.
31. The first letter is from the year 1787, while the second is from 1788. See the correspondence between Rabbi Menachem Mendel with the Chassidim of Lithuania, and the letters of Rabbi Avraham of Kalisk starting in the year 1784. Also, Glitzenstein, *Sefer Hatoldot*, vol. 2, 452.
32. See in detail Etkes, *Rabbi Shneur Zalman of Liadi*, 72.

in writing, according to what we have today in print, were disseminated in 1793, yet part of them had already been implemented long before then.[33] Limitations on visitors and students to Liozna already began appearing fifteen years prior. They had been only allowed to visit after properly preparing themselves and being dedicated to their studies for a set period of time.[34]

In an effort to ease the restrictions placed upon the visits of Chassidim to Liozna, a larger study hall was built in 1796 that was capable of handling more people. In the regulations, it is stated: "But someone here in the summertime does not have any permission to visit in the following winter. However, if the new, larger study hall is ready, then they will be allowed to come."[35]

Those visitors to Liozna who had means to do so would rent a place to stay in the home of one of the local Chassidim. For younger Chassidim and the poor who came to spend time in his court, Rabbi Shneur Zalman established an organization for guests that raised funds and provided free meals and housing. In order to cover the costs, Rabbi Shneur Zalman would turn to his followers "to provide for the needs of the simple poor – from among the larger Chassidic brotherhood – who traveled to us for months, or even years, and sustain them with bread and food every day of the week."[36]

The rules reveal the tremendous state of the Chassidim, as well as the breadth of Rabbi Shneur Zalman's influence. His efforts were not limited to the realm of spiritual guidance; he even implemented structures for organization and daily life. He guided community activists working on behalf of the good of Jewish congregations. He involved himself in finding avenues for others to make a livelihood, raising monies in support of communal projects and Jewish women in general, along with selecting towns for Chassidim to go to live.[37]

An interesting additional example of his unique style of leadership

---

33. Ibid., p. 73.
34. Glitzenstein, *Sefer Hatoldot*, vol. 2, 383.
35. *Igrot Kodesh – Alter Rebbe*, letter 50 (24 Adar, 1796), 175. See also letter 28, 95.
36. Ibid.
37. Concerning this, see in detail in *Sefer Hatoldot* in several places, 2nd ed., ch. 9, "Askanut Tziborit."

was his attention to the education of women. Rabbi Moshe Feinstein is considered to have been one of the greatest deciders of Jewish law over the last hundred years. His great-grandmother Rachel lived in Liozna. The story told is that she was intellectually gifted and longed to learn Torah. In those days there were no Torah schools for girls, and there was certainly no option of Talmudic studies for them. Her father went to the Maggid of Liozna himself and asked him what to do about his daughter. How could she utilize her abilities?

In a highly irregular move, Rabbi Shneur Zalman agreed that the gifted girl could attend the same class with the best students in Liozna, "while sitting in the back of the classroom."[38] Interestingly, one of the outstanding students in the class was Rabbi Shneur Zalman's grandson, who was destined to continue his work as the third Rebbe of Chabad.

According to research on rhetoric, the ability to organize is one of the most important ingredients in winning over others.[39] In other words, Rabbi Shneur Zalman's leadership ability comprised more than just a talent for giving deep Torah classes and talks; it also revealed talent in organizing the daily lives of the Chassidim around him. On the other hand, despite his involvement in communal life, in every free moment he asked for quiet, so that he could enter into Torah study and deep intellectual contemplation. The never-ending issues facing the Chassidim gave him neither peace nor an opportunity to go into his studies as much as he had wished.

In words he wrote in 1795, he admitted to Chassidim his desire "to quickly escape this land and speedily make way on my journey to rest." Why did he wish to leave it all behind and make his way to his place "of rest"? Because of the burden of the community. "Being that my shoulders are unable to bear the weight of all the people, who together stand around me from morning to night; giving my downtrodden soul no rest for knowledge and awe of the Creator."[40]

We find similar words from Rabbi Shneur Zalman two years prior,

---

38. Moshe Feinstein, *Igrot Moshe*, vol. 8, 5; printed by his son and son-in-law after his passing.
39. Michael S. Kochin, *Five Chapters on Rhetoric: Character, Action, Things, Nothing, and Art* (University Park, PA: Penn State University Press, 2009).
40. *Igrot Kodesh – Alter Rebbe*, letter 43, 142.

in 1793. The reason for those words was the sheer number of people pouring out their bitterness and suffering to him. Their approaching him disturbed him from his intensive intellectual and spiritual pursuits.

> My heart knows just how truly bitter is my poor soul – whose value to me I myself evaluate and also literally perceive with my heart. I literally see the commonly found great confusion in my mind and heart. And how many times I despise living my life like this, and many times resolved in my heart to uproot my presence in this country.[41]

When writing the regulations, Rabbi Shneur Zalman opened with a request "from the depths of my soul": do not violate these rules and do not come to Liozna without permission. From the way in which the request is presented, it's easy to see that the public had a hard time upholding them. As a result, he was left with no choice but to insist on strict enforcement of the regulations.

> I place my request before all of my dear, beloved members of the Chassidic brotherhood in general, and especially those involved in holy efforts – the administrators...to them I repeat my request with all my heart and soul, to adhere to them with a sharp eye and monitor, literally, the saving of my life by preventing God's nation from traveling here. And to warn them against embittering and distressing my soul by traveling here at an inappropriate time...[42]

The regulations conclude with severe penalties for those failing to abide by them:

> Know that anyone who violates any of the aforementioned will not only be judged by Heaven – which I didn't bring about and thus have no ability to forgive – but they will also have assessed a personal financial penalty to be paid to the charities for the Holy Land...

His preference to be a person of intellectual contemplation and live in the world of thought can also be discerned from the fact that even after he had become the Rebbe, he did not take pleasure in offering his

---

41. *Igrot Kodesh – Alter Rebbe*, letter 35, 114.
42. *Igrot Kodesh – Alter Rebbe*, letter 35, 111–18.

Chassidim guidance on material matters.[43] In the mentioned letter, he demonstrates his preference to flee from his lonely position of helping those with life difficulties and those seeking guidance in material affairs. He explains that his role is not to provide such advice, but to offer spiritual instruction. Rabbi Shneur Zalman's clear lack of desire to be involved in the physical affairs of the Chassidim has several reasons. One had to do with the broad scope of tasks already on his shoulders.

"Could you imagine Moses sitting in judgment of cases all day long? What would be of his Torah study?" Rabbi Shneur Zalman would quote from the Talmud.[44] "But to provide advice to everyone in matters that aren't aspects of Torah and fear of Heaven, such a thing was never done."[45]

In his mind, the role of a leader was always and always will be guiding the congregation in spiritual-psychological matters, and not handing out guidance concerning their material affairs. Even the sages of the Mishnah and Talmud, who were knowledgeable of all of the secrets of creation, were never asked for guidance in material affairs.

Come now, let us debate. Remember the days of old; reflect upon the years of other generations. Has such a thing ever been, and where did we see such a custom in any of the writings of the Sages of Israel, either the early or later ones – a common, established practice of asking for advice in material matters in order to know how to conduct oneself in the physical world? Even the greatest early scholars such as the Sages of the Mishnah and Talmud, for whom no secret was withheld and for whom the pathways of the firmament radiated . . . [46]

According to a testimony that was preserved, given Rabbi Shneur Zalman's desire to be involved in his learning despite the breadth of tasks incumbent upon him as leader, even those who lived in Liozna took

43. This is despite the fact that the Chassidim continued to ask him questions about those issues and the Rebbe answered them. See the Lubavitcher Rebbe, Sichah of Shabbat Parashat Shoftim, 1991, footnote 101; see also the summary chapter.
44. Talmud, *Shabbat* 10a.
45. *Igrot Kodesh – Alter Rebbe*, letter 35 (1793).
46. Tanya, *Iggeret Hakodesh*, siman 22.

care to avoid seeing him.[47] Throughout the week, a person had three opportunities to see him. The first was during public Torah readings on Mondays and Thursdays, when the Rebbe would typically be the reader. The second chance was when he said words of Torah at specific times in the room next to where he received his Chassidim. And the third time was on his way to the mikveh.[48]

Not only did the public seek out Rabbi Shneur Zalman to hear advice and guidance, but according to descriptions, his appearance was authoritative and resonated in quite a presence. Based on verbally transmitted reports among the Chassidim, Rabbi Shneur Zalman was very strong, tall, broad shouldered, and had big hands. He also possessed a thick, melodious voice. The Rebbe would pray at great length using the intentions for the prayers arranged by Rabbi Yeshayahu Halevi Horowitz, who was known as the Shelah. He would pray from the prayer book compiled by the Shelah, word by word, with great care in pronunciation and grammar.[49] On Shabbat, a large crowd would gather to hear his words of Torah, which he would deliver with a melodious style.

Rabbi Shneur Zalman's day was scheduled down to the detail, and he took great care to utilize every moment. From a letter his grandson sent to his son, we can understand the huge importance he ascribed to schedule implementation and time utilization. The grandson, the Tzemach Tzedek (future third Rebbe of Chabad), was educated and raised by Rabbi Shneur Zalman after the boy's mother suddenly passed on in the beginning of 1792.[50] The Tzemach Tzedek writes the following:

> When I was three years old, I was instructed by my grandfather – Rabbi Shneur Zalman – to be scheduled and organized. When I was five, he told me that I should invest effort in being scheduled and organized more than in being a Torah scholar, since it was one

---

47. From the testimony of Shimon which appears in Glitzenstein, *Sefer Hatoldot*, vol. 2, 2nd ed., 560.
48. Ibid.
49. See *Torat Menachem*, vol. 1, 1950. See also Rabbi Yosef Yitzchak, *Sefer Hasichot 5704/1944*, 131; and *Sefer Hasichot 5707/1947*, 99.
50. The story of the passing of Devorah Leah appears in chapter 5, "The Battlefield."

of the fundamentals upon which rests all aspects of intellect and character traits.[51]

IMPRISONMENT

In the coming years, the Chassidut that Rabbi Shneur Zalman led would know trying times in the struggle with its opponents, the Mitnagdim. The Chassidim would be subjected to humiliation, public floggings, bans, attacks on their livelihood, slander, destruction of their homes, and ransacking of their property. As mentioned in the introduction, due to the rapid spread of Chassidut in White Russia under his leadership, and as a prominent leader in the movement, Rabbi Shneur Zalman drew the most excitement, more so than any other Chassidic leader.[52] Rabbi Shneur Zalman was arrested twice due to slander and accusations from the Mitnagdim.

In the years leading up to his arrest, Rabbi Shneur Zalman told the Chassidim of the efforts he was investing in trying to calm the unrest.

> If I had the possibility of ending this with them, without a doubt I'd do it, as there is no greater mitzvah than making peace among Jews … but what can we do that we haven't already done? So much effort already invested in this and without results; we've tried and done our part …[53]

In the winter of 1772, when he was twenty-seven years old, Rabbi Shneur Zalman attempted to temper the Vilna Gaon's opposition to Chassidut. He went and knocked on his door along with his mentor and friend Rabbi Menachem Mendel of Vitebsk. They had hope that the meeting would be crucial for the future of Chassidut. The two students of the Maggid of Mezeritch sought to influence the senior rabbinical leaders of the time and help them see that the commonly held negative view of Chassidut was inaccurate. If they had at all noticed problematic behavior among the Chassidim, it was within a small, marginal group that deviated

---

51. Rabbi Yosef Yitzchak, *Kuntress Hatzemach Tzedek u'Tnuat Hahaskalah*, 4n8 (New York: Kehot, 1957).
52. See Etkes, *Rabbi Shneur Zalman of Liadi*, 313.
53. *Igrot Kodesh – Alter Rebbe*, letter 52, 182.

from the true path of Chassidut. Twice the two great Chassidim stood
at the Gaon's door, and twice he evaded them, recoiling from having
any kind of discussion. The following is the testimony of Rabbi Shneur
Zalman:

> Right from the beginning we announced our intentions and traveled
> to the home of the Gaon and Chassid, to debate with him and address
> his complaints about us. ... The door was closed on us twice.[54]

According to one version of the story, when the Gaon heard that the
Chassidim were already on their way to him, he went to a suburb of
Vilna and waited until the two visitors had left the city.[55]

During his experiences dealing with the opposition to Chassidut, the
confidence Rabbi Shneur Zalman had in himself and his path was clear
to all. And while he requested that the Chassidim avoid confrontations,
he never backed off from his path. He continued pursuing opportunities
for face-to-face discussion and debate of the issues in order to prove to
the Mitnagdim and to the Gaon first and foremost that their approach to
the Chassidim was mistaken. Not only did Rabbi Shneur Zalman want
to disprove their erroneous view of the Chassidim, but he also wanted
to demonstrate just how accurate the teachings of Chassidut were
concerning their view of the Creator and His relationship with creation.[56]

But his efforts toward dialogue and reconciliation did not bear fruit.
In 1798, the czar's general prosecutor received a letter that outlined three
fundamental accusations against Rabbi Shneur Zalman. The first was
that he was rebelling against the czar. The second accusation was that he
presided over and promoted a lifestyle of "idleness and debauchery."[57]
The third crime was inciting the youth to steal money from their parents.
The claims attempted to arouse the authorities' suspicion that not
only was Chassidut a new religion, but it even supported subversive
elements – as well as the Ottoman Empire – by sending monies to the
Holy Land, which was then under the rulership of the Turks. The letter

---

54. *Igrot Kodesh – Alter Rebbe*, letter 52, 182.
55. Mordechai Wilansky, *Chassidim v'Mitnagdim – L'Toldot Hamiflos she'Beneihem b'Shanim 1772–1815* (Jerusalem: Mosad Bialik, 1960), vol. 1, 198.
56. See *Igrot Kodesh – Alter Rebbe*, letter 8, 27; letter 45, 156; letter 52, p. 181.
57. Etkes, *Rabbi Shneur Zalman of Liadi*, 248ff.

was sent in relation to the escalation of conflict between the Chassidim and the Mitnagdim.

As noted in the introduction, the event that soured the relationship and led to the slanderous letters against Rabbi Shneur Zalman was the passing of the Gaon. Some of the Gaon's students in Vilna decided to get revenge against the Chassidim for their opposition, so they quickly resolved to renew the bans and blocks they had instituted against the Chassidim and to add new ones. The coming months would witness powerful persecutions against the Chassidim. At the same time, they decided to turn to the ruling authority for help in wiping out the threat presented by the Chassidim.[58]

The slander led to Rabbi Shneur Zalman's arrest and transport for investigation in Petersburg. He answered all their questions in Hebrew, which was then translated into Russian. The extant original handwritten responses provide a rare glimpse into his broad view, or at least the view he wanted to present to the investigators. Among the topics covered, he addressed questions concerning prayer, the value of Torah, the path to achieving purity, and the use of bodily movements in prayer. He explained to the investigators the contribution made by Chassidut to Jewish congregations following the cessation of the phenomenon of purchasing rabbinical positions from local ruling authorities. He described the nature and quality of his Torah talks, which had transformed him into a leader of the movement, and he attempted to firmly implant an appreciation for the importance of the teachings of Kabbalah in Jewish thinking, as an integral aspect.

Rabbi Shneur Zalman continued to explain to the investigators the sources of his livelihood. Business was his primary source, he explained. His wife dealt in types of grain in the market and maintained a tavern that sold spirits and other products. In addition, he received some payment from the community, noting that it was customary among all congregations to support their spiritual teacher or mentor.[59] He also discussed the monies sent via Chassidim to their brothers in the Holy Land in order to support their settlement there.

58. For more details on this, see ibid.
59. Etkes, *Rabbi Shneur Zalman of Liadi*, 268.

The incarceration united the Chassidim and brought out their sense of obligation and commitment to Rabbi Shneur Zalman. They came together to take upon themselves a series of initiatives both physical and spiritual in order bring about the release of their rabbi. A committee was chosen to oversee specific actions. Public fasting on Mondays and Thursdays was instituted, with minimal eating on other days. Psalms were to be recited daily, and monies were raised to support the efforts to speed up the release.[60]

After fifty-three days, on 19 Kislev, which was November 16, 1798, the decision was made to let Rabbi Shneur Zalman go. Along with him, additional Chassidim who had also been arrested were freed. For Rabbi Shneur Zalman, the incarceration represented a turning point on high concerning the effort to spread the teachings of Chassidut. If everything occurring to a person has meaning, then the jailing and release held meaning for the entirety of Chassidut. Until today Chabad Chassidim celebrate that day, 19 Kislev, as a holiday of redemption and Rosh Hashanah for the birth of Chassidut. It was seen as the day on which heavenly permission was granted to continue to spread the teachings of Chassidut as a primary tool for bringing the arrival of Mashiach and the ultimate redemption.

A second jailing occurred less than two years after Rabbi Shneur Zalman was freed from his first incarceration. Along with being put in jail, authorities conducted a search of Rabbi Shneur Zalman's home and confiscated 103 handwritten manuscripts in order to check if they were free of anti-government content.[61] This time, Rabbi Shneur Zalman sat in jail for eighteen days. In the end he was freed, however he was initially refused permission to return to Liozna. He was asked to remain in Petersburg so that the senate could continue with their investigation of the conflict and to rule once and for all on the government's position concerning Chassidut.[62] The requirement to remain in Petersburg distressed the Rebbe and interfered with the flow of Chassidic life in his community. In a letter written in 1801, he appealed to the czar to be allowed to return home. In response, he merited an official document

---

60. See Glitzenstein, *Sefer Hatoldot*, vol. 2, 198–99.
61. *Igrot Kodesh – Alter Rebbe*, 56.
62. Regarding the second arrest and release see Etkes, *Rabbi Shneur Zalman of Liadi*, 307.

granting his request and allowing him to return home, free to move as he pleased throughout White Russia.

DECREASING STRUGGLES

According to Chassidic sources, while Rabbi Shneur Zalman was still in Petersburg, he met with a local member of the aristocracy who invited him to move to one of the towns he owned, Dubovna or Liadi. In exchange, he promised to intercede on the Rabbi's behalf with the czar and help him be able to leave Petersburg. Rabbi Shneur Zalman agreed. In Av, 1801, the Rebbe and many of his Chassidim moved from Liozna to Liadi, and there they reestablished the Chassidic court.[63]

Over the next ten years, the confrontation between the Chassidim and the Mitnagdim faded. The Chassidic movement grew and prospered, but also suffered from internal struggles and disagreements. The victory of the Chassidim over the Mitnagdim in the dealings with the government became overwhelmingly clear three years after Rabbi Shneur Zalman's second arrest. The Chassidim won official permission to continue to act in accordance with their approach. This merit was anchored by a collection of special laws enacted by the government of Alexander I concerning the Jews.[64]

The reduction of hostilities between the two sides also expressed itself in a strengthening of connections between the leaders of the camps. Rabbi Chaim of Volozhin, the greatest and most senior of the Vilna Gaon's students, established a famous yeshiva in Volozhin. In the years following his first arrest, Rabbi Shneur Zalman formed a relationship with him based on mutual respect. The two kept up the connection and cooperation.[65]

LOVE AND DEMANDS

From among the dozens of letters written by Rabbi Shneur Zalman to his Chassidim, even at times when they faced confrontation from outside or from within Chassidut, one can clearly see two different internal

---

63. See Glitzenstein, *Sefer Hatoldot*, vol. 2, 2nd ed., 237.
64. See Wilansky, *Chassidim v'Mitnagdim*, vol. 1, record 28, 295, in Etkes, *Rabbi Shneur Zalman of Liadi*, 309.
65. See *Igrot Kodesh – Alter Rebbe*, letter 104, 391.

processes undertaken by the rabbi. The two nearly complete opposites were given expression by Rabbi Shneur Zalman. On one hand, his letters reveal the tremendous love he had for each and every Chassid and for all Jews in general. This love was also perceptible in his writing style and the expressions he chose to use. His letters would typically open like this: "My beloved ones, my brethren and friends, who are unto me like my soul." He often added to this a blessing using the following format: "And my soul and delight will request them to pour out all their blessing forever..." And he would end the letters with descriptive words such as "From he who loves you with all his heart and soul"[66] or "As is their wish and as is the wish of he who seeks their welfare with all his heart and soul."[67]

At the same time, his relationship with his students features firmness and clear demands upon them to accomplish true spiritual achievements. He demanded that they avoid stagnation, be impervious to financial challenges, and more. He passed on to the Chassidim that spiritual development needs to be their primary focus in life, never marginalized by material challenges. His demanding relationship with the Chassidim wasn't a contradiction to the tremendous love he showered on them. In fact, the strong approach forged the foundation of that very love. Many of his letters, as mentioned, deal with his tremendous demands concerning the collection of charity monies earmarked for causes. It stands to reason that had they not felt that Rabbi Shneur Zalman's demands sprang not from concern for himself but solely directed toward the benefit of the cause on behalf of which they labored, they wouldn't have responded and contributed so much money out of the very little they had.

As a spiritual leader, Rabbi Shneur Zalman lacked the strength to impose sanctions. After all, his acceptance of the mantle of spiritual leadership had been voluntary. However, the lack of ability to formally enforce never held him back from instituting policies that kept people out of his lessons or his court whenever an incident occurred that deviated from acceptable conduct. When it came to the personal spiritual work of his students, anything failing to meet the high standards he

---

66. For example, *Igrot Kodesh – Alter Rebbe*, letter 7.
67. *Igrot Kodesh – Alter Rebbe*, letter 34, 111.

insisted upon created an immediate response. The source of his authority was the power of his approach and the dedication the community felt toward him as their rebbe. For example, in a letter from 1801, Rabbi Shneur Zalman informs the Chassidim to be careful to avoid *kalut rosh* (frivolity) or *letzanut* (mocking behavior). Of anyone who failed to avoid this, it was demanded that "he stay far away from my border and not see my face." Mockery, emphasizes Rabbi Shneur Zalman in one of his letters, prevents one from experiencing true joy, the kind that enlivens "the downtrodden." He so seriously condemned behavior that hurt another's or one's own spiritual efforts that he went on to request that the Chassidim inform him of any inappropriate behavior: "Furthermore, I ask of my brethren and friends, anyone who witnesses another violating the aforementioned, do not bear the disgrace of your colleague – inform me."[68]

THE FINAL JOURNEY

As the summer of 1812 approached, Napoleon began his invasion of Russia with a huge army of seven hundred thousand soldiers. Rabbi Shneur Zalman publicly supported Alexander against Napoleon. He even enlisted emissaries from among his loyal followers to support the Russian army by spying on the movements of the French. The information gathered in these spying missions was transmitted to the Russian commander stationed in Vitebsk.[69]

At first, Rabbi Shneur Zalman didn't want to leave Liadi in order to avoid causing distress to the Jews of White Russia. However, as the French army continued to approach, he was left with no choice. The cruel war, which claimed the lives of many citizens, pushed Rabbi Shneur Zalman, his family, and the families of the Chassidim living in Liadi to flee from the invaders. Napoleon's soldiers left behind them a trail of utter destruction and held a policy to force the locals to support the invaders. Jews, vulnerable and helpless, were the first targets of abuse.[70]

---

68. *Igrot Kodesh – Alter Rebbe*, letter 68, 258.
69. See the discussion in Etkes, *Rabbi Shneur Zalman of Liadi*, ch. 10, "Bein Napoleon l'Alexander."
70. See *Igrot Kodesh – Alter Rebbe*, 237–47.

At the peak of the harsh Russian winter, several months after the beginning of Napoleon's invasion and a bit before the crushing defeat of his army, Rabbi Shneur Zalman passed away in the town of Piyana, an isolated village without Jewish residents. Before his passing, he requested to be buried in the small Jewish cemetery in Haditch in the Poltava Region, about 180 kilometers from Piyana. The grueling 180-kilometer trip from Piyana to Haditch in the month of January in the depths of winter was undertaken by three escorts, one of whom was Rabbi Shneur Zalman's grandson.

The struggle of needing to cope with the opposition of the Mitnagdim to the Chassidim, the inner conflicts, his arrests, and his passing are elaborated throughout coming chapters. The purpose of this chapter was to offer an overview concerning the personage of Rabbi Shneur Zalman and the aspects of his personality, and to point out aspects that influenced his approach.

The next chapter deals with the structure of the soul as outlined by Rabbi Shneur Zalman. Familiarity with the soul's structure enables people to assess their current states and spiritual tendencies and to understand the reasons for their behavior. Rabbi Shneur Zalman uses this discussion to gradually provide his readers the tools they need to handle common spiritual issues.

CHAPTER 3

The Inner Battle

A *yechidut* is different from a meeting with a psychologist, although they both seek to offer personal treatment and life guidance. The patient enters the rebbe's room with an overwhelming sense of awe and respect, with tremendous anticipation and hope, gratitude, and a readiness to hear, absorb, and apply the rebbe's advice. Although the rebbe knows the patient to the greatest possible extent, the *yechidut* time is not used for dialogue. The anticipated advice is given, and the Chassid follows it when he departs to work on himself.

Understandably, training and preparation to become a rebbe is different from that of a psychologist. However, concerning the fundamental aspects that apply to the patient, there are similarities between the task of the psychologist and that of a rebbe. If we were to describe an interaction with Rabbi Shneur Zalman as if he were a psychologist, the first step would involve assessing the state of the person by observing the patient's behavior, categorizing his struggles, and locating their sources. Next, he would outline the appropriate treatments, that is, the ideal state of living. Lastly, the rebbe would point out the path needed in order to obtain the student's proper state of being.

One of the core questions in a contemplative person's mind, and surely, too, for philosophers and psychologists, is what is the nature of mankind? Are people naturally good, or perhaps they are fundamentally bad? Do they tend toward being social or prefer alienation and seclusion, only being forced to join with others by external factors? Moreover, our perception of human nature is directly linked to the environment of the person observed. Times of war, suffering, and savagery generally cause us to see human nature differently than times of tolerance, brotherhood, and responsibility. In this light, what was relevant in Rabbi Shneur Zalman's environment? How did he assess human nature? Did his own life experiences affect which behaviors he noticed and influence the formulation of his approach, or perhaps his treatment was solely based on the understandings presented in the Kabbalah?

A detached review of Rabbi Shneur Zalman's biography indicates a single preeminent relationship which, if explored, would be helpful in dissecting his teachings on the structure of the soul. That was his relationship with Rabbi Avraham of Kalisk. Something that disturbed Rabbi Shneur Zalman was the conduct of Rabbi Avraham and his Chassidim. Rabbi Avraham of Kalisk was a former student of the Vilna Gaon who became enchanted with the ways of Chassidut and transformed into a passionate Chassid of the Maggid of Mezeritch, who was successor to the Baal Shem Tov. Rabbi Avraham married the Maggid's sister and moved, as mentioned earlier, to the Holy Land along with Rabbi Menachem Mendel of Vitebsk during the Chassidic immigration of 1777. When Rabbi Menachem Mendel passed away in 1788, Rabbi Avraham became the leader of the Chassidim in Israel.

In 1786, Rabbi Avraham of Kalisk repeatedly pleaded with Rabbi Shneur Zalman, with support from Rabbi Menachem Mendel of Vitebsk, to accept the leadership of the Chassidim in White Russia.[1] His actions were inspired by a deep appreciation of Rabbi Shneur Zalman's unique personality, abilities, and faithfulness to the path of Chassidut. Rabbi Shneur Zalman insistently refused to accept the mantle of leadership, but Rabbi Avraham continued to push. "Doing work for the public's benefit is of massive value," Rabbi Avraham argued. "It outweighs all counterarguments." As for the inherent difficulties and challenges, the

---

1. See Etkes, *Rabbi Shneur Zalman of Liadi*, 23ff.

work itself draws down on the person tremendous strength to help him overcome the weight of the burden.[2]

The greatness of Rabbi Avraham and his support of Rabbi Shneur Zalman in becoming the leader of Chassidut in White Russia only increased Rabbi Shneur Zalman's frustration with him in the following two significant events. The first and foremost, which Rabbi Shneur Zalman felt caused serious damage to Chassidut, was the conduct of Rabbi Avraham and his Chassidim in the twenty years prior to the spread of the Tanya. Already during the lifetime of the Maggid of Mezeritch, Rabbi Avraham was known as someone who emphasized behavior described as unique and passionate. He surrounded himself with Chassidim who clung to his approach and exhibited irregular behavior. In the year 1770, Rabbi Avraham led a group of thirty-five passionate Chassidim in the region of Shklov. Their activities and style of behavior featured wildness and lack of stability. They mocked Torah sages who were not Chassidim, walked on their hands with their feet in the air, spoke in a joking and depraved manner, and give off appearances of being irreligious. The logic behind their behavior was to bring themselves to a state of humility and self-negation and thereby crush their arrogance and ego.

In one particular event, one of Rabbi Avraham's more intense students entered the city of Shklov and requested permission to give a public Torah talk. He was tested by the community's leaders and found to be overflowing with Torah knowledge. He was invited to speak. For an hour, the Chassid spoke before the congregation, weaving together many ideas and mixing in understandable explanations. When it appeared he was about to wrap up, his talk's focus shifted in a way that shocked the audience. He suddenly began to degrade and scorn the great Torah leaders of the day.[3] The entire city went into turmoil. Members of the community that were exposed to the Chassidim of Rabbi Avraham feared reprisal. The contrast between the Chassid's brilliance on the one

---

2. See the letter sent from Israel: *Igrot Kodesh – Alter Rebbe*, addendum 7 (winter 1786).

3. As shared in *Hatamim* 2 (1936): 62–63.

hand, and his brazenness on the other, pushed the community to spread word of his behavior and call for strong opposition to Chassidism.

In the eyes of this community, Rabbi Avraham's group of Chassidim became representative of the totality of Chassidut. The sages of Shklov wrote a letter to the Vilna Gaon, the respected rabbinical leader. They insisted it would be simple to label the Chassidim they had exposed as being heretics, as had been done in the past with the followers of Shabbtai Tzvi. In the view of Rabbi Shneur Zalman, the Shklov community's complaint had the potential to become highly influential, as the Vilna Gaon formulated his anti-Chassidic view based on their testimonies of Rabbi Avraham's Chassidim. Indeed, the complaints seemingly served as the foundation for fierce opposition to the Chassidic movement. The stain caused by Rabbi Avraham's Chassidim remained on the entire movement and caused tremendous damage that wouldn't fade for a long time.[4] It led the community of Vilna and many others to begin warring against the Chassidim.

The behavior of Rabbi Avraham's Chassidim angered many Chassidic leaders in eastern Europe, including the Maggid of Mezeritch. Due to the tensions, Rabbi Shneur Zalman, the youngest of the Maggid's disciples at the time, got involved in the case. He suggested to his rebbe that Rabbi Avraham should be allowed to come visit the Maggid's court. The Maggid followed his recommendation and received Rabbi Avraham. However, he rebuked him for the path he had chosen for himself and his followers, while expressing reservation about the frivolity, mockery, and brazenness they had embraced.[5]

The second incident Rabbi Shneur Zalman had with Rabbi Avraham occurred years after Rabbi Shneur Zalman accepted leadership. It involved Rabbi Avraham's fight against the printing of the Tanya. The main reason given by Rabbi Avraham for this fight was his opposition to publicizing secrets of Kabbalah. Not only did he share his reservations with the Tanya's author, but his letters against the book were spread among the Chassidim at large, and they included complaints against Rabbi Shneur Zalman.

---

4. See the sources cited in Glitzenstein, *Sefer Hatoldot*, vol. 1, 2nd ed., 253–58; also Etkes, *Rabbi Shneur Zalman of Liadi*, 227.
5. *Igrot Kodesh – Alter Rebbe*, letter 89 (Elul 1805), 344.

Professor Immanuel Etkes, who analyzed the dispute in depth, argues that the method of protest chosen by Rabbi Avraham indicates that there were others who supported him in his attack against Rabbi Shneur Zalman. In the words of Etkes, Rabbi Shneur Zalman, who began his approach "as a junior leader serving under 'the Rebbeim in the Holy Land,' transformed into an innovative, independent, and powerful leader in a just a few years' time." Etkes continues: "It stands to reason that Rabbi Avraham was not pleased with this development, and even opposed it."[6]

The dispute didn't remain only in their exchange of letters. It also pulled in other Chassidic leaders who took sides in the disagreement. Rabbi Levi Yitzchak of Berditchev openly supported Rabbi Shneur Zalman and his activities. In opposition, however, were Rabbi Baruch of Mezhibuz, the Baal Shem Tov's grandson, and Rabbi Asher of Stolin, the son of Rabbi Aharon Hagadol of Karlin, who supported Rabbi Avraham.[7] Rabbi Shneur Zalman's response to the attack against him was measured. At first, he refused to believe that Rabbi Avraham would say such harsh words.[8] Following many accusations, violations, and insults, he penned a long and deep response that expressed his astonishment and dissatisfaction with Rabbi Avraham's leadership.

> Baseless hatred only arises out of gossip and slander. For it is not a person's nature to literally experience baseless hatred toward someone who hasn't caused any harm; not in action or in words.... He has...mistreat[ed] us and delude[d] us into false plots, deviating from that which is already well known to everyone.[9]

He writes further about Rabbi Avraham forgetting the efforts he put in to restore his relationship with the Maggid:

> I'm further shocked how you could forget the fact that I traveled together with you to the holy congregation in Rivne to the Maggid

---

6. Etkes, *Rabbi Shneur Zalman of Liadi*, 330–31.

7. For more details on those involved in the disagreement, see Etkes, *Rabbi Shneur Zalman of Liadi*, 365–78.

8. See *Igrot Kodesh – Alter Rebbe*, 20.

9. *Igrot Kodesh – Alter Rebbe*, letter 89, 333–39.

of Mezeritch, in the summer of 1772. And your fear of our Rebbe
prevented you from entering the city fully, and instead you waited
for him at its entrance. You asked that I and Rabbi Menachem
Mendel appear... and ask him to speak positively on your behalf to
our Rebbe, that he should grant you permission to go to him.... Our
eyes saw and our ears heard sternly with you about your approach
to your leadership of the Chassidim in Russia.... How is it possible
to deny well-known things and switch darkness for light and light
for darkness?[10]

One can assume that Rabbi Shneur Zalman's astonishment is based, at
least in part, on the question of how such problematic behavior could
occur within a senior Chassidic figure. Specifically regarding Rabbi
Avraham's opposition to spreading the Tanya, Rabbi Shneur Zalman
wondered how such a giant in Torah and Chassidut could make pointless
arguments against him that, in his own words, "denied the facts on the
ground."[11]

Chassidim tend to assume Rabbi Avraham's opposition to Rabbi
Shneur Zalman's intellectual approach primarily stemmed from having
a different approach to serving God.[12] In their eyes, Rabbi Avraham was
considered a completely righteous tzaddik, one of the great disciples of
the Maggid of Mezeritch. His interests would seemingly be different
from those of a regular person. However, if we see Rabbi Avraham not
just as a great Chassidic leader, but also as a human being like all men,
then Rabbi Shneur Zalman's words indicate one of two possibilities.
One is that Rabbi Avraham failed to learn enough Chassidut and work
on himself sufficiently. As a result, his character development didn't
advance properly. Alternatively, another possibility is that we don't
properly understand the inner structure of the soul. The popular view of
the psyche's makeup typically separates out behavior and is insufficient
in its treatment of the topic. Meaning, that structure of the psyche
necessitates the presence of an additional force that influences some
people's behaviors. Such people are likely to stumble and lust after their

---

10. Ibid., 344.
11. Ibid.
12. See the discussion on this in Etkes, *Rabbi Shneur Zalman of Liadi*, 383.

desires for pleasure, honor, and glory – even if they are viewed as scholars, rabbinic leaders, and spiritual mentors.

THE TANYA'S INNOVATION: TWO SOULS

It is understood that a person has two drives. There is a drive to accomplish holy things, called the *yetzer hatov*. Then there is a drive to do unholy things, called the *yetzer hara*. How is one supposed to handle that? By learning Torah and fulfilling mitzvot. The more effort one invests in this, the more one improves and uplifts oneself. And the more a person is thereby elevated, level after level, from the level of the *rasha* or wicked person toward the level of the *tzaddik* or completely righteous person, the closer one gets to the Creator, and the more one is freed from unhealthy tendencies.

The Ramchal, Rabbi Chaim Moshe Luzzatto, who died in 1746, a few months after Rabbi Shneur Zalman's birth, outlines this logic in a very clear and convincing way. His book *Mesilat Yesharim* imparts wisdom from the Kabbalah and is categorized as a classic work of ethics and musar. It details the levels one passes through to reach closeness to Creator. There is no dispute about the goal, which is to refine one's character. One obtains this goal by going against one's drives and cravings. The more one is pulled toward the vanities of the world, toward the physical world of bodily pleasures, the more distanced one becomes from the Creator. And the more one turns one's back on physicality, the more one readies oneself for closeness and connection to the Creator.

According to this way of thinking, we can compare the process of self-refinement to developing a muscle. The more one practices, the easier it gets. From this perspective, a person of faith who lives in the world of Torah is like a professional runner who easily covers distances that most people find difficult. The temptation and strength of the inner drive is developed in stages.

There are those who describe the process of repentance and drawing closer to Judaism as traveling from darkness into light, like having a revelation or experiencing spiritual illumination that transports a person from one place to another.

Does the process of self-refinement and personal growth really occur in such ways?

According to several examples, it's not necessarily so. The problem with the aforementioned view is that it does not guarantee success, and it doesn't fit with commonly found behavior. The central innovation of the Tanya is not in the study of measurements, but in the fact that the soul is composed of an inner conflict that will always occur, no matter how much you work on yourself, and therefore the opportunities for victory are found at every moment anew. From time to time we are reminded that even people completely submerged in the world of Torah – famous rabbis, Torah scholars – slip up. They fall prey to the seduction of their evil inclination and cravings, succumbing and becoming unable to withstand a love for honor, or faulty decision making born of self-interest. At the same time, there are those who are far from the world of Torah study and the observance of mitzvot, but in certain moments demonstrate self-sacrifice, powerful faith, and dedication.

For many people, seeing an apparent gap between the values of Torah and behavior that seem to contradict those values is intolerable. This happens when there is an assumption that people who observe ritual have reached illumination and cannot fall. This assumption has always been a major contributor to heretical thoughts and people distancing themselves from a life of Torah and mitzvot. It made common views of religion enter a state of crisis. Religion was seen as a system of ethics that was divorced from the facts on the ground, and this led to tremendous frustration and disappointment.

A person who accepts upon himself the obligations of Jewish law tries to live up to the traditional standards of observance. This is important because when communal leaders, rabbis, and Torah scholars fail to conduct themselves in a way of *tocho k'baro*, meaning the outside matches the inside – when there is a gap between the rituals they are promoting and their personal behavior, when they abstain from character development, or they fail to do it correctly – then the community is likely going to notice the disparity, and it will arouse doubts about faith.

Faith, however, isn't supposed to be dependent only on the behavior of rabbis. A person of faith needs to create a deep and solid inner and independent structure born of a grasp and understanding of the relations between the world and the Creator. But, in actuality, people often do not experience independent thought. They must not take on a system of faith which they pretend is their own but is completely divorced from what they believe in. Otherwise, when other people see inauthentic behavior, it impacts the state of their faith as well.

Rabbi Shneur Zalman formulated a unique outlook. According to his approach, the gap between Jewish obligation and actual behavior is not a result of defect in character. Rather, it is a fundamental part of the framework of the psyche. For this reason, faulty character traits typically are not surprising, nor do they weaken one's faith. According to the discussion in the Tanya, it's clear that an observant person or a repentant one does not thereby immediately enjoy complete happiness and peace of mind. He still has his work to do and battles to win. Based on Rabbi Shneur Zalman's logic, we can conclude that even a person who chose to observe Torah and mitzvot grapples with issues of meaning and purpose and struggles to understand his or her role in the world and the direction of history.

Searching, questioning, investigating, and checking are all significant parts of Jewish thinking, but these processes don't automatically produce a sense of stability. Faith and repentance as described in the Tanya are part of an infinite process full of continuous rising and falling: times of exaltedness and closeness to the Creator and times of sadness and emptiness, times of discovery and feeling, and moments of distance and exhausting challenges to one's spiritual connection. The process of faith as laid out in the Tanya is comprised of self-awareness of one's constant inner battle, the battle between self-serving drives and righteous service of the Creator.

How does Rabbi Shneur Zalman handle the duality he identifies within a person? What creates a lack of accord between the values that a person claims he holds by and wants to adopt and his actual behavior?

Rabbi Shneur Zalman begins by defining the source of a person's lack of stability. His dissection of the framework of the psyche is revolutionary, brilliant, and original. Granted, he indicates sources for his approach,[13] and his ideas are a product of other Jewish works. Nonetheless, Rabbi

---

13. The sources indicated in the Tanya are the works of Rabbi Chaim Vital, *Sha'arei Kedushah*, vol. 1, sha'ar 1–2; *Eitz Chaim*, sha'ar 50, ch. 2; and as written in Yeshayahu: "The souls which I have made" (Yeshayahu [Isaiah] 57:59).

Shneur Zalman expressed them in a unique way and ushered in a revolution in our understanding of the human psyche and its interaction with reality.

Rabbi Shneur Zalman's line of thinking recognizes that few people live a linear life in which they face an issue, overcome it, and continue moving forward. Rather, most people face turmoil and conflict, a state of flux with perpetual advancements and retreats.

Dr. Jekyll and Mr. Hyde, the heroes of the famous story by Scottish author Robert Louis Stevenson, are an extreme example of the battle of the souls. Dr. Jekyll is a scientist and respected doctor who concocts a chemical transformation that enables his hidden, dormant soul powers to emerge. These powers, which are based on total selfishness, reveal a completely different person – Mr. Hyde – who is especially violent. Even without having to rely on empirical scientific knowledge, we can see how a person expresses extreme inner fluctuations between wanting to give to the world and wanting to receive from the world, between freedom and seeking out what's good and true, and intensely felt existential anxieties. Religious experience and faith do not develop along a linear path. They cycle continuously between progress and slipups.

How can we get a clearer picture of these drives at work in a person? Rabbi Shneur Zalman's explanation of the structure of the psyche brings clarity to the elusive concept of the soul. According to his framework, a person is more than just one soul, one body, and powers that are active within the soul. A person is comprised of two souls and one body.[14]

The concept of two souls enables us to explain the inner conflict in a different way. These two souls are engaged in a constant battle: Who will control the person? The wavering and lack of consistency on the soul level is not produced by opposing powers grappling within the person. Rather, it's a war between two different souls.

The difference between the idea of having two drives, the *yetzer hatov* and the *yetzer hara*, or having two full souls, is substantial. Our drives pull us in two different directions – good or the opposite – and their battle provides us some context for appreciating our inner conflict.

---

14. "Every Jew…has two souls…which are two life-forces…" Tanya, *Likkutei Amarim*, ch. 1.

However, the concept of a conflict between two souls is far deeper and gets more to the core. The two souls are two kinds of perspectives and identity, each having its own complete personality that analyzes the world and seeks to live in its own distinct way. The fact that we have two souls battling against each other teaches us that the inner conflict is more than just between doing good or bad; it's a war over a person's being and identity.

The first psychological suggestion from Rabbi Shneur Zalman is that knowing the framework and makeup of the psyche is essential for treating yourself and overcoming suffering, depression, anxiety, and lack of meaning and purpose. Deep and fundamental change requires a working knowledge of the framework of the soul and its potential. Insight into the soul's faculties is like a window that enables a person to get to know himself better and thus to become empowered to overcome the drives he faces.

Awareness of the inner battle between the souls is the first step on the path of dealing with spiritual-emotional struggles because it reveals the source of the issue, the mechanism generating the inner turmoil. Rabbi Shneur Zalman's approach provides a person with tools, advice, and guidelines for undertaking a process of inner change and improvement, yet the choice of whether or not to pursue it remains the person's alone. For this reason, step one is for the student to learn about the structure of the psyche.

In order to heal oneself, Rabbi Shneur Zalman insisted that a person have detailed and thorough knowledge of his own soul potential. He began his book with a description of the soul's structure, consistent with the scientific style of the time. Enlightenment thinkers were fascinated by approaches that emphasized precision, certainty, and clarity, and that were founded on mathematical principles. They aspired to apply these same principles to the other fields of science. Logical thinking, based on fundamentals and axioms from which rational arguments were built, served as cornerstones for understanding the world. The scientific revolution generated by Galileo's ideas emphasized the deconstruction of complex bodies into their most fundamental parts in order to understand how each one works. Only after recognizing all the parts is it possible to appreciate the full object's functioning. This method, applied throughout the scientific community, was also applied to the fields of philosophy and the social sciences.

In Rabbi Shneur Zalman's letters, one can recognize several of the scientific revolution's fundamental principles. His approach was highly technical, precise, clear, and detailed, aimed at teaching without looking to impress or excite. His description of what occurs inside the soul isn't academic, philosophical, or intellectual, as one finds, for example, 150 years later with Rav Joseph Ber Soloveitchik. In his writings, Rav Soloveitchik also discusses the soul's duality and the conflict between what he calls the "man of faith" and "majestic man." However, the duality is primarily theoretical and lacks a technical, detailed description of the framework of the soul.[15] Rabbi Shneur Zalman's depiction of the soul's structure is meant to be applied in practicality. He establishes fundamental principles and factors and then afterward opens up essential layers of logic. The theoretical logic guiding his book could be described as follows: just as it's impossible to fix an electrical appliance unless you know how it works, so, too, it's impossible to treat the soul without knowing the components it possesses.

TIIE FIRST SOUL: THE NATURAL SOUL

Who are the two souls? Their nature is described in a general way throughout the book's chapters. Here, we will provide a first general encounter with the souls.

> One soul originates in the *kelipah* [shell of superficiality that hides the true nature of the world] and Sitra Achra [literally, "other side," referring to forces that resist God's dominion over the world], and it is clothed in a person's blood in order to give life to the body; as it is written, "For the soul of the flesh is in the blood." From [this soul] stems all the undesirable characteristics, deriving from the four evil elements within it...[16] The second soul in Israel is truly "a part of God above."[17]

---

15. See Rav Joseph B. Soloveitchik, *The Lonely Man of Faith*, Tradition 7, no. 2 (summer 1965).
16. Tanya, *Likkutei Amarim*, beginning of ch. 1.
17. Tanya, *Likkutei Amarim*, beginning of ch. 2.

One soul, the first one, is called the *nefesh hativit* (natural soul), since it expresses the natural, basic physical aspect of a person. It's also referred to as the *nefesh habahamit* (animal soul), because of its involvement in fulfilling the body's needs.[18] Additional names for this soul that appear in the Tanya include the *nefesh hachiyunit* (animating soul) and the *nefesh habasar* (fleshly soul), since it gives life to the body. These terms all point to the same thing: the physical aspect. This soul is best characterized as a person's sense of ego and independent existence. At the center of its being is self-awareness, the "I," the urge to exist, the thirst for life, and the desire to fulfill its desires and drives. The natural soul causes a person to sense his own being and experience himself as an independent creation. It can be said that the life force of the body and the natural soul's sense of independence are two sides of the same coin. The perceived life force of the body is expressed in a person's awareness of self, or the "I."

The natural soul is the dominant figure in a person's management and is characterized by attraction to physical things, a desire for honor, achievements, and success. The natural soul's association with a strong sense of "I" consciousness and its interaction with the world is constantly guided with the dynamic of give and take. It pushes a person to interact with his surroundings in harmony with his own personal interests. These relationships are assessed according to how much the person receives or needs to give, regardless of whether the giving or receiving is counted in terms of money or emotional currency. And this is a natural interaction because the person actualizes his natural and primary side: his needs.

Now, the natural soul is not inherently bad. It can show love and giving, but always with some strings attached, some personal interest involved. The love toward one's partner, for example, depends on looks, success, or how much the partner gives. The love also depends on the

---

18. As our sages stated: "Six things were stated concerning man; three indicate that he is like the ministering angels, and three that he is like an animal... eating and drinking like an animal..." (Talmud, *Chagigah* 16a). Rabbi Shneur Zalman Gopin counts the natural soul separately from the animal soul. According to his explanation, the animal soul is not a separate soul, but rather the animalistic behavior of the natural soul. While the natural soul seeks to obtain its needs, the animal soul expresses traits connected to ego and not to natural ambitions. See Gopin, *L'Daat et Hamiddot* (New York: Kehot, 2014), 67–68.

personal state of the one giving it. Generally speaking, a successful person has more love for others; the individual for whom things are going well has more to give. But should that same person begin to slip and lose status, life begins to appear bitter and gloomy, and the person holds back from showing love.

The natural soul's positive expressions can exist for a variety of personal reasons. The soul has an inherent impulse for kindness and compassion. There are people who unhesitatingly give help and support as soon as they are asked.[19] Some have other motivations for giving: a desire for the honor their acts will bring them. Such people do good deeds because they want others to know about it, or to gain notoriety for their abilities, fortune, and graciousness. Some people give in order to get spiritual rewards in this world or the next. Their belief in the system of reward and punishment motivates them to be good people. Some do kindness for the immediate benefits they receive: they can't bear to see the suffering of the needy recipient, so they exert themselves in acts of kindness to stop the suffering. For example, because they can't stand to see the dismal state of the impoverished in their city, they make generous donations to charity organizations that focus on getting people out of poverty. This is ultimately kindness done by the giver in order to obtain personal satisfaction. Doing acts of kindness stimulates pleasure, and thus one's personal interest is the motivation for giving.

While the natural soul is not necessarily bad, generally speaking it does contain negative traits, primarily taking and receiving without giving. The self-centered approach to interactions that motivates the natural soul's actions also obstructs one's relationships with others and with the Creator. From the perspective of the animating soul, a person cannot achieve true understanding of and identification with another person. Why? Because others are always viewed in terms of how they serve personal interests; we reach out to them because it is effective and beneficial. Even one's connection with the Creator, from the animal

---

19. The inherent positive traits associated with the Jewish people – compassion, kindheartedness, and bashfulness – don't necessarily derive from the godly soul. Rather, they are kindnesses that derive from the natural soul. See Tanya, *Likkutei Amarim*, ch. 1. For comparison, see Tanya, *Iggeret Hakodesh*, siman 12.

soul's perspective, is always for a gain and benefit, since the Creator is there to fulfill needs. That's why we turn to Him. The classic example is that of the thief who prays to God for success in his efforts before undertaking his exploits.[20]

Given its egocentric tendencies and the centricity of the "I" within it, the natural soul is the source of negative character traits. And this is so despite the fact, as mentioned, that the soul itself isn't wicked or bad. Rabbi Shneur Zalman identifies four archetypal negative traits that are produced by the natural soul and cause damage to the person and his surroundings. They are mentioned here in brief and then handled in greater detail in chapter 7, which discusses treatment for soul tendencies.

The first category of negative traits is anger and arrogance. These traits express pridefulness and an emphasis on the "I." A person becomes angry because of an inflated sense of self, a feeling that "I" am the only existence in the world. Anything deviating from that worldview is a nuisance and disrupts the person's calm. Anger and arrogance are traits that nourish themselves. They take hold of a person until the anger breeds more anger and the arrogance more arrogance.

The second category of negative traits is the drive for physical pleasures, a craving for delight and enjoyment. When the pleasure is unregulated, it's likely to push a person to unethical behaviors, a lack of self-control, and, ultimately, self-expressions that lead to the abyss in order to obtain the pleasures.

The third category of negative traits outlined by Rabbi Shneur Zalman is mockery and boasting. Alongside them we can include idle chatter and spoken words that are empty of real meaning and significance. Depravity, mockery, and boasting are traits that are empty of value. These traits possess an aspect of harming others, even if unintentionally. Mockery is characterized by not taking responsibility – destructively revealing private confidences. A person who makes fun of others is fickle and

---

20. "The thief calls out to God just before he goes in to steal" (Talmud, *Berachot* 63a). An additional example comes from the explanation of the verse from Devarim (6:5), which is mentioned daily during the Shema prayer: "And you will love the Lord, your God, with all your heart [*b'chol levavcha*]." Rabbi Shneur Zalman points out that instead of *libcha*, meaning "your heart," it reads literally "your hearts," meaning with both of your drives. Tanya, *Likkutei Amarim*, ch. 9.

flighty, behaving like one bereft of essence or abilities.[21] Based on that same principle, a person who boasts is not necessarily arrogant. In general, boasting is simply baseless, as it relies on something that isn't of a person's own making: skills are divinely given to a person to use for good. In contrast, an arrogant person boasts about possessions or status.

Finally, we have the fourth category of negative traits: sadness and depression. Sadness is a trait of contraction. It drags a person down. It puts the person at the center of a self-consciousness worldview, against a backdrop of feeling that things aren't going as planned. People suffering from sadness express a sense of heaviness by putting the "I" at the center of everything.

Sadness, which is a natural tendency in the soul, not only contracts and reduces a person's stature, it also pushes the person to serve and rely only on him- or herself. In a state of depression, it's as if the person denies the Creator's existence, unable to hold firm to the belief that things will work out. Sadness prevents a person from seeing anything outside of the self. As a result, the person fails to properly focus on the task at hand.[22]

Everyone has some amount of all four archetypal negative traits. Rabbi Shneur Zalman has a clear view of what the preferable traits consist of. In Judaism, good and bad traits are not a result of value judgements, but rather of absolute ethics: godly ethics. Anger, for example, in most cases is negative. It's possible to use anger to achieve tangible results, but its source, the egotistical sense of "I" which means that because things are not going as I wanted them to, I have permission to be angry, is negative. Typically, anger is categorized as idolatry, since its hallmark is the distance it generates between a person and the Creator as well as the person's surroundings.[23] A person experiencing anger does not accept that all that happens is directly a result of God's will. Anger therefore testifies to a lack of faith.[24]

---

21. *Sefer Hamaamarim*, Kuntresim, vol. 2, 306a.
22. Rabbi Shneur Zalman draws a parallel between these four negative traits and the four general elements common in nature. See Tanya, *Likkutei Amarim*, ch. 1.
23. In a select few cases where the anger is precise and focused, and part of the process of elevating the spiritual dimension over the physical, it can be a positive. Positive anger is addressed in chapter 7 and in Tanya, *Iggeret Hakodesh*, siman 25.
24. See Tanya, *Iggeret Hakodesh*, siman 25.

The origin of the natural soul, the animal soul, is described as *kelipah*, which means shell, peel, or husk. *Kelipah* is the external wrapping that covers the fruit. Getting to the fruit and revealing its inner dimension requires its removal. There are stronger and weaker forms of *kelipah*, meaning, they cover more or they cover less.[25]

Rabbi Shneur Zalman lists two categories of *kelipah*. One has some space in the coverage that makes it possible to reveal the inner dimension, the spark of the Creator. The good and holy in such *kelipot* can be revealed, even if it takes great effort. For example, a person may strive toward a professional accomplishment motivated by an ambition for fame and fortune, yet even so, the person may thereby experience desirable inner growth. Then there are *kelipot* in which the power of the Creator is very hidden and, thus, the good they possess cannot be revealed.[26] For example, when a person hurts another person without cause, it's not possible to thereby reveal the inner power that sustains each human being. There's no reason for a person to invest soul energy in things associated with such *kelipot*. They're impossible to rectify.

Another commonly used name for the drives associated with the natural soul (such as anger, pride, hunger, frivolity, and melancholy) is Sitra Achra. This technically translates as the "other side," and it is the aspect of the universe that is not holy or part of the sacred inner dimension. In the world of the other side, every expression is aimed at *disconnection* from the Creator and increasing consciousness of independent self. The physical life force of a person – the body and animating spirit – naturally derives from the Sitra Achra, the side that isn't holiness.

It should be pointed out here that according to Rabbi Shneur

---

25. *Zohar* 2:140b.
26. The *kelipot* are divided into four categories. In Chassidic writings, each of the *kelipot* characterizes an unhealthy spiritual state. For example, "a stormwind" represents unregulated, disorganized actions produced by pressures and excitement. Such behavior causes a person to lose track of the core point, causing things to deteriorate. See the Tzemach Tzedek's *Ohr Hatorah*, Bamidbar (Numbers), vol. 1, Hosafot-Parashat Naso, "Ko Tivarcho," 93. In contrast to the first three impure *kelipot* (*shalosh kelipot hatemei'ot*), *kelipat nogah* can also be transformed into good. One can free up the good it contains and raise it above the bad. The meaning of *nogah* is that the *kelipah* is not hermetically sealed, a small amount of light can radiate and shine from it. See Tanya, *Likkutei Amarim*, ch. 1, p. 6.

Zalman's view, things relating to the natural soul such as Sitra Achra or impurity, concepts seen in Kabbalah as indicative of darkness and wickedness, become in his writings natural descriptions of the soul's tendencies, descriptions that are not aloof and distinct from life, but are easy to grasp and even identify with.

THE SECOND SOUL: THE GODLY SOUL

Intellect can lead a person to the Creator. One can contemplate the order found in nature and wonder who oversees it all. Contemplation on the order found in the universe and the conduct of the creations typically leads to the independent conclusion that there is a Creator Who looks out for His creations. There's Someone in charge. But Rabbi Shneur Zalman doesn't suffice with this kind of intellect. For him, there is something deep and fundamental in a person, and it isn't just intellect or contemplating the external, visible dimension of the world. Rather, a person possesses a literal portion of the Creator.

The second soul is called the *nefesh elokit* (godly soul), because it's directly derived from the Creator.[27] The Creator embedded part of Himself into a person in the form of the godly soul, not as He created everything else in the creation – in a general, encompassing way – but rather as deep and significant inner potential. If the animal soul is characterized by egocentrism in which the person's self is at the center of everything, the approach of the godly soul is the opposite. It's characterized by giving, lack of grandiose self-importance, and a drive to return to its source: a craving for the Creator.[28] From the beginning, it has no interest in physical pleasures. They only interfere with contact between the soul and the spiritual realm. It has no desire for them. Instead, it wants connection with the Creator. The most central feature of the second soul is that the person does not believe the self to be the

---

27. Even though the animal soul's source is also godly. According to the Baal Shem Tov's approach, it's impossible for there to be anything in creation that isn't from God, including a person's body. However, the animal soul descends various levels on its way into this physical world, and thus its distance from the Creator is seemingly much greater.

28. Tanya, *Likkutei Amarim*, ch. 18–19.

core and center of all of creation. Everything does not orbit around the individual, who does not subscribe solely to a give-and-take relationship with the world.

Just as the natural soul generally produces negative traits, the godly soul is like its mirror opposite, producing positive traits. In place of anger and arrogance, the second soul arouses a thirst for the Creator. It's full of warmth and appeal. Instead of generating arrogance and anger, it inspires a desire to recognize how God is the source of everything. In place of cravings for pleasure, it seeks nothingness, spirituality, and transcendence. Replacing the mockery and boasting are expressions of self-nullification (focus on one's mission rather than on one's self), lack of self-importance, and a desire for inclusivity. Instead of sadness and laziness, one finds a soul that inspires joy and enthusiasm.

This is not to say the animal soul is limited to only expressing itself as drives and lusts for pleasure. It can also be refined, intellectual, and attain its own spiritual achievements. However, even with such experiences of ascension, it remains rooted in self-absorption. It testifies to man's being a biological creature of a level not so distant from that of an animal. The person driven by the *nefesh habahamit* is above the animal kingdom but still within its grasp. In contrast, the godly soul represents the highest level within a person, in which the mortal has some similarity to the Creator. Yet the godly soul is called the second soul because it is the second to appear within a person.[29] It isn't naturally inherent to us, and we do not immediately identify ourselves with it.[30]

RELATIONSHIP BETWEEN THE SOULS

How can the relationship between the two souls be best described?

There is the animal soul of fluctuation, stress, struggle, worries, and urges, opposed by the longing to soar, give, and be refined and clean.

---

29. There's an additional reason the godly soul is called the "second soul": it descended into this world for the sake of refining the natural soul and not for its own benefit. See *Torat Menachem*, vol. 45, 1966, part 1, 311.

30. The godly soul only starts to reveal itself in a person at the age of bar mitzvah. Therefore, it's the second soul. See *Zohar* 1:179; and the Rebbe Rashab, *Sefer Hamaamarim 5670* (1910), 63.

These are the difficult and common expressions of the souls in a person's life, expressions that most people try to hide from others. Furthermore, they appear even more challenging to a person who feels obligated to be exalted, holy, and refined. It's so challenging, in fact, that Rabbi Shneur Zalman chose to describe their relationship as a battlefield.[31]

In one of his discourses, Rabbi Shneur Zalman describes the battle-field scene between two animal souls in the arena.[32] The two are cast upon the battlefield in order for one to vanquish the other. God watches over their battles with pleasure. For Him, their warring is a form of delight.[33] What is it, exactly, that gives Him enjoyment? It is the efforts of the combatants to endure and conquer, for one to overcome the other. It's natural to assume that the more the war is invigorated, dynamic, unexpected, and, most importantly, causes identification with the side of one of the combatants, the greater the pleasure.

When the balance between the combatants in the arena is off, the battle is uninteresting. Everyone knows that a big, strong person can triumph over a weaker one. Therefore, God steps in, holding the leg of one combatant to give a chance for the weaker one to win. Sometimes, despite a significant power imbalance between the combatants in the ring, the outcome is unexpected. One overcomes the other in a tremendous display of strength and determination, showing resourcefulness and employing a strategy that upsets the odds.

In the teachings of Rabbi Shneur Zalman, the combat is obviously not literal, but only an analogy. The picture of a battle that he describes in detail is reminiscent of many aspects of the gladiator fights waged

---

31. See *Maamarei Admor Hazaken* (5566/1805), vol. 1, 335ff. Even earlier sources discuss their interaction – see Talmud, *Baba Batra* 75a; *Vayikra Rabbah* 13:3; *Yalkut Shimoni*, Iyov 247, 826.

32. The outcome is for the future, but already the battle is being waged in the present. But if the war primarily occurs in this world, why are the battles described as those which will occur in the future? According to the Lubavitcher Rebbe, the power to be victorious in the war derives from the essential level within the person, which will be revealed in the future. See "Shabbat Parashat Shemini," *Torat Menachem*, vol. 5, 1952, part 2, 167.

33. The concept of a king's inner delight is discussed many times in various works of Chassidut. See Tanya, *Kuntress Acharon*, 6; *Likkutei Torah*, Beshalach 1–2; Shir Hashirim 12–13. Also, see *Emek Hamelech*, sha'ar 1. The word *sha'ashu'im* is found in several places in Tanach – for example, Tehillim 119:92.

in ancient Rome. The movie *Gladiator* can help with the visualization. Maximus Meridious, the captured Roman general, refuses to fight. He lacks motivation now that his wife and son have been murdered. But when the time comes, he has no choice. He's thrown into the fight, bound by chains to another fighter who had treated his wounds and saved his life. Refusal to fight would cost both their lives, his and the slave's, and deprive him of an opportunity for revenge. In order to succeed, Maximus not only has to win, but he has to also win the hearts of the audience and gain their delight. He wasn't expected to win. An insurmountable number of obstacles were placed before him. But with the help of extraordinary prowess born of his skill and experience, he successfully reaches Rome and his victory, winning over the crowd and causing the caesar, Marcus Aurelius, to come down to him and acknowledge him. Ultimately, it was his prowess that saved his life and brought him back his freedom.

In Jewish literature, the penultimate battle before God, called in Aramaic *kynegia*, is that fought between the Leviathan (a mystical giant sea creature) and the Shor Habor (a giant wild ox).[34] Who are the animals, the dueling life forces according to Rabbi Shneur Zalman's teachings, fighting to control the human being? Using this analogy, the two souls are those who wage war against each other inside a person over the right to direct the person's conduct. The soul that does not place man at the center of attention – that is, that caters to the opposite of our natural awareness of self, and instead considers focus on God as its direct source – is embodied in the Leviathan.[35] The natural soul – the source of our animalistic tendencies, depression, anger, pursuit of lusts, and mockery, which derives from the Sitra Achra (the "other side") – is the Shor Habor.

---

34. Talmud, *Baba Batra* 74b.
35. The Leviathan expresses connectivity. On the statement "This Leviathan that You formed in order to play with" (*Avodah Zarah* 3b), see Rabbi Shneur Zalman's discussion in *Likkutei Torah*, Shir Hashirim 1d. The word *Leviathan* is related to *"yilaveh ishi"* (Vayetzei 29:34; in Rabbi Shneur Zalman's *Torah Ohr*, Toldot 17d; Vayetzei 23b; and other sources), which indicates connection and being escorted. The general point is that the creatures of the sea exist in a state of constant presence within their source. The sea, in the teachings of Kabbalah, is called "the hidden world," while dry land is called "the revealed world."

Describing this dynamic complex of battles helps us understand why we experience two approaches. Why do we rise and fall, retract and give, smile and frown, or become sanctified or animalistic? The answer: our inner fluctuations are part of the inner fighting. Combat is given to us in order to be victorious. The spiritual challenges a person experiences throughout his life are, in part, due to the duality in the soul's structure.

In the description of the *kynegia*, God is responsible for the setup and the relationship between the souls. Generally speaking, God is also responsible for each side's prospects of victory or defeat. He decides who will be favored by Him, the egocentric side or the side trained in giving and holiness. Typically, the animal soul is stronger and has better prospects for winning. Gladiators can only win by implementing tremendous bravery. Rabbi Shneur Zalman supplies his readers with historical examples. When David was king, God altered the relationship between the souls so that holiness would vanquish the Sitra Achra. The same occurred in the time of his son, King Solomon. However, for large chunks of the history of the Jewish people, people's wild energies and natural dimension overpowered holiness, both in the world and within each person.[36]

A tangible demonstration of the conflict between the souls can be found during the time of prayer. Rabbi Shneur Zalman emphasizes that according to the *Zohar*, prayer is a time of war.[37] During prayer, the one praying is likely to whip up a raging battle between the souls within. For the most part, during prayer a person needs to concentrate and remove the mind from extraneous things while attempting to focus on things related to the Creator's unity and oneness. The person seeks out a quiet place in which to talk to God. Prayer is an attempt to connect with the Creator,[38] which is why the word for prayer, *tefillah*, also means a bond and connection.[39]

---

36. *Maamarei Admor Hazaken* (5566/1805), vol. 1, 335.

37. "Prayer is a time of war," *Zohar* 1:240b; 3:243a. Also quoted in *Likkutei Torah*, Parashat Ki Tetzei.

38. Rabbi Shneur Zalman, *Torah Ohr*, Terumah 80a. It should be mentioned that the purpose of the "war" during prayer is to arouse and inspire the animal soul in a process known as "the sword of peace." See *Padeh b'Shalom* 1979, 9 Kislev, ch. 6, and footnote 42.

39. Like a person "who repairs [*hatofel*] an earthenware vessel" – i.e., binds it together (*Keilim* 3:5).

Right there in the middle of prayer, which is supposed to be the experiential pinnacle of connection between the worshipper and the Creator, all kinds of disruptive things attack the person and his peace of mind. An assortment of worrisome thoughts and ideas that had sunk into the back of his consciousness suddenly pops into his mind right when he tries to concentrate on his prayers.

The message stressed by Rabbi Shneur Zalman is that as much as a person seeks to be sanctified, elevated, victorious, and a part of what shines and radiates in life, so does the opposing side rise in response and make it so much harder. The pull of the physical world draws the person back into confusion and negative thinking. Once one fighter exerts itself, the other tries to respond with at least as much force.[40]

Because of the inner construction of a person, which is complete with two full souls, all efforts to rise in aspects of ethics and faith are met with a wave of challenges and battles, difficulties, suffering, isolation, and indecision. This, emphasized Rabbi Shneur Zalman, is true for the individual as well as the congregation attempting to collectively take on the challenges facing them. He wrote this to the members of the congregation in Kapust, a town in White Russia, where the community suffered from those who opposed Chassidut:

> My dear brothers and friends, strengthen yourselves greatly... that one's prayers be reinforcing, as a person grappling with his enemy needs to raise up all his strength, power, and might.... And as we find in warfare: all the soldiers need to gather in one place, and strengthen each other together, and not be dispersed and isolated. The same applies to prayer – at least ten, all as one...and let each one help his brother.[41]

Against this backdrop, Rabbi Avraham's opposition to Rabbi Shneur Zalman comes into focus. The effort to transcend and sanctify can be opposed by the threat of slipping, all due to the battle between the souls.

---

40. "When one is gaining the upper hand, the other likewise exerts itself with all the resources of its strength." Tanya, *Likkutei Amarim*, ch 28.

41. *Igrot Kodesh – Alter Rebbe*, letter 71, 263. The letter is believed to have been written before 1801.

WHY FIGHT?

For most people, the war waged between the souls is never ending. It's a constant battle with almost no breaks. Rabbi Shneur Zalman offers an additional depiction of the war: a battle between two kings where each does his utmost to rule the body and direct it according to his will. The body, seemingly neutral, is described in the Tanya as a small city with each soul seeking victory and the opportunity to have the body fulfill its wants.

> For the body is called a "small city." [The two souls, in relation to the body,] are like two kings who wage war over a city, which each wants to capture and rule. That is to say, [each king wants to] direct its inhabitants according to his will, so that they obey him in all that he decrees upon them. Similarly, the two – the godly soul and the animating animal soul, which originates from *kelipah* – wage war against each other over the body and all its organs...[42]

Describing the two warring souls as being God's gladiators isn't very flattering to people. You could even say, treading very lightly, that it fails to present the relationship between God and man in a complimentary manner. The description raises two fundamental questions. The first is, what's the point of the battle? To express it differently, of what gain is never-ending combat? Why does life need to be a series of fights, lacking peace and calm? Why can't life be not like a battlefield, but rather a place of harmony, relaxation, and equanimity, where one can grow without slipups and losses?

The second question is no less controversial. What could be funny or delightful about dilemmas, soul upheavals, and the inability to rise, climb, and elevate?

The answer to the first question is this: The point of battle is the accomplishments one can obtain in war. On the one hand, war not only leads to separation and division, but is likely to damage a person's ethical and refined core. War generally awakens people's darkest drives and loosens their reins. Anyone attracted to combat is likely to experience

---

42. Tanya, *Likkutei Amarim*, ch. 9.

a loss of morals and values. However, in the eyes of Rabbi Shneur Zalman, battle also develops the two fighters. Rabbi Shneur Zalman cites a battle found in the Tanach. Yaakov fights with Esav's angel. As part of the wrestling, they grab each other and try to subdue the other, which causes them to kick up dust.[43] The fight forces the combatants to figure out their opponent and respond to him, compelling them to improve and advance. Should one of them approach the battle in a state of laziness and heaviness, he'll be easily defeated, even if he's stronger. At the same time, if he shows up full of inner confidence and positivity, his chances of winning are far greater, even if he's the weaker of the two.[44] Confidence, decisiveness, determination, and inner faith are more than just critical ingredients in any fight; they are also core principles that can be learned and improved from one fight to the next.

According to Rabbi Shneur Zalman, the dust they kicked up represents elevation of the lowest elements. Dust, generally speaking, stays on the ground. But something happens during the fight. A change occurs. The confrontation sharpens their powers and creates the ability to move and advance from lower to higher levels. As a person begins to rise, he also takes with him his immediate surroundings. This rhythm can be compared to the process of dialectical thinking: from the conflict, development is born. One force challenges the other, and together, as they grapple, they form new synthesis and advancement.

As expressed in Chassidut, the godly soul has no need for rectification and purification. As a piece of the Creator, it is already whole. But it descends down into this lowly world in order to refine the body and the animalistic natural soul. During its battle with the natural soul, it also elevates a person's animalistic side. In return, the godly soul itself becomes elevated to a higher level than the one from which it originally descended. Regarding this, Rabbi Shneur Zalman repeatedly employs the concept of "the advantage of light" seen specifically when it "comes from out of the darkness."[45] One way of understanding this is that even

---

43. See "Vayabek Ish Imo," *Maamarei Admor Hazaken* (5567/1806), vol. 1, 159; "19 Kislev, 5721," *Torat Menachem*, vol. 29, 1961, part 1, 242.
44. See Tanya, *Likkutei Amarim*, ch. 28.
45. For example, see Tanya, *Likkutei Amarim*, ch. 12 and 13, and in many other places.

a small amount of light suffices to push away darkness. In other words, every expression of the godly soul has the power to illuminate dark parts of this lowly world.

Now it's clear why a person is given inner battles for the purpose of attaining elevation. Battles between the souls lead to growth and revelation of one's hidden potential. When a person succeeds in revealing something after investing great effort, it becomes a source of great pleasure, as well as internally engraved and full of importance. For that reason, and for the invested effort and the resulting elevation, a person is embroiled in combat all throughout life, says Rabbi Shneur Zalman.

What still remains unclear is God's delight from the battles. Delight – that is, the enjoyment derived from playing a game – is not a form of mockery. Rather, it's an expression of joy and pleasure. God can have great joy from our victories in these battles. Why? Because He'll be focused on the fact that the people He made have beaten and overcome the sense of independent existence that permeates reality and makes it seem that there is no God. It's not the battles that give the Creator joy and pleasure, but the victories. The ultimate purpose of war is for the good to beat the bad and for holiness to overcome the profane and the superficial. In Rabbi Shneur Zalman's words, the purpose is "in order to punish the wicked and give reward to the righteous."[46] People who win the daily battles in life are elevated. The elevation experience is what arouses them to feel joy. Delight and pleasure are not from battling, but rather from the good side's victory. The conflicts express a point of connection with the Creator, not a distance from Him.

The difference between the animal soul and the godly soul in Rabbi Shneur Zalman's teachings isn't one of instinctual, on-the-spot emotional reactions versus intellectual reasoning. According to his own testimony, the issue of the soul and the nature of its relationship with the body is a topic that occupied him since his youth. The concept of the battle between the souls came to him in stages as he engaged in intensive study and obtained complete proficiency in all areas of Torah. When he reached the conclusion that fully addressed the nature of the battle, he said he felt he had "discovered the path of true life":

---

46. Tanya, *Likkutei Amarim*, ch. 22.

As I researched and understood there had to be an animal soul, God helped me find the paths by which to recognize it and to differentiate whether the drive toward any given thing from among all the world's permissible things that a person craves and wants originates from the godly soul or the animal soul.[47]

This true path in life, and the description of our inner world as a battle-field, even without a more detailed picture of the combatants, already has a lot of meaning and significance for our lives. These are things that find expression in Rabbi Shneur Zalman's psychological approach and the personal growth work he recommends to his readers which help people win their battles and overcome a lack of spiritual balance.

One insight is that there is *no victory without exertion*. The path to overcoming the drives of the animal soul, depression, anger, lust, and laziness on the way to revealing the godly soul demands work, prepara-tion, and training. It's impossible to win if you're not an expert fighter. The battles occurring in the soul are part of the difficult war that requires God's assistance as well as the efforts of the warriors.[48] For example, sadness is a natural trait. On the other hand, joy comes as a result of one's efforts at self-help. Take a person who is just not naturally happy. The only way to happiness is to put in the effort to adjust these faulty views on life and reality, and to prepare oneself for battle. It's more natural to wake up in the morning and be subjugated to your natural traits, to sadness and nerves. If you notice a happy person, recognize that this is someone who has put in effort and contemplation to transform the natural state of depression to one of joy.

A second insight is that *we must fight*. It's not optional, it's essential. We have to go fight on the front lines, join the battles, and do our work. This is because within the framework of the inner war between the godly and natural souls, it's impossible to have any neutral territory. You can't overcome your depression without supporting an alternative to replace it. Emptiness is untenable within the soul. Immediately, a drive, desire, emotional block, or lust comes along and fills the gap left by the

---

47. See Rabbi Yosef Yitzchak, *Sefer Hasichot 5705/1945*, p. 127. See Glitzenstein, *Sefer Hatoldot*, vol. 1, 69.

48. For more on this, see *Torat Menachem*, vol. 5, 1952, part 2, 169.

tendency you just outed. A person cannot overcome challenges without some focus on obligation and action. If one does not place effort into developing the *nefesh elokit*, one will avoid participation in the war by caving and surrendering to animalistic drives.

An additional insight to bear in mind is that *victory is always temporary*. Every day, there are victories in battles, but not in the war. In the soul's battle for control – the animal soul in one direction and the godly soul in the other – there are no heroic victories in which one soul is defeated. Victory is always short-lived. A person without emotional fluctuations, without an inner conflict, is generally a person who has ceased growing and fulfilling life's purpose.

This tells us that the inner work prescribed by Rabbi Shneur Zalman is never-ending. While the Tanya was written in a technical and unemotional style, it still expresses the huge storm happening in the soul throughout a person's life. We live in a battlefield from which we can't escape. The conflict continues until we die. We can't take a break from dealing with it. At any moment, we can get hit with a deluge of unfocused thoughts, like sadness or rage, which threaten to pull us down. The danger surrounding an older person who has succumbed to unhealthy tendencies toward depression and rage is no less than that confronting a young person, and may even be greater.

The final insight that should be mentioned is that the explanation of the battle between the souls contains crucial advice that has relevance to our daily lives. The first piece of advice emerges from understanding the complexity of our human nature and has the potential to free a person of extraneous pressures. It is this: when it comes to spirituality and ethics, our growth and development is not linear. Inside of us are two souls fighting it out, and the result is inner thrashing. Sometimes we'll raise ourselves up high, transcending our situation and striving to impact our surroundings. A little while later we may crash internally and, as a result, pull back our hands and hearts. The knowledge that this is normal for the soul helps us realize that *inner fluctuation is a natural part of creation*. It's not our fault there's a war raging inside us. Realizing that we are imperfect and unable to be perfect makes it all easier. While the burden we bear is huge, and so much is expected from us, it's understandable that we'll have slipups and failures. We can push ourselves to actualize our potential, yet we shouldn't feel disappointed by our shortcomings. The bottom line is that the mission in life is the striving and the winning. We can all rise up, be better, and love more. However, if we wake up and suddenly realize we aren't truly doing that, or that our own parents aren't on that level, feelings of disappointment don't have to shatter us.

It is a natural reaction to be disgusted by hypocritical people or by those who announce their adherence to values, only to later be caught failing to live up to that standard. However, this reaction is only possible due to a lack of understanding of the true structure of the soul. Someone learning the Tanya's depiction of the structure of the soul may no longer feel as surprised by such things, since it is understandable that the soul experiences constant conflict. There are battles between various desires and the desire to be holier. It's only natural we'll sustain losses and defeats. It's natural to find people who fight so hard and win at certain times, only to then find themselves slipping into foolish behavior. It's not worthwhile nor desirable to lose. In fact, it's forbidden to lose, but there's no reason to become more worked up than necessary.

No less uncommon is the disgust a hypocritical person has for him- or herself. Without the concept of two souls, an unstable, fluctuating person is likely to think there is something wrong with him or her. Failures and stumbling are an intermediate point between one's potential for unhealthy conduct, which is an inseparable part of the person, and what's far worse: deciding to fully actualize that aspect. But negative potential is not an unfixable stain. The future is completely in our hands and up to us.[49]

The second advice that arises from the discussion of the conflict between the souls is actually the very opposite of what we are likely to imagine. Our duality helps us identify the source of human sickness and evil, yet also our unique *human potential*. It teaches us that we can be free from difficulties, inner pitfalls of the soul, and external dimensions. We can rise above our physical tendencies toward a higher dimension.

---

49. For this reason, it's mentioned that God says: "I don't ask you to do things according to My ability, but rather according to yours," *Bamidbar Rabbah, parashah* 12:3. Therefore, our difficulties are proportional to our abilities – "the load given depends on the camel" (Talmud, *Ketubot* 67a, in the beginning).

The very fact that we possess a part of the Creator in fact reveals to us, according to Tanya, that our difficulties, challenges, and all that we struggle with can help us rise above the state in which we find ourselves.

Rebbe Nachman's Chassidim call this insight "the secret of the good point," in a concept based on his writings. They emphasize how the ability to recognize this potential is a significant indication of a person's growth and development. Without knowing the point of perfection in oneself, one won't be able to see it in others. Everyone has a higher source, a point of good, and the following choice to make: meditate on it and be empowered, or hide from it. From Rabbi Shneur Zalman's perspective, appreciating that everyone has the inner war that they need, and that they have the ability to be victorious, makes it easier to handle the intense challenges that come with worries, pressures, and anxieties.

THE PRINCIPLE OF DUALISM

It's not hard to imagine the notion of warring souls being one of the most appealing Chassidic concepts which captured the hearts of its audience from the time of the Tanya's printing up until today. The principle of dualism won people over and became something with which they could identify. Those who either heard it or read it could recognize in themselves Rabbi Shneur Zalman's description of the typical state of the soul. Armed with teachings about the battle between the souls, people who encountered doubts or a lack of solidity understood why it was so and kept these from being blown out of proportion. The idea of a godly soul indicates a person's infinite, positive potential. Even if a person lost battles, stumbled, or sinned, with the right conceptual framework one can see such a failure in context, accept it, and use it to prepare for the next fight.

Since the Tanya was written by Rabbi Shneur Zalman, the idea of one war and two souls has continually appeared in a variety of styles in many authors' works, both religious and not religious. Martin Buber, for example, used it to analyze interpersonal relationships. Winner of the Israel Prize Professor Shlomo Giora Shoham added an additional layer by using the approach of theoretical dualism to dissect the traits of companies and cultures.[50]

---

50. The works of Shlomo Giora Shoham include *The Myth of Tantalus: A Scaffolding*

THE INNER BATTLE · 77

Rabbi Shneur Zalman did an amazing job of describing the inner workings of the psyche. Still, the theoretical knowledge that we have two souls is not enough. The practical challenge comes when we try to apply that knowledge to determine which behaviors are produced by the natural soul and which are generated by the godly soul. The general distinctions utilized in the Tanya serve only as a stepping-stone for a deeper discussion.

---

for an Ontological Personality Theory (St. Lucia: University of Queensland Press, 1979) and *Valhalla, Calvary and Auschwitz* (Cincinnati: Bowman and Cody Academic Publishing, 1995).

CHAPTER 4

Soul Colors

$\mathcal{T}$he concept of two battling souls adds a new dimension to our understanding of the structure of a human personality. But, as mentioned, there's still a component missing from the picture. In order for this approach to enter the patient deeply, Rabbi Shneur Zalman needed to present a detailed view of the soul. More detail and depth to the portrait of the soul's structure means an improved ability to know how to handle challenges generated in the modern era. Knowing the complete picture of the soul is an important asset in examining the patient. In Rabbi Shneur Zalman's words, it's a procedure that, upon completion, can provide the reader of the Tanya with "tranquility for his soul,"[1] remove unnecessary doubts, worries, and confusion, and clarify what type of personality he's received, what his dominant traits are, and where he should focus his energies.

This is exactly what Rabbi Shneur Zalman did. He provided a detailed technical sketch of the soul's structure and of its capacities, of how they become revealed, and of the method by which they change and develop over time.

In his book *Chayei Olam*, Rabbi Adin Even Yisrael Steinsaltz writes:

---

1. "Compiler's Foreword" to the Tanya.

It used to be that the opening page of volumes of the Talmud featured the following disclaimer due to censoring: "Everything that is written here about Gentiles is not referring to Gentiles of today, rather to Gentiles in the past..." In our generation, we find a similar message on the opening page of books – an unseen statement.... We need to erase these pages and their message that material you're about to read is talking about someone else; that it really applies to "them," or "they," or others. Anything but us. And this unfortunate issue applies to books of ethics or volumes of Talmud – the message needs to be the very opposite: it's only speaking to me; it's all written for me, and I'm obligated by it. Above all the message is: this is talking to me.

Rabbi Steinsaltz's words are in harmony with what Rabbi Shneur Zalman is communicating to us. All of these words, these ideas he's presenting, are actual, relevant, practical, and necessary to us. The message found in those pages of the Talmud was true in the past and today, and likewise, everything described in Torah books, be it ethical teachings, books on personal holiness and growth, or legal works, exists within each one of us and was written for us.

Similarly, Rabbi Shneur Zalman isn't looking to present abstract theoretical ideas from the teachings of Kabbalah and Chassidut. He assumes the reader already knows the fundamentals and basic ideas of several concepts, or that he will go learn them. Rabbi Shneur Zalman's general approach is to stay rooted in the practical meaning and application of the ideas and not to engage in a theoretical discussion of the relationship between the souls and between body and soul.[2]

---

2. This is hinted at in the order in which he presents ideas to readers of the Tanya. In the first part of the book, *Likkutei Amarim* or *Sefer shel Beinonim*, Rabbi Shneur Zalman deals with the framework of the soul in depth. In the second book, *Sha'ar Hayichud v'Ha'emunah*, he primarily focuses on understanding the oneness of the Creator. The printed version of the Tanya features several hints to Rabbi Shneur Zalman's vacillating between which of the two should come first. Apparently, he initially thought it better to begin specifically with recognizing God's oneness. However, he ultimately changed the order and began with the structure of the soul. One of the indications of this is that there are citations in *Sha'ar Hayichud v'Ha'emunah* that read, "as will be explained later" (ch. 6, 10–11); yet the point was already discussed in the first section of Tanya. (See *Iggeret Hakodesh*, vol. 5, 187; vol. 22, 48; and other

This focus contributed to Rabbi Shneur Zalman's approach becoming one of the accepted therapeutic approaches of the modern era. Even masters of Kabbalah and Chassidut look to the well-defined and detailed structures presented in the Tanya and related literature for clarity about the soul. In this way, Rabbi Shneur Zalman accomplished what he often sought to achieve: to help people reveal their inner identity, become more spiritually secure, achieve victory for the godly soul, and overcome the spiritual maladies produced by the animal soul.

A good example of this includes centers that train coaches and healers according to the wisdom of Chassidut – primarily based on the framework of the soul as it's described in the Tanya. They actualize his ideas and writings. Found all over the world, these centers offer various programs, including those specifically designed for helping professionals such as psychiatrists, psychologists, social workers, and educators. The courses apply the teachings of Kabbalah in order to explain the inner workings of the soul and to present unique treatment approaches.

The response from students and practitioners is impressive: Rabbi Shneur Zalman's system works. Practitioners come away with tools for treating stress, anxiety, depression, alienation, lack of meaning, and a wide variety of other such personal issues.

As we find with any set of processes, stage one separates the system into parts. Learning generally starts with a generalized framework of the soul and of its abilities according to the teachings of Kabbalah and Chassidut. Next, students learn how to test and determine personality types and to identify conflicts and crises. After discovering what's interfering with a balanced expression of the soul's faculties, the applicable therapy is outlined based on the Tanya's approach.

---

places.) A possible explanation for *Sefer shel Beinonim* coming before *Sha'ar Hayichud v'Ha'emunah* is that Chassidut was intended to go beyond providing a conceptual framework and offer a person help with his daily problems. Rabbi Shneur Zalman isn't looking to reveal the structure of each personality or secrets of creation according to the teachings of Kabbalah – unless they have bearing on the reader's life. For more readings on the need for working on oneself, see Rabbi Yosef Yitzchak, *Igrot Kodesh*, vol. 6, 78; *Torat Shalom*, Miluim, p. 33; *Sefer Hamaamarim* 5710 (1940), 197; and other sources.

THE CHASSIDIC METHOD

This chapter, which deals with a more detailed exploration of the soul's faculties, is more technical. But before jumping into the structure of the soul, there's an important question about Rabbi Shneur Zalman's model that needs to be addressed. How does he know what the soul looks like, and what its relationship is with the body? What are the sources for his theoretical approach regarding what goes on inside a person? What observations or research, if any, are his ideas based on?

Borrowing from the common approach to research, there are many ways to get to know the soul. The researcher can gather evidence, conduct observations, question and talk to people, and distribute questionnaires in order to confirm or reject the models and theories he's developed about the soul and its ability to handle situations. Sigmund Freud, the father of psychoanalysis, who had a major impact up until today even despite challenges to his system, saw the soul, the body, and their relationship to each other through a theoretical lens.[3] For Freud, observation and experience needed to be the sources for knowledge about the soul, just as they are the sources for the development of the natural sciences. The intellect and soul are objective subjects to be scientifically investigated like any other field of inquiry.

Rabbi Shneur Zalman, however, didn't view the soul like material in a test lab. Despite the fact that he'd collected a tremendous amount of material from personal meetings with Chassidim, these didn't serve as the basis for the treatment method he devised. Nor did his own private contemplation provide the foundation for his psychological approach. Therefore, how did he figure out the workings of the soul? What did he base them on? From where did he learn such a precise depiction of what the soul encounters across a wide range of experiences? What is

---

3. For example, see the exact quote in Peter Gay's book, in which Freud announces his intention was "to furnish a natural-scientific psychology, that is, to represent psychical processes as quantitatively determined states of specifiable material particles, and thus make those processes graphic and consistent." Peter Gay, *Freud: A Life for Our Time* (New York: W.W. Norton, 2006), 79. Cited in Hebrew edition: *Freud: Parashat Chaim l'Zmaneinu* (Tel Aviv: Dvir, 1993), 75. And see Baruch Kahana, *Shvirah v'Tikkun: Model Chassidi l'Psychologia Klinit* (Jerusalem: Rubin Mass Publishers, 2001), 15.

the evidence for the world of ideas that he outlines in describing the aspects of the soul's expression?

Rabbi Shneur Zalman shares that his understanding of the soul is not a product of observation, experience, or personal contemplation. His description of the soul is based on the unique methodology developed by Chassidut, the translation of the language of the Kabbalah, and primarily of the work of the Arizal, into a practical understanding of the soul.[4] The teachings of Kabbalah make it possible for a person to gain a far better understanding of the Creator and His relationship with Creation. Chassidut took advantage of the opportunity and utilized the teachings to gain a greater appreciation of knowledge of the soul.[5] The perspective offered in Chassidut is based on an analysis of the faculties active in the soul and a recognition of the capacities by which the Creator directs the world.[6] This invites us to think about how God created the world and continues to direct it, and this gives us insight into the soul's efforts within the body: there is a parallel between how the Creator's power is reflected in creation and the way the soul is reflected in the body.

Here's the core point at the heart of the unique approach to spiritual treatment espoused by Rabbi Shneur Zalman in particular and Chassidut in general: God created man in such a way that his soul and body reflect the way that God created and runs the world. Awareness of the Creator and His connection with the world, gained from the teachings of Kabbalah, provides insight about the soul. And in this case, the opposite is also true: awareness of the soul grants insight into the Creator, to a certain extent. As we see in Rabbi Shneur Zalman's words:

---

4. The teachings of the Arizal and the *Zohar* are mentioned many times in Rabbi Shneur Zalman's writings. In addition, there is a tradition that the sources which strongly impacted Rabbi Shneur Zalman's approach were the Maharal of Prague, the Shelah, and the Maggid of Mezeritch. See *Likkutei Amarim*, Chassidut Mevueret, 6.

5. According to Chassidut, some of the sources for this include the Book of Iyov (19:26), which emphasizes that "from my flesh I perceive Godliness." In Tanya, see *Likkutei Amarim*, ch. 51. In large part these words are a continuation of what's written in Bereishit (Genesis) 1:26: "Let us make man in our image and likeness." We also find in "Patach Eliyah," the introduction to the *Zohar*: "We can learn about the higher things from the lower things."

6. Tanya, *Kuntress Acharon*, siman 4.

The verse "And from my flesh I will behold Godliness" speaks of a partial understanding of Godliness by [contemplating] the soul which is invested in the body...[7]

THE INNER ESSENCE

What can the Chassidic approach teach us about the soul? What did Rabbi Shneur Zalman have to say to a simple textile merchant in White Russia or a bartender in a village tavern that is also relevant for us today?

There's a well-known Chassidic story that can help us understand Rabbi Shneur Zalman's message. Zalman Senders was a very successful Chassid of Rabbi Shneur Zalman who lived in Shklov.[8] He was a Torah scholar, wealthy, and had many refined and positive personality traits. He was free of arrogance and generously distributed charity. Many people would invest monies with him, acknowledging his tremendous success in business. Profits earned from this money were immediately delivered to the investors, without charging any fees for his efforts. One day, the Chassid's dealings hit a snag, and he lost all his money and that of his family, as well as everything others had invested with him. With a heavy heart, he traveled to his Rebbe. He entered Rabbi Shneur Zalman's room and told him everything pained him. He described how it all came about and the great financial loss he had suffered. "I don't care if I remain poor," he told Rabbi Shneur Zalman, "but I need to stand by my responsibilities and fulfill my charitable obligations." The entire time he spoke, Rabbi Shneur Zalman sat with his head between the palms of his hands and his elbows resting on the table. When the Chassid finished lamenting his situation, Rabbi Shneur Zalman gave him a deeply piercing look and, with a melody, said: "You're telling me what you need...but you haven't thought about what you're needed for."

The Rebbe's words shocked the Chassid, and he fainted. *What does the Rebbe want from me? Aren't I a good person, with a refined character, who only sought to fulfill my obligations and help the people I promised to help?* Sometime later he recovered, and then he understood. By lamenting to

---

7. Tanya, *Iggeret Hakodesh*, siman 15.
8. See Zalman Ruderman, *Sippurei Mofet: Baal Hatanya* (Kfar Chabad: Ufaratzta, 2008), 77–84.

Rabbi Shneur Zalman about his financial state, he had chosen to present to him what he lacked in life. He had failed to overcome an exaggerated sense of self and personal importance. He'd overlooked the inner point of wholesomeness and goodness that he should have sought to connect with instead.

The story continues with the Chassid remaining with his Rebbe in Liozna for another two weeks. He met again with Rabbi Shneur Zalman, who praised him for the personal growth work and perspective change he'd achieved and gave him parting blessings. The Chassid soon overcame his financial troubles and restored his wealth. He was able to fulfill his obligations, but with a different outlook on life. Rabbi Shneur Zalman expected the Chassid to find joy and continued growth after the crisis.

The story's core message also has to do with Rabbi Shneur Zalman's teachings on the soul. In general, Rabbi Shneur Zalman sought to show his audience that they possessed an inner spiritual dimension independent of the physical ups and downs they experienced. There are no lacks, absences, or separations in such a dimension – only wholesomeness, stability, and unity. This dimension, according to Rabbi Shneur Zalman's approach, is something people need to learn how to reveal practically, by their actions, words, and thoughts. This aspect of a person we can call the "essence of the soul" or the inner "I" – not to be confused with the egocentric "I."[9]

Rabbi Shneur Zalman teaches that we can't reveal the essence of the soul, the deep and innermost dimension. The godly soul's essence can't

---

9. The comparison made by the teachings of Kabbalah and Chassidut, between the way in which the Creator directs and impacts the world and the faculties of the soul, is aimed at highlighting a core point. It's designed to show us the connection between a person's essence, the deep, inner "I," and another person's being. There is a process by which the Creator, so to speak, "descends" and "draws closer" to the world. It's a similar process to the way in which the essence of the soul is revealed in stages and establishes a connection and dialogue with the world around. The purpose of outlining the structure of the soul is to assess this process and instruct a person in how to stay connected to the soul's essence, to avoid an interaction with the world that is distant and dissociated from one's inner dimension. Similarly, the inner essence of the *sefirot* descends various stages in order to power creation. For more on this, see Rabbi Yoel Kahn, "Eser Sefirot: Shlavim b'Yachas HaBoreh el Habriah," in *Sugiyot b'Chassidut*, 145–55.

be limited, defined, or understood. It's abstract.[10] However, in our lives we can reveal a lofty level, step by step through the conscious faculties of our soul.

There is a significant difference between the method by which many psychological approaches relate to the essence of the soul, through what they commonly refer to as the subconscious, and the way the teachings of Chassidut relate to that same concealed dimension. The essence of the soul, the inner "I," isn't viewed by the teachings of Chassidut as a primitive instinctual element to be curbed by the intellect and emotions. A person does not hide skeletons in the subconscious that need to be worked through. Rather, our hidden and subconscious abilities are holy and spiritual dimensions of the soul which we try to sensitively reveal and which can fill us with hope and faith.

In a letter written after being released from his first imprisonment in around 1799, Rabbi Shneur Zalman advanced a detailed description of what that inner being is, that essence of the soul that transcends intellect. According to his system, within the subconscious and the essence of the soul that's beyond logic lies a sublime spark, a spark of God: "The inner core point of the heart is . . . an aspect of radiance from the supernal level of *chochmah* [wisdom], which is above *binah* [understanding] and *daat* [knowledge], in which is invested and hidden actual light from the Creator . . . and this is the idea of there being a spark of Godliness inside of every Jewish soul."[11]

The message delivered to Rabbi Shneur Zalman's readers is that they have an essential dimension that's transcendent and that endows them with tremendous potential: the potential for mankind to reveal a spark of the Creator which leads to emotional well-being and a life of meaning and purpose, a life of victory for the godly soul. Psychologically speaking, this means that a person no longer needs to go searching for personal perfection, but rather to connect to that inner point, and then, naturally, the person's being and nature change. Rabbi Shneur Zalman doesn't wage war against the natural soul and its egocentric drives. Instead, he

10. As described by the Lubavitcher Rebbe: "At its core, the soul is a small spark from the lowest level of the Creator." *Torat Menachem*, vol. 25, 1959, part 2, 92.
11. *Igrot Kodesh – Alter Rebbe*, letter 65, 245.

connects a person to the inner being and personal life's purpose, and then, the darkness, jealousy, anger, and coarseness are automatically banished.

According to this approach, recognizing the soul and treating spiritual maladies depends on a person's intellect, emotions, and actions. If a person contemplates and meditates in such a way that his soul capacities become expressed, one of two things can occur. Either his faculties will express his essence, the being of the godly soul, or, they will distance and cut him off from it. Becoming distant from one's inner essence, from the "inner point of the heart," is likely to cause spiritual problems.

As you recall, Rabbi Shneur Zalman presents a person with a choice between a material and transitory life or eternal life. Choosing the eternal is a result of connecting to the inner lofty dimension in the soul and revealing this choice in your practical daily life.

Rabbi Shneur Zalman doesn't have to prove to us that we possess a natural soul. The relationship to that soul comes naturally. It's easy to see how people have a tendency to view everything around them with self-interest. Our first, natural, and primary impulse is to look for the benefit in everything, including our relationships with partners, family, and even with the Creator. This drive is the result of making our sense of independent existence, our own "I," the focus of life. Our personal interests naturally serve as a set of terms and rules for connecting and drawing closer to others.

On the other hand, the existence of the godly soul and the lofty human potential to rise in life are things that need to be uncovered and exposed. Therefore, there are still questions that should be clarified: How is a person's soul expressed? What are its faculties? What is its source? How is its structure different from that of the natural soul? From where does it receive its capacity? Understanding how the soul's faculties evolve from its essence can help resolve these queries. The framework of the soul reveals a lofty, deep inner dimension in our connection with others and in daily routines, while allowing us to overcome egocentric tendencies. It enables us to reduce the distance between the "I" and others. We gradually transform from separate, independent individuals to people connected with others and our surroundings.

FACULTIES OF THE SOUL

Rabbi Shneur Zalman's map of the soul is based on several systems of faculties. This chapter will focus on two of them. One system is intellectual faculties. The second is the emotions.[12]

The teachings of Kabbalah tell us that the inner framework by which the Creator made and runs the world comprises ten *sefirot*. These are the attributes by which the Creator manifests Himself. The first three *sefirot* are *chochmah, binah,* and *daat,* three levels of divine intelligence. The remaining seven *sefirot* (*chesed, gevurah, tiferet, netzach, hod, yesod,* and *malchut*) correspond to divine "emotions," as it were.[13]

Rabbi Shneur Zalman wrote that just as the divine attributes are divided into ten *sefirot,* likewise the human soul: "As is known, the soul comprises ten *sefirot*."[14] In total, the soul has ten faculties that combine to form the structure of the intellect and emotions. The ten faculties in the soul parallel the ten *sefirot*.[15] That is, the faculties of the soul, like the *sefirot,* are divided into three intellectual faculties and seven emotional faculties. The three intellectual faculties are the first three faculties in the ten *sefirot*.

To a certain extent, the connection the *sefirot* have with God is comparable to the connection between the faculties of the soul and the soul itself. The soul's potentials delineate the ways in which one person is revealed to another. So, for example, a person known for his *chochmah* (wisdom) is called a *chacham,* while one known for his *chesed* (kindness) is called a man of *chesed.* However, wisdom and kindness aren't the essence of the soul, but rather descriptions that express a person's core abilities that get revealed to others.

---

12. An additional system is that of the general faculties, which will be addressed in the coming chapter; these include the means of expression for the intellect and the emotions.

13. There is a disagreement among the Kabbalistic masters whether the *sefirah* of *keter* is included in the ten *sefirot*. For a general discussion of the topic, including sources, see *Maamarei Admor Hazaken al Ketuvim* (5569/1808), 216.

14. *Igrot Kodesh – Alter Rebbe,* letter 45, 154.

15. Since the soul bears the form of ten *sefirot,* a human is called a "miniature world." Now, given that every soul has a complete set of faculties – in the image of the Creator – we're taught that "When one saves a Jewish life, it is as if one saved an entire world" (Talmud, *Sanhedrin* 4:5).

From the time of his first arrest, Rabbi Shneur Zalman emphasized the central importance of deeply studying the ten *sefirot* in the teachings of Kabbalah:

> The wisdom of Kabbalah that I began to learn with my Rebbe, and later on from texts, is the knowledge of ten *sefirot* and their names; and how, through them, the Creator directs and enlivens the higher and lower worlds.[16]

Rabbi Shneur Zalman insisted his students learn the structure of the *sefirot* and how the structure of the soul's faculties parallel them. One of the reasons for this is that knowing the structure of the soul's faculties is at the heart of recognizing and dissecting the soul from various perspectives. Knowledge of their makeup enables a deep probing of personality, analysis of dominant and weak traits, revelation of the interrelationships between the capacities active in the soul, and, primarily, determination of whether the person's actions are an expression of his inner being or concealment and distancing from it.

Another reason Rabbi Shneur Zalman invested so much in explaining the structure of the soul is that there is, so to speak, a whole range of connections between the soul faculties a person develops in life and the powers the Creator brings to bear in the world. This notion is illuminated by Rabbi Shneur Zalman's words in his final hours. It was Saturday night after Shabbat when he passed from this world at the age of sixty-seven. His grandson stood by him and prayed the evening prayers with a somber melody. When he finished praying, his grandfather called to him. He mentioned an idea to him that was based on a passage in the *Zohar*, about the events occurring in the higher worlds being an outcome of what happens down here in our physical world. "According to the measure demonstrated by a person below, so is he shown from on high."[17] The grandfather shared with his grandson that a person determines the kind of energies he receives from on high. This means that being happy seemingly causes God to be happy. And this brings a person increased blessings.

---

16. Quoted from *Igrot Kodesh – Alter Rebbe*, letter 58, 221.
17. *Igrot Kodesh Admor Hatzemach Tzedek* (New York: Kehot, 5747/1877), 222–26.

As stated in the *Zohar*:

Come and see: This lowly world is always ready to receive.... The higher world only gives in accordance to the state of the lower world; if it's in a state of joy then, in response, abundance flows from on high. But if the state of the lower world is one of sadness, then, in response, the flow of blessings is reduced. Therefore, "Serve God with joy,"[18] since a person's joy attracts a parallel joy from on high.[19]

This principle is strongly featured in the teachings of the Baal Shem Tov, who often emphasized the verse "God is your shadow,"[20] meaning, God is like a person's shadow. Whatever a person does, God also, so to speak, does. According to this logic, sadness in our world arouses sadness above. Joy invites physical blessings to come and join it. We understand from Rabbi Shneur Zalman's words to his grandson that prayer accompanied by a morose melody at such a time was not recommended. In truth, Rabbi Shneur Zalman's state at that point was cause for worry and concern, as will be discussed in the last chapter. He was fleeing Napoleon's armies and was sick and weak. Nevertheless, he insisted on directing his grandson to be protective of joy and to remove fear and worry from his heart.

Rabbi Shneur Zalman explains in the Tanya that the soul is like a rope that begins in the higher realms. The direction a person chooses to shake the rope in this world determines the influence and energies raining down from the higher realms.

Scripture states: "Yaakov is the rope of [G-d's] heritage." The analogy compares a Jew's soul to a rope, with one end above and the other end below. Pulling the lower end causes the higher end to be moved and pulled as well; as much as it can be pulled. It is exactly so with regard to the root of the soul of man and its source...[21]

Concerning this point, it's worthwhile to mention that exploring the soul in light of the teachings of Rabbi Shneur Zalman and his successors is

18. Tehillim 100:2.
19. *Zohar* 2:179b.
20. Tehillim 121:5. Also see *Keter Shem Tov*, Hosafot, siman 78.
21. Tanya, *Iggeret Hateshuvah*, 6.

considered to be an act of learning deep and lofty wisdom. Its wisdom is connected to wisdom about the Creator, which forms the core of Kabbalistic and Chassidic teachings. This chapter doesn't pretend to reveal clear rulings or present comprehensive summaries of every aspect of the ten *sefirot* and the ten faculties of the soul. Rather, it explains very generally the Chassidic approach based on the teachings of the soul's structure, and the process of how a person can reveal their inner essence while relating to reality and to others around them.

1. Intellect

The first system of inner faculties discussed by Rabbi Shneur Zalman in the Tanya includes the three intellectual powers that are invested in the mind and that direct our conduct. The intellect occupies an extremely important position in Rabbi Shneur Zalman's teachings and serves as one of the most significant weapons in the war of the souls. It can be used to vindicate the godly soul's approach or that of its opponent. Through the intellectual faculties, people can change themselves, impact their emotions, or restructure problematic approaches. Intellectual contemplation produces and develops new insights and breaks a situation down into its causes, details, and components. Detailed knowledge influences a person's perspective and enables him to adjust his emotional reaction to the current situation.

While the *middot* (emotional traits) are responsible for feelings, the *sechel* (intellect) includes tools for comprehension, innovation, and processing. The first component of the intellect is called *chochmah* (wisdom). The second faculty is called *binah* (understanding). And the third is *daat* (knowledge), the ability to connect. Together, *chochmah*, *binah*, and *daat* form the acronym *chabad*, which was adopted as the name for the Chassidic movement formed by Rabbi Shneur Zalman.

Ideas spring from *chochmah* (wisdom) into the mind. As if in a flash, the faculty of *chochmah* offers our first grasp of a thought, the beginning of revelation, and the first stage in the birth of new ideas. However, it does not provide a fully developed idea. The glow of the idea flickers, waiting for assistance and clarification. *Chochmah* possesses the potential of the entire intellectual process to come, like a seed has all the potential for a tree and its fruits. A person has some additional intellectual stages to pass through on the path to developing the seed, or the idea. Without such stages, the seed will likely be nothing more than an idea that came and went.

Therefore, after the idea is sparked in the mind, the next stage unravels and dissects the hidden parts that were concealed in the point of *chochmah*. This is a process expressed by *binah* (understanding). It actualizes the potential that is found in the flash of the original concept. While *chochmah* is a momentary flash, *binah* is expansion and explanation of what was conceived. With it, an idea is investigated, pulled apart, and opened up by getting into all the details and by inferring one thing from another. Through *binah*, a person takes the idea that popped into his mind and moves it closer to comprehension using tools such as examples, logic, and connection. With *binah*, we work to grasp the idea, investigate its possibilities for implementation, and apply it to the facts on the ground.[22]

Alternatively, we can see *chochmah* as creativity. A person without *chochmah* will struggle to experience flashes of insight, new approaches, and unexpected ideas. Rabbi Shneur Zalman writes that the word *chochmah* is connected to de-emphasizing the self and ego. In order for ideas to spark up, a person needs to be humble. Arrogance prevents a person from learning new things.[23] It leaves him too self-involved and without space available for novelty to well up. Someone deceived into believing he knows everything becomes rooted in place and unable to recognize new things. *Binah* is the ability to further develop that flash of creativity. A lack of *binah*, however, leaves the person with a pile of *chochmah* ideas that lack application or are out of touch with reality. Failing to develop our ideas is akin to wasting them. They never find expression in our lives.

The third intellectual faculty is that of *daat* (knowledge). It's the power of deeply connecting, binding, and uniting with the subject due to persistent ongoing involvement. *Daat* binds the point of *chochmah* and broadens *binah*, resulting in the formation of a deep emotional

---

22. There are three dimensions to *binah*: depth, width, and length. See the Mitteler Rebbe, *Ner Mitzvah v'Torah Or*, Sha'ar Yichud, 109b.

23. Regarding *chochmah* being *bittul* (nullification), "*koach mah*" (the power of what), see Tanya, *Likkutei Amarim*, ch. 3, 18, and other sources.

connection with the topic. The persistent focus reveals new angles, both expected and unexpected.[24] Comprehension that lacks *daat* remains cold and distant, devoid of feelings toward the topic or others. It fails to inspire action or to connect the person to what he understood in his mind. An example of lacking *daat* would be if a speaker delivered a talk in an abbreviated fashion with short points. The lack of explanation blocks him and the audience from forming a connection with the ideas he's sharing. The focused delving-in of *daat* helps transform cold intellectual understanding.[25]

The Tanya spends considerable time on the topic of *daat* and its great influence in our daily lives. According to Rabbi Shneur Zalman, the primary technique for working on oneself is not to deal with traits and feelings directly. The challenge is to find the proper way to utilize the intellectual faculties of *chochmah, binah*, and *daat* in order to influence the emotions.[26] Specifically, the importance of *daat* is related to the logical underpinnings of Rabbi Shneur Zalman's approach. According to his line of thinking, the intellect is the source of the emotions – therefore in order to overcome undesirable feelings one needs to address his intellect. Emotional arousal depends not only on our understanding of the subject matter, but also on our connection to it.[27] This bond is the product of *daat*, which serves as the link between *chochmah* and *binah*, and between the emotions.

A clear example of *daat* presented by Rabbi Shneur Zalman is of

---

24. The source for understanding *daat's* influence on the development of feeling can be seen in *Zohar* 2:177b. It's further explained in the Tzemach Tzedek's *Derech Mitzvotecha*, Mitzvah Ha'amanat Elokut 2:46a. The subject of the acronym for Chabad (*chochmah, binah,* and *daat*) is discussed in many sources. See Tanya, *Likkutei Amarim,* from the beginning of ch. 3.

25. The concept of *daat* in godliness is that of a strong understanding, recognition, and sense. See "Sichah Shabbat Parashat Vayishlach, 14 Kislev, 5718," *Torat Menachem,* vol. 21, 1958, part 1, 194; and in other sources.

26. For a comparison to the teachings of the Baal Shem Tov, see Glitzenstein, *Sefer Hatoldot,* vol. 1, 51.

27. See Tanya, *Likkutei Amarim,* ch. 42. On the subject of *daat* and connection, see also chapter 3. *Daat* is not only comprehension, but is also related to having heartfelt feelings. See *Likkutei Torah,* Bamidbar 2d; Tanya, *Likkutei Amarim,* ch. 20. For more on the relationship between intellect and emotions, see Tanya, *Likkutei Amarim,* ch. 13.

that within a marriage. When describing the bond between Adam and Eve, the Torah says: "And Adam knew [*daat*] his wife, Eve."[28] The word *daat* is used to express unity and connection. Love is a feeling that's only produced by getting to know someone deeply. It requires constant maintenance and always focuses on details, knowledge of the traits that characterize the object of one's love. This isn't merely informational knowledge, but rather an emotional bond fueled by a detailed awareness. Part of connecting to people is learning about them and getting to know the details of their life.[29] When a couple lacks constant involvement in their shared life, their love will likely lack zest and passion. Accordingly, *daat* is significant when it comes to marital relationships.

Another example of the application of *daat* is the way operating room surgeons don't get emotional when a new patient arrives. Thanks to *daat*, we think about things connected to us and have feelings for those things specifically. Without that connection, we quickly forget things, and they fade without leaving a trace. This principle can help us appreciate what many operating room workers in Israel described during Operation Protective Edge in Gaza. They reported having a harder time treating wounded young soldiers than they did treating other patients. The reason is the connection formed, via *daat*, to the soldiers and their circumstances.[30]

Anyone studying a page of the Talmud will quickly see that one of Judaism's significant defining traits is its process of learning and deduction, which includes deliberation, discussion, hair-splitting contemplation, and rebuttals. All of that scholarship is for a specific purpose: intellectual exertion is a vehicle for exciting emotion. The external emotions are subdued when the mind is active and revealed when the mind ceases to dominate.[31] In situations where we have some involve-

---

28. Bereishit 4:1. See also Tanya, *Likkutei Amarim*, ch. 3, 43.
29. "The core of *daat* is not merely comprehension, etc." Tanya, *Likkutei Amarim*, ch. 43.
30. People have an emotional reaction to events they feel connected to, without making any special efforts. However, building a connection to an abstract idea requires a person to invest great effort. See *Likkutei Sichot 6*, Parashat Yitro 2, paragraph 4.
31. "As is known, while intellect is in an active, revealed state it is impossible to reveal the emotional traits." *Torat Menachem*, vol. 9, 1953, part 3, 137.

ment, the intellect will work to arouse our emotions and strengthen our feeling of connection.

It's Rabbi Shneur Zalman's view that learning has the power to strengthen one's faith. Pure faith, he holds, can raise a person up, but faith is often distant, general, and just beyond our reach. Therefore, it often fails to find its expression in our daily lives.

In-depth Torah study can transform generalized faith into a more significant form, one that inspires an emotional bond, down to the details, via the power of *daat*.[32] When viewed in this way, the intellect can be described as a guide. Its role is to teach the emotions where to travel, how to reach their desired destinations, and to understand historical events that occurred along the way. While the intellect points the way, it doesn't command the traveler or make demands. It helps a person develop feelings, but it does not dictate the emotion.[33] Therefore, when a person experiences an emotional drive or attraction to something, the intellect doesn't interfere, but it can point in a more appropriate direction or guide a person to consider other things that will serve to disconnect from that attraction.

A person who develops his faculty of *daat* (knowledge) is called a *bar daat*, a person of intelligence. A few generations ago, there was a Chassid who told a relatively unknown story about Rabbi Shneur Zalman. To him, the story was miraculous, and he used it to demonstrate how much the Rebbe was a *bar daat*. In this case, a *bar daat* is a person who constantly lives in a state of full consciousness, and from doing so, derives his self-control.

One Friday afternoon, Rabbi Shneur Zalman visited the bath house as part of his preparations for Shabbat. With his head in hot water, he scrubbed his head for an entire hour. One of the Chassidim, who didn't realize it was the Rebbe, had fun with the scene he saw. Apparently, he began to laugh and gave a forceful slap to Rabbi Shneur Zalman's head. For the storyteller, the miracle was the fact that Rabbi Shneur

---

32. Rambam, *Mishneh Torah*, Hilchot Yesodei HaTorah 2:11: "What is the path to love and fear of God.... And the explanation of all the principles featured in these two chapters is called Maaseh Merkava."

33. For an example of a trail guide, see Gopin, *L'Daat et Hamiddot*, 161–62.

Zalman didn't pick up his head. Instead, he continued scrubbing his head and completely ignored the blow. According to the story, Rabbi Shneur Zalman kept his head down in order to save the Chassid from embarrassment.[34]

2. Emotions

What is a human being? According to Chassidic thought, the core of a person is not the body, deeds, or thoughts. Rather, a person's essence is most expressed in feelings and emotional traits.[35] A person is happy or sad, enjoying or suffering, craving or satisfied. And while the emotions are influenced by the efforts and actions of the intellect, in the moment we're experiencing a feeling, it is truly the dominant force. Furthermore, the majority of spiritual issues confronting a person are emotional.[36]

The beginning of our self-expression to others is the emotions. The intellect is also an expression of our character, albeit a limited one, and during our intellectual efforts we are involved with something external to ourselves. However, when we are trying to understand something, we still don't emerge from ourselves completely. We are still separate. For this reason, the intellect is associated with coldness.

Thoughts, speech, and actions all express the soul. But emotions are the engine that drive a person to connect to others. Thus, a very intellectual person, or someone who is highly intellectually expressive, will tend to be less social and more introverted. Intellect offers a more

---

34. Rabbi Yitzchak Ginsburg, speaking on 24 Tevet, 2000, in Ramat Aviv.
35. Regarding the emotions being the main part of a person, see *Likkutei Sichot* 24:118, in the explanation of the comparison featured in the verse "for a person is a tree of the field." A growing tree refers to the emotional traits, which are the crux of the person. It is specifically the emotional traits that express the essence of the soul. A person's primary spiritual work is that of refining the emotional traits. Footnote 28 in *Likkutei Sichot* 24:118 says: "See the continuation of *Maamarim* from 1902, vol. 3, 'Generally speaking, a person is the aspect of emotions'; likewise 'A person is a tree of the field.'" See also *Torah Ohr*, Yitro 72c.
36. In the teachings of Chassidut, the soul's faculties are divided into beginning, middle, and end. The intellect is the head, the highest part to which a person needs to rise. The faculties of action comprise the end, and along with the emotional traits, they comprise the essence of the person. Similarly, the ten *sefirot* are also divided into beginning, middle, and end.

removed perspective on things, while the emotions form connections.[37] They are characterized by warmth and passion. Why? Because when a person feels, his soul extends out to another until they become the core of the experience. As the soul gets closer to another, it's moved to draw closer or go further away.

THE SEVEN *SEFIROT* IN THE SOUL

In total, there are seven emotional traits that combine to form the full spectrum of feelings or *middot*. The traits most focused on in the Tanya are the "intellectual *middot*," the emotional traits that are generated by our intellectual efforts. Their strength and intensity is guided by the intellect. The second type of *middot* are ones that are more practical and action-oriented, aroused indirectly by the mind and in harmony with a person's nature and character.[38]

The *middot*, the emotional traits, can be learned and analyzed from a great many vantage points. In one of his letters that was later incorporated into the Tanya's fourth section, Rabbi Shneur Zalman suggests a method for appreciating the *middot*: compare them to the process of a father sharing an idea with his son.[39]

The father gets to thinking, and this arouses within him feelings of love and a desire to teach his son. The love and desire to give are part of the attribute of *chesed*. *Chesed* (kindness) is followed by *gevurah* (strength). *Gevurah* is the power to set boundaries, a trait that slows down and limits the attribute of *chesed*. An example of *gevurah* can be understood when a father cannot transmit ideas as he understands them

---

37. By that measure, just as relating to another is the beginning of feeling, the attribute of *chesed*, so, too, does the creation of the world on a conscious, revealed plane begin with *chesed* – the Creator's desire to give to the world. The teachings of Chassidut commonly quote the verse "The world is built with *chesed*" (Tehillim 89:3). See Tanya, *Sha'ar Hayichud v'Ha'emunah*, ch. 1. It is also quoted in several other places in the Tanya.

38. Regarding *middot* that are natural, emotional, and logical, and how they parallel the stages of pregnancy, nursing, and intellect, see Sholom DovBer Schneersohn, *Hemshech Ayin-Bet*, vol. 3 (Brooklyn: Kehot, 1977), 1225.

39. Tanya, *Iggeret Hakodesh*, siman 15. The *middot* described there are those of the intellectual soul.

himself. He needs to limit the flow of ideas in order to match his son's level, and in order for them to be appropriate for his needs and abilities. Therefore, he shares the details and points via stories, analogies, and examples. Without this, the son won't understand and may even lose the desire to learn.

Rabbi Shneur Zalman describes the process of transmission from father to son:

> ...and each of the particular attributes in man derives from one of these seven attributes, for they are the root of all the attributes...: the attribute of *chesed*, which is a drive to give good to all without limit; and the attribute of *gevurah*, which seeks to restrain giving, or to withhold it altogether in certain cases...
>
> For example, when one wishes to share and teach an intellectual subject to his son, if he will tell it to him in its totality, exactly as it appears in his own mind, the son will be unable to understand and absorb it. Rather, he needs to arrange it for him in a different order and context, every word properly spoken.... So, too, does the father need to adjust the insight or the subject he wishes to share with his son, and to divide them into many parts, relating them gradually, with skill and discernment...[40]

Gevurah's restraint and contraction is produced by being calculating, and by a desire to securely control the dosage received by the son. *Gevurah* is also likely to include concern, a form of fear, that perhaps too great a love for the son will lead to sharing more than what he can handle. While these assessments and concerns place contractions and limitations, the two of them are still characterized by reduction and separation, and not openness. *Gevurah* (fear, control, and contraction) is the very opposite of *chesed*.[41] *Chesed*, like love, has to do with the giver and sharer. A father wants to give. *Gevurah* and contraction relate to the recipient or, in our

---

40. Ibid.

41. In Kabbalah, one of the common approaches to the structure of the soul's faculties is to arrange them in three lines: right, left, and middle. *Gevurah* and *chesed* belong to opposing lines that complement each other, while the middle line brings balance between them. The right line is the line of *chesed* and giving; it expresses the desire to give kindness. The left line is the line of *gevurah*, judgment, and contraction. It reigns

case, the level of the son. In its purest form, *chesed* that is free of any balancing interaction with other traits will express itself without limits. Such a state emphasizes the giver. *Gevurah* comes, and it reduces and limits this giving with an eye to the precise capacity of the recipient. In other words, the focus passes from the giver to the receiver. These two first core traits, *chesed* and *gevurah*, are representative of the process by which emotions are revealed, from the essence of the soul outward to another person, from the giver to the receiver.

The next trait is *tiferet*, the attribute of compassion. It's an intermediary trait that is characterized by emotional wholesomeness, i.e., a desire to give, independent of the giver's love or the recipient's need. *Tiferet* is an intermediary attribute, a mediator between *chesed* and *gevurah*. *Tiferet* emerges from the integration of *chesed* and *gevurah*. It "imports" a desire to give from *chesed*, tempered by limitations and boundaries that stem from *gevurah*. The result is giving even to someone undeserving, with compassion and an effort to adjust the giving and kindness to the recipient.[42]

The next three middot, *netzach*, *hod*, and *yesod*, are more action-oriented. They also express a relationship with the outside world and with others, but in addition to being accessed by contemplation, they are inherent and natural, like energy flowing from a very high source. Returning to the example of a father and son, the father wants to share an idea in a way that is adjusted to fit the son's traits, but the process is likely to get blocked by obstacles. For example, the father may be short on time due to other commitments, or the son may be resistant to input. The challenges can lure the father into weakening his desire and giving up on his plan. The traits of *netzach* and *hod* push the father to seek counsel and strategize ways to overcome the inner and outer challenges. The essence of these two traits is a drive to overcome obstructions and vanquish anything standing in one's way, and to actualize ideas. *Netzach* and *hod* block the inner capacities from convincing the father that the son is not yet ready for the learning process or that external challenges are likely to interfere.

---

in the influence from *chesed* and adjusts *chesed* to fit the vessels of the recipient. The middle line provides balances between the lines, between giver and receiver.

42. See "Shabbat Parashat Va'etchanan," *Hemshech Ayin-Bet*, vol. 1, 353.

The sixth faculty is *yesod*. The *sefirah* of *yesod* expresses connection, a bond that produces a thirst that opens up the channels of intellect and improves the way things are expressed. When a person is closed and shut off, even if he really prepares himself intellectually, he won't be able to properly and fully express himself. His words will come out truncated and ungraceful because they lack a relationship with the content being learned. *Yesod* is responsible for the connection between father and son, a bond that also invites the father to share a greater flow of level-appropriate ideas.[43]

Finally comes *malchut*, which packages the idea. It is the revelation of the soul's capacities to the outside world, associated with the faculty of speech. In the mind and even within the emotions, a person understands something about another person or something about the world. However, it's all still in the realm of the individual's understanding and feelings. Comprehension and feelings are connected to one's personality. The attribute of *malchut* constitutes a form of disconnect from a person's own character, thus enabling a full relationship with another. In intellect and emotion, the other person impacts you and you are affected by the other, yet with *malchut*, you impact the other. All of our soul faculties are connected to our personality, but *malchut* expresses a spiritual development in which the person "exits" or "leaves" the self in order to establish a dialogue with the other. *Malchut* is discussed at length in the teachings of Chassidut.

Following this introduction, the anatomy of the soul should be clearer. A person has intellect and emotions. Their relationship forms our character and personality. However, the picture gets more complicated when you add in the war between the souls.

Both the more animalistic part of a person and the more godly part feature intellect, emotion, and the rest of the soul's ten faculties. The faculties of the natural soul are a mirror image of the godly soul's faculties. The natural soul's faculties do not directly stem from the Creator as do the faculties of the godly soul. Instead of ten *sefirot*, the natural soul is comprised of ten impure crowns. They act on a person like external

---

43. For further examples, see the Lubavitcher Rebbe, "Shabbat Parashat Chayei Sarah, 5720" *Torat Menachem*, vol. 27, 1960, part 1, 141.

forces and pull him far from his inner being, as Rabbi Shneur Zalman describes.[44] While the powers of the natural soul express disconnect between one's inner being and external conduct, the godly soul's powers express the connection between the intellect and emotions, and the essence of the soul.

The aforementioned view has significant implications for treatment. Since our corrupted traits derive from the natural soul, such as arrogance, pride, sadness, and anxiety, and are outside of our inner being, they are only discussed in brief, if at all, in Rabbi Shneur Zalman's Tanya. His general approach dismisses involvement in them. In his eyes, a connection to the essence, to wholesomeness and goodness, automatically gets rid of the negative. Any involvement in depression, for example, only amplifies it. The way to get out of negative traits is by connecting to a positive, proper, and accurate grasp of reality.

For Rabbi Shneur Zalman, there's one mechanism by which we can measure the capacities that are active in the soul: whether there is separation from the Creator or connection with Him. The godly soul allows for the process of connection to the Creator as well as to one's inner being, while the natural soul embodies separation from the Creator and the true essence of our soul.

Seeing our behavior in terms of degrees of separation from God provides Rabbi Shneur Zalman a foundation for describing what good and bad really are. Bad, or evil, has to do with disconnection. Every evil thing derives its sustenance from kelipah and the Sitra Achra, the other side which is far from holiness, yet plays itself as the main character and turns a blind eye to anyone or anything else. Evil is connected to a one-dimensional, egocentric view of life. On the other hand, goodness relates to a person's sense of unity and connectedness with the world.

Everyone has a mosaic of faculties, but there are some traits that are particularly dominant and come to define one's personality. Personal growth and working on our own self involves dealing with those traits.

---

44. "The soul of Sitra Achra derived from kelipat nogah, which is clothed in man's blood, consists of ten 'crowns of impurity.'" Tanya, Likkutei Amarim, ch. 6. The total number of crowns comes to eleven (including keter), and opposing them are the eleven spices in the incense burned in the Temple, and the eleven skin curtains in the Tabernacle. See Rabbi Yosef Yitzchak, "Shabbat Parashat Mikeitz, 1926," Sefer Hamaamarim.

We can't change the dominant drives of the animal soul. A person of *chesed*, a social person who enjoys giving, cannot transform into a person of *gevurah*, someone who contracts, who engages in inner spiritual pursuits divorced from the outside world.

Rabbi Sholom DovBer Schneersohn, the fifth Rebbe of Chabad, states:

> One's inherent nature will never change.... A person of *chesed* will never transform into a *gevurah* person.... Similarly, a person who naturally embodies *gevurah* will never change and become inherently endowed with *chesed*.... And this is so no matter how hard one tries to change one's nature...[45]

A person with a particular nature has a choice: express it in a healthy, inner way, or do so in the opposite way, which will likely be negative and expressive of the traits of the external dimension or, as expressed in Kabbalah, the *kelipah*.

For example, if you use the framework of the *middot* (character traits) to generate a psychological picture of a personality, a person dominated by the trait of *chesed* (kindness) will have a personality characterized by loving others. Such an individual will love being around people and derive pleasure from giving to others. This is a person who easily connects. In contrast, the problematic or *kelipah* expression of doing *chesed* is a person whose love of others is a product of self-love. Such a person is social, liked, and enjoyable to talk with, but is motivated to take, and

---

45. See Rabbi Sholom DovBer Schneersohn, "Shabbat Parashat Beha'alotecha, 1904," *Hemshech Ayin-Bet*, vol. 1, 93. "The *middot* are a simple expression of their source, as mentioned above." See also the Lubavitcher Rebbe: "It is human nature for everyone to have a particular path, according to their inborn character. For example, a person born when the dominant constellation is Mars (which relates to *gevurah*) will naturally tend toward a position of *gevurah*, a contraction, and not relate to *chesed*. And one born at a time connected to *chesed* will feature a nature expressive of *chesed*, and not at all of *gevurah*. Furthermore, those who work hard on themselves and achieve a change in their nature – e.g., expressing different conduct at appropriate times – even though they are naturally endowed with *gevurah*, nevertheless, their efforts connect them to acts of *chesed* (at appropriate times). Still, this fact itself is part of their nature, but it is nature that's been altered by efforts at personal growth." *Torat Menachem*, vol. 17, 1956, part 3, 13.

not to give. A narcissist such as this will invite friends to a new house in order to brag and not out of a true desire to share. A true person of *chesed*, however, identifies with others and knows how to be sensitive to their pains and joys. But a self-loving person, whose attribute of *chesed* is distorted, will struggle to identify with others in this way. Yet the narcissistic *chesed* doer won't transform into an offensive person, either. The negative impact on others will be concealed and subtle. The *kelipah* of *chesed* doesn't necessarily feature intentional, humiliating harm. It can even seem sweet to others, but all the while the offender is completely focused on the self and on personal needs.

An additional example would be a *gevurah* (strength) personality, which is characterized by a constant inner withholding. Unlike the *chesed*-oriented person, these types are never accepting of what appears on the surface. Rather, they dig deeper and look to reveal hidden layers. Their goal is to be abstract and to express their desire to rise higher spiritually. *Gevurah* personalities have a harder time connecting to their environment. They are always seeking something and are not necessarily living in harmony with what is happening in the moment.

The distorted dimension of *gevurah* isn't a state of inner seeking for unhealthy things. Instead, it's expressed as frustration due to the holding back. The lack of inner satisfaction is experienced as bitterness, a lack of happiness, criticism, guilt, and avoidance. The lack of a pathway for expression leads to searching to fill in what's missing, resulting in feeling no pleasure in life or with current reality. On the other hand, a positive expression of *gevurah* would be having a deep desire to understand things, to search, create, and explore.

Even when properly formed, the *middot* are not fully revealed as they are. They differ from person to person in the quality and strength of their expression. They become intertwined and interconnected with each other and thereby balance each other. So, for example, a father who loves his son must be able to institute boundaries. The two traits of love and fear become enmeshed and together work positively on behalf of the child's development.

In a talk from 1812, Rabbi Shneur Zalman offered an analogy that helps us appreciate the beauty generated by the partnering of the *middot*: "When a person's attributes are too good, it ceases to be beautiful. Just as it's not beautiful when his traits are too wicked. Rather, a person whose traits are properly balanced and mixed together is called beautiful."[46]

Rabbi Shneur Zalman presents the classic example of the schools of Hillel and Shammai to describe the concept of interdependence and balance in the *middot* (character traits). Hillel and Shammai were the two leading sages of the last century BCE, who founded opposing schools of Jewish thought. While the school of Shammai typically expressed stringency, measure, and precision, there were topics regarding which they were more lenient. And the school of Hillel, though typically lenient, had other areas in which they were strict.

> Now, every Jew needs to comprise both these traits [*chesed* and *gevurah*] ... Thus, we find various matters that demonstrate the leniencies of Beit Shammai and the stringencies of Beit Hillel. This teaches us why Beit Shammai, whose soul was rooted in the Supernal "left," always decided stringently regarding all Torah prohibitions. Whereas Beit Hillel, who derived from the Supernal "right," would find arguments for leniency in order to permit the things prohibited by Beit Shammai... nevertheless, in numerous matters, even Beit Shammai were lenient. This is due to the inclusiveness of their soul's root, which is compounded of the "right" (*chesed*) as well. And, likewise, the root of Beit Hillel's soul was also compounded of the "left" (*gevurah*).[47]

The more a trait tries to reveal itself as an independent entity, without inclusion that leads to its expression alongside other traits, the more it stands to reason that its expression will include emotional problems that derive from *kelipah*. Without the balance present among a person's *middot*, individual traits are likely to generate soul expressions that push the person away from other traits. For example, a person gripped by anger and nerves will express one trait: *gevurah* of the animal soul. He or she will not be able to express other traits.

---

46. For a different version, see "V'Rachel Haitah Yefat Toar," *Maamarei Admor Hazaken* (5572/1812), 108.
47. *Igrot Kodesh – Alter Rebbe*, letter 13, 245.

WHOLESOME COMPLETENESS

The godly soul's primary challenge is to reveal the person's actual inner being and express the concealed, hidden part of the soul. The godly soul fulfills its vision by expressing a person's wholesome completeness.

The goal to express our inner being has practical implications in how we view ourselves. In this context, lacks aren't viewed as blemishes. A person is fundamentally whole. Expressions of the natural soul conceal this, but don't cause damage to our wholesomeness. Just as a person doesn't feel incomplete for lack of wings, so, too, are inappropriate behaviors not a cause for concern that something might be permanently missing or flawed. Rather, the lack is part of the structure of the life given to us by the Creator so that we will reveal our full and complete being, our inner essence.

In Rabbi Shneur Zalman's outlook, this goal can be seen as a form of inner return. A part of the human purpose in the world is to sense one's inner completion and express it. On the other hand, disconnection from such internal examination is described by Rabbi Shneur Zalman as alienation from the inner spark of godliness that is one's true self.

> And not every person merits to attain that level.... Because that dimension is present by him, but in a state of exile and captivity. Moreover, it parallels the exile of the Shechinah (Divine Presence), since it is the godly spark that is present within the godly soul.[48]

It's important to highlight that each soul's connection with the body and capacity for expression are different. The animal soul activates the body directly, while the godly soul has to work through the animal soul. The natural soul is responsible for instinctual expressions and the connection with the body and can also be used as a tool for the godly soul.

Rabbi Shneur Zalman's psychology doesn't describe a war in which one side seeks to annihilate the other, but rather, a battle between two souls for control. The goal of the fight is to determine which side will influence a person's actual conduct and thinking. The godly soul's mission is to influence the path of the natural soul and train it. On its own, the godly soul lacks the capacity to influence physicality; it needs the

---

48. Ibid., letter 65, 245.

natural soul in order to have an impact. The animal soul is a necessary and natural element, but it conceals God's presence in a person and in the world when it acts independently. However, as soon as the godly soul is victorious in the war for control, the natural soul transforms into its servant.[49]

Therefore, to a certain extent the comparison made in the previous chapter to the soul's war is liable to be deceptive. The two souls are not like arena fighters. Rather, the warring souls are more like horse and rider. They aren't distinct polar opposites, but they are connected to each other. The godly soul tries to guide the animal soul and work through it. It seeks to transform the animal soul into its chariot. The godly soul is unable to be expressed in physicality without the help of the animal soul, who often rebels, challenges, and refuses to carry the rider.

Seemingly, the godly soul should come across as being stronger. Its potential is far greater, since it is sourced directly in the Creator. However, the animal soul's influence upon us can be felt more powerfully due to its direct connection with the body and its love of physical and tangible pleasures, while the godly soul loves the abstract and spiritual instead. The result is that the godly soul has to constantly work and push to express itself. Without proper awareness, opposition, and guidance, the corrupt attributes of the animal soul are likely to wield great strength.

According to Rabbi Shneur Zalman, the goal of the dominion of the godly soul over the animal soul, like that of a rider on a horse, is the realization of man's purpose. A person's mission is to express God's presence in the world by way of the godly soul influencing the animal soul.

How is the battle expressed practically? How are the godly soul's abilities expressed in our daily lives? After Rabbi Shneur Zalman finishes his discussion about the faculties active in the soul, he moves on to describe the way they become revealed.

---

49. Tanya, *Likkutei Amarim*, ch. 23, 35.

CHAPTER 5

The Battlefield

CHARACTERISTICS OF VICTORY

Can a person really change? According to research on the process of socialization, the more a person matures and grows, the harder it becomes to change the general shape of the person's conduct and thinking. What is Rabbi Shneur Zalman's position on this? As a Chassidic leader, he held the view that people can change. A person has to be in motion, seeking to get outside of himself, to develop and flourish. Rabbi Shneur Zalman did not want to see years passing by while people remained stuck with the same issues of anger, fear, pride, judgment, and criticism. It's a mistake to think that change is a sign of weakness or that cynicism, outbursts, and mockery have a protective effect. According to Rabbi Shneur Zalman's collection of discourses and teachings, a person's mission is to change.

Chassidut not only honors the desire to change, but also acknowledges the power of the soul's faculties deep within the person, as well as the characteristics of the battle. We aren't blank slates; there's a nature embedded inside us, and our emotional traits reveal this nature.[1] Therefore, we can assume that Rabbi Shneur Zalman does not expect people to change their character in the first stage of work, but he surely expects ultimate victories in the inner battle. Man's true test is to be doggedly insistent on victory in an arena that probably appears repetitive,

---

1. For example, see *Torat Menachem*, vol. 17, 1956, part 3.

at first glance. At the end of a long journey of victories, a person is likely to achieve inner changes. This is how a person can change the nature of his character.[2] These victories also enable a person to prevent any external, *kelipah*-influenced expression of his traits, while encouraging more positive revelations. For example, one may transform anger and insult into passion and warmth, or convert bitterness and introversion into deep inner searching.

What do we mean by victory? Simply put, being more happy than depressed; decreasing fear, pressure, and a lack of faith and trust; removal of negative thoughts; learning to avoid being led to undesirable places by one's thoughts; strengthening one's self; boldly restraining from negative speech; avoiding laziness and being involved in fruitful activity; overcoming addictions; and increasing mutual responsibility. We could say that Rabbi Shneur Zalman's challenge was to help his audience become connected to the true, inner reality, to inspire them to be among those who connect with others and make a positive contribution rather than causing division and being takers. Victory has to involve people becoming less self-absorbed, its primary expression being to make others, not oneself, the main focus. Victorious people are those who listen and truly see others, who identify with their pain and their struggle. Victorious people are connected to themselves. They view themselves and make decisions free from the influences of public opinion, trends, or what others think.

These small victories, the conquests in battle, are a person's mission in life, according to the Tanya. The purpose is not found only in the large-scale accomplishments of the Jewish people or in a society as a whole, but rather in each person's daily wins over everything that comes their way. From Rabbi Shneur Zalman's perspective, these victories are the greatest disseminators of godliness and the Creator's majesty.[3] Rabbi Shneur Zalman sees the subjugation of the animal soul's drives as a central feature of *avodat Hashem* (serving the Creator) as well as of rectifying and transforming one's character traits.[4]

---

2. This is discussed at greater length in Sholom DovBer Schneerson, "Shabbat Parashat Beha'alotcha," *Hemshech Ayin-Bet*, vol. 1, 509, 674.

3. Tanya, *Likkutei Amarim*, ch. 27.

4. The Rebbe Rashab expresses this directly: "For this reason we were given a godly

Scottish economist Adam Smith, who lived in the same time period as Rabbi Shneur Zalman, outlined his view of the proper system for maintaining a thriving economy: when all people work to further their own interests, everyone benefits. According to Smith, without government interference, companies thrive and grow. It's as if there is an invisible hand supporting economic competition and guiding everything toward success for the economy and for all the businesses involved. This would be on the condition that each individual pursues self-interest.[5] In other words, personal interests help promote common interests. Rabbi Shneur Zalman's approach, however, is the opposite of Smith's. Rabbi Shneur Zalman wants people to work on their characters and improve themselves by overcoming their personal interests and instead connecting and identifying with others. At the same time, there is one aspect of his teachings that has some similarity with Smith's idea of the "invisible hand." When everyone works toward self-improvement, the overall situation and society as a whole is healed. Self-refinement is the most crucial assignment a person has, and the purpose for which we are created. National interests are advanced by each and every person's individual efforts at self-improvement.

GARMENTS OF THE SOUL

Now that the pathways of victory have been described and outlined, we need to ask the following question: How do the battles between the animal soul and the godly soul play out? According to Rabbi Shneur Zalman, there are three battlefields on which the souls' capacities are expressed, that is, three places which demand conquest and victory: thought, speech, and action.

In these three arenas, the powers of the souls battle and find expression. There are no other battlegrounds. Soul capacities can only be expressed in thoughts, in spoken words, and in actions. For example,

---

soul – to vanquish the natural soul. And this is the purpose of creation: the godly soul's powers overcoming and suppressing the natural soul's powers. If the natural soul weren't needed in order for us to work to subjugate it, it would never have been created..." See the Rebbe Rashab, *Kuntres u'Mayan mi'Beit Hashem*, ch. 1, maamar 13.
5. Adam Smith, *The Wealth of Nations* (Oxford: Oxford University Press, 2008).

no one sees our feelings, but rather, people perceive the ways in which those feelings are expressed. Only revealed emotion can be experienced by others via actions and words. For the one who loves, feelings are revealed in thoughts and in strong desires that push aside any other thoughts. Generally speaking, the way we perceive ourselves and the deep potential active within us is through thought. Still, there are times in which we reveal how we feel in words and actions. Speech and action are a part of our communication and connection with others and with the world around us.

In Rabbi Shneur Zalman's teachings, thought, speech, and action are called the garments of the soul. The garments do not express anything of their own. Rather, they express the capacities of the soul, the comprehension of the intellect and emotions, and sensitivities of the *middot*.[6] But the garments are not a part of the essence of the soul or its inner intellectual and emotional faculties. They are something additional, the same way a person's clothes are not a part of one's inner dimension. Just as a person can choose how to dress to attend an event, so too, says Rabbi Shneur Zalman, a person has the freedom to choose the kind of thoughts, words, and actions to use. They can be positive, optimistic, and focused – or the opposite.

The following quote from a Chassidic discourse delivered by Rabbi Shneur Zalman in 1806 explains the difference between the garments of the soul (that is, thought, speech, and action) and the faculties of the soul (that is, the intellect and emotions):

> There is a difference between these faculties (ten powers of the soul: intellect and emotions) and the three garments – thought, speech, and action. The faculties are called connected and united garments, bound to the essence of the soul. Even though they are the soul's faculties and not its essence, nevertheless, they are totally bound up and united with it.... Such is not the case with the three garments of thought, speech, and action – they are completely separate garments.
>
> This is like physical clothes which are a separate entity from the

---

6. See Rabbi Yoel Kahn, *Machshevet Hachassidut* (Kfar Chabad: Sifriyat Eshel, 2005), 57.

person wearing the clothes. He can choose to wear them or remove them, since they are totally separate from him and worn only at his choosing. But they have no true closeness and connection with him, since they are a foreign entity and separate from him. He can change from one to the other by simply removing one and putting on another, etc. The same cannot be said about the body in which the soul is enclothed. . . . [7]

Categorizing thought, speech, and action as garments emphasizes their actual distance from the soul's essence. Clothing is foreign to our being, while the limbs are a part of us. We use clothing in order to show ourselves publicly, and through them, others can gain a sense of who we are. For example, wearing an expensive jacket sends a particular message. On the other hand, sloppy clothing broadcasts a different message. Either way, the message isn't necessarily true. I can wear an expensive jacket without being a wealthy man. The same applies to the soul's garments. Every joke or story we tell and every thought passing through our minds reveals something about us. But what we choose to express doesn't have to be in sync with our understanding and feelings. That's why, for example, a person can hate someone yet still speak well of him. In such a case, the words are not expressive of what is in the soul's faculties.

According to what we have explained until now, the garments are likely to be expressions of a person's disconnect from his true essence. It is for that reason that Rabbi Shneur Zalman sees so much value in them. As he writes:

> Even though they are called merely "garments" of the soul, nevertheless, their quality is infinitely higher and greater than that of the soul itself.[8]

The soul's garments are external elements, and this endows them with an advantage: they can be changed or replaced. The soul's faculties and traits are difficult to change, but they can be expressed in ways that differ from their natural tendencies. It's the soul's essence that is

---

7. See *Maamarei Admor Hazaken* (5567/1806), vol. 1. For a different version of this, see "Patach v'Amar 'Ahnt Hu Chad,'" 47.

8. Tanya, *Likkutei Amarim*, ch. 4.

resistant to change. A person who controls anger or restrains kindness and unconditional giving in response to the needs of the environment hasn't changed who he or she is. The only change that's immediately available is in the soul's garments.

This is what leads to Rabbi Shneur Zalman's view that the garments of thought, speech, and action are where a person's battles truly occur, where the natural soul and the godly soul engage in fierce combat, and where one needs to be victorious. It's there in the garments that the godly soul's potential can and must vanquish the drives of the natural soul. Such victories enable a person to grow and develop and to express the strength of the godly soul. We don't choose our nature, but we do get to select how we'll behave, what we'll say, and on what we'll focus our thoughts. This is in our power in each and every moment.

Rabbi Shneur Zalman's goal is to demonstrate that the garments are more than merely something external that a person utilizes as needed. Rather, since a person's thoughts, words, and actions are garments of the soul, they should truly suit the soul. When we speak words of affection, those words are more than just an outcome of the love felt in our hearts. The soul's faculty of love itself is expressed through the words. Victory, then, is when a person chooses garments that are true to the soul's exalted and lofty being. Defeat is choosing soul garments that disconnect us from our inner essence and are not expressions of the soul's potential in thoughts, words, and actions.

In the Tanya, Rabbi Shneur Zalman describes the battle and victory found in the soul's garments as follows:

> The three garments of the animal soul – namely thought, speech, and action – which derive their vitality from *kelipah* do not prevail within a person over the godly soul to the extent of clothing themselves in the body, neither in the brain nor in the mouth or in any of the other 248 organs, to cause them to sin and to defile them, G-d forbid. Only the three garments of the godly soul alone manifest themselves in the body.[9]

An advantage to the garments being external in comparison to the soul is their greater potential for change and broader ability for expression

---

9. Ibid., ch. 12.

compared with the intellectual and emotional faculties of the soul.[10] Rabbi Shneur Zalman offers two examples to illustrate the advantage held by the garments over the intellect and emotions. The first example is what happens when a person of average intelligence hears ideas from a wise speaker. The simpler man can later publicly repeat each and every point he heard, and the audience will believe he's an intelligent man. He's merely being glorified for having wonderfully wise garments. In truth, he lacks the intellectual ability to create ideas like those shared by the wise man, whom he had previously heard. The second example is that of a person who is wicked on the inside, yet who exercises restraint and only expresses good deeds, so that acquaintances come to believe he or she is a good person.[11]

The simple person who repeats the wise man's words is not only glorified by another's wisdom but actually penetrated by it. Intense involvement with wise words eventually transforms this simple person into a wise one, according to Rabbi Shneur Zalman. The same applies to a person who tends to back away from his or her environment. If such a person becomes accustomed to doing acts of kindness, he or she will eventually transform into a kind person, to the extent that the essence of the person – the character and tendencies – change. These two examples demonstrate how habits can lead to change and to periods in which, through effort and perseverance, hidden traits are exposed and become dominant.[12]

We learn from these two examples that a person whose natural traits are less than ideal can improve the inner dimension by working with the soul's garments. Though they may be external to the soul and influenced by its present state, they can also have their own impact, just as a person's clothes impact movements and expressions. Arrive at a

---

10. The *keilim* (vessels), the intellect, and the emotions are limited relative to the garments. Regarding the advantage of the garments over the vessels, see an example in *Torat Menachem*, vol. 15, 1956, part 1, 123. See also *Torat Menachem*, vol. 4, 1952, part 1, 268.

11. Printed in *Maamarei Admor Hazaken Haketzarim* (New York: Kehot, 1981), 144. See "Shabbat Parashat Beshalach, Tu b'Shevat, 5720," *Torat Menachem*, vol. 27, 1960, part 1, 352.

12. See "Shabbat Chol Hamoed Sukkot, 5721," *Torat Menachem*, vol. 29, 1961, part 2, 43.

party with inappropriate clothing, and you'll feel uncomfortable and express that in your conduct. The potential wielded by the garments is the impact of the external on the internal. If a person strives to avoid being judgmental and, instead, to spread warmth and affection, this behavior may initially seem forced. However, with the passage of time, the developing positive habits become second nature. Habituation has the power to embed new capacities in a person even though they previously did not exist at all.[13] Habits have a significant impact. For a person who isn't naturally consistent in a specific trait or behavior, repetition can become habitual and be adopted to overcome an inherent tendency. At the same time, unhealthy habits will likely reveal concealed aspects that were better off unexpressed.[14] A person regularly exposed to cynicism and criticism will close up, lack sensitivity and care, and be unable to identify with others.

Why can't the soul's faculties be revealed as they are? Why does the soul need garments?

It's hard to properly express ourselves when we're in an emotional and agitated state. Our intention becomes detached from our words. That lack of calm also makes it difficult to concentrate and focus on learning. In order for the soul's potential to find expression in its garments, it has to undergo compression. Its power needs to be contained and fitted into the garment. This *tzimtzum*, contraction, is part of the process by which the soul's faculties are revealed externally, both to the person himself and to those around him. Distinguishing between the soul's faculties and its garments enables the faculties to communicate expression and revelation to others.

When we're unable to express our emotions, it leads to a piling up of bitterness, frustration, and dissatisfaction, and a turn to aggressive

13. "Furthermore, habit reigns supreme in all matters; it becomes second nature." Ibid., ch. 14. Regarding faith: "This is also implicit in the word *emunah* (faith), which is a term indicating 'training,' to which a person habituates himself, like a craftsman who trains his hands." Tanya, *Likkutei Amarim*, ch. 42.

14. Moshe Shilat points out that the index to the Tanya arranged by the Lubavitcher Rebbe lists five places under the term *hergel* (habit). These sources in the Tanya discuss various benefits and types of habituation and consistency. See Moshe Shilat, "Regilut, Hergel v'Hatmada," *Maayanotecha*, April 25, 2012, http://www.toratchabad.com/contents.asp?aid=90373.

behaviors that vent the frustration. There are faculties pushing for expression. Without a pathway for expression, a sense of deprivation and lack of wholesomeness will grow.

When the soul's faculties are powerfully radiating but lack a means of expression, we call that *tohu* (chaos). Chaos results when strong soul faculties – which may be understood as being intense lights – have no path to expression or are being incorrectly expressed. A *tohu* state of consciousness involves having unsatisfied desires and drives and an inability to distinguish between real and imaginary needs or compulsions.

An aspect of this process to bear in mind is the fact that our garments surround and protect us. Without them, we experience a lack of ability to express ourselves, which becomes a threat to our existence. The garments ensure that the soul's capacities are contracted and balanced. At times, we find ourselves taken over by strong emotions such as anger, fear, or depression, and changing garments is one of the methods for dealing with such powerful expressions of the natural soul.[15] In this way, the garments offer protection for both one's self and others. Just as clothing covers over and conceals us, so do the soul's garments cover and conceal it. We also pick the clothes that we're wearing, and thus they express what we choose to reveal. The garments can cover up unhealthy expression and assist in building positive social connection. They can protect people with sensitive souls and provide a buffer against direct contact with our traits. And the garments can also help a coarse person to become more refined. They grant us the opportunity to reveal our soul powers and traits in an orderly fashion that is clear and contextually appropriate.

Teachings of Chassidut emphasize the verse which states: "[The world] wasn't created as chaos [*tohu*]; it was formed to be orderly and settled."[16] According to the teachings of the soul's structure, *tohu* is rectified, and has *tikkun*, literally meaning that it is fixed or purified from sin, by adopting garments in which the lights and their vessels can settle.[17] In general, lights are the faculties of ths soul that seek to express

15. The source of the animal soul is the world of *tohu*. For example, see "Kuntres u'Mayon mi'Beit Hashem," ch. 2, maamar 13.

16. Yeshayahu 45:18.

17. *Tohu* and *tikkun* are two fundamental concepts in the teachings of Kabbalah and Chassidut, which are also levels in the structure of worlds and in one's grasping

themselves. The vessels contain the lights within them and allow them to be revealed. In a state of *tohu*, there is a mismatch between lights and vessels. In a baby, for example, the intellect is underdeveloped and the lights shine without vessels. A baby is unable to express thoughts in orderly speech and therefore cannot control the vessels. A baby whose desires go unmet bursts into tears, and no amount of verbal explanations will help. With maturity, the child develops the capacity to realize that a particular desire is not productive: this is a mode of *tikkun*, in which there are vessels to accommodate the lights. The world was created in order for man to express lofty levels of light via his body, actions, thoughts, and words, and thereby make the world a better place: to give *tikkun* to the world, to fix it and make it good.

Rabbi Shneur Zalman provides an extensive discussion of the garments in order to show his audience how to utilize them to express the soul's faculties. Each garment has its own characteristics; however, the essential aspects are the same for everyone. The garments that indicate victory for the godly soul are those which connect us to ourselves, our environment, and those around us. They help us be connected and attached, not cut off and isolated. Furthermore, they prevent any one particular trait such as anger, stress provocation, and the like, from total takeover and dominance in our lives.

CHALLENGES OF USING THE GARMENTS

1. Thought

Out of all three garments, thought has several aspects that make it our most important and yet challenging arena of battle. In the Tanya, the concept of thought appears no fewer than fifty times, which testifies to the centrality and importance of our efforts here. The primary task in our thought work is to formulate a proper and spiritually healthy approach to our view of self and the world. It's also incumbent upon us to avoid thoughts that drag us into a place that cuts us off from an accurate view of reality.

What is a spiritually healthy and proper view of reality? This doesn't

---

the Creator. They are explained in many sources, for example, *Likkutei Torah*, Shir Hashirim 9c.

refer to moral and ethical differences of opinion, but to our inner processes. Rabbi Shneur Zalman describes the common phenomenon that
occurs in our lives, which is that we're often exhausted by our thoughts.
They ceaselessly flow and create an intense struggle. We try to concentrate on something of importance, but our thoughts frequently pull us
into the dark abyss. We may not be willing to admit it, but our thoughts
expose us to things that we ourselves may find revolting. Nearly everyone
contends with such flows of thought. Most people experience thoughts
that would be labelled as shameful or even dangerous if revealed publicly.
Furthermore, most of the worries that swamp us are caused by our
incessant thoughts.[18]

What is the source of these problematic thoughts? The main battles between the intellect and emotion, between mind and heart, and
between the animal soul and the godly soul occur in our thoughts. When
the animal soul claims victory, the flow of thoughts are likely to be those
that drag us down into troublesome areas, forbidden things, unethical
issues, and certainly into an unfocused state, which all translate into
wasted time and energy. We are not our thoughts. As explained, thought
is only a garment. However, our thoughts tow our innermost and loftiest
dimension into those inappropriate places.[19]

Due to the battle waged by the souls within our minds, thought
is exhausting and constantly moving. The fatigue is a product of the
grappling of the intellect and emotion of the animal soul on one side
and of the godly soul on the other. The combatants tire as they each seek
total control over thought.

One of the examples of the battle waged in thought that Rabbi

---

18. "Like the waters of a river that flows constantly at a powerful pace," as expressed
by the Lubavitcher Rebbe in his private study, "Motza'ei Shabbat Noach," *Maamarim
Melukatim*, 1978, vol. 1, 246.

19. Thoughts flow and also sweep along with them a person's higher elements, the
part of God that we all possess. This is the godly soul. We all have a part of God in
us. This is the innovation of the Tanya: that the Creator is not above or on the side
but a part of us. In the teachings of Chassidut, the discussion about the movement
of thought is based on the expression found in Shir Hashirim: "The king is bound in
the tresses" (Shir Hashirim 7:6). This notion is quoted in Tanya, *Likkutei Amarim*,
ch. 45. According to the commentary of Rashi, "in the tresses" means "in the flow of
water, in the pools constructed in Israel in order to water the flocks."

Shneur Zalman discusses at length is what can happen during the time of prayer.

According to his approach, we should not become disappointed if during prayer, we experience "cravings and other foreign thoughts." Such foreign, extraneous thoughts are a natural occurrence and not evidence of our blemishes. In fact, the opposite is true. Such thoughts attest to the inner war taking place inside us, the battle between the souls, in which each seeks total dominion over our thoughts. As he writes:

> The foreign thought that occurred to him derives from the *kelipah* of the left part of the heart, which wages war…against the godly soul within him. It is known that it is the way of combatants and similarly of wrestlers that when one is gaining the upper hand, the other likewise exerts himself with all the resources of his strength in order to prevail. Therefore, when the godly soul exerts itself and musters all its strength in prayer, the *kelipah* also gathers strength to counter it, aiming to confuse and topple the godly soul by means of a foreign thought of its own.
>
> This refutes a common error. When a foreign thought occurs to some people during prayer, they mistakenly conclude that their prayer is worthless. For, had they prayed properly and correctly, no foreign thoughts would arise in their minds. They would be correct if we had but one soul, the same soul that prays being also the one that thinks and ponders on the foreign thoughts. But, in fact, there are two souls, each waging war against the other in the person's mind – each of them wishes and desires to rule and pervade the mind exclusively.[20]

Unlike speech and action, thought never ceases, because thought is the garment most connected to the soul.[21] For this reason, Chassidut refers to thought as *levush pnimi* (an "inner garment").[22] The connection

---

20. Tanya, *Likkutei Amarim*, ch. 28.

21. Thought isn't necessarily the highest of the soul garments. Speech seemingly should be greater, since it partially derives from elemental dimensions of the intellect. See Tanya, *Iggeret Hakodesh*, siman 5. For more on this subject, see Yehiel Harari, "Hamashma'ut Hapnimit Shel Hadibbur," in *Yom Huledet*, 3rd ed. (Ashkelon: Hitbonenut Publishers, 2012), 139ff.

22. Concerning the three types of thought, see *Likkutei Torah*, Shir Hashirim, p. 34c.

of thought with the soul enables it to reach deeper into the soul than either speech or action can, and, thus, its impact on the soul is typically immediate.

Due to the tremendous importance of thought in our relationship with ourselves, Rabbi Shneur Zalman quotes the words of our sages: "Thoughts of doing a sin are harder than the sin itself."[23] It is harder on the soul because it takes the soul down. Of course, the actual performance of a sin is worse than thinking about doing it; however, undesirable thoughts blemish the soul in a far more intense way than the deed. As a result of the damage caused by negative and unintentional thoughts, Rabbi Shneur Zalman asks his readers to be vigilant of the battles fought in this arena. We can't prevent negative ideas, worries, and desires from popping into our thoughts, but we can choose to replace them with alternatives. It seems that it's natural for such thoughts to show up; they are typically attacks from the animal soul. The speed with which we detach from those thoughts and from wallowing in them in our minds is the primary test we face.

We cannot completely stop the flow of our thoughts, but the ideas they contain can be exchanged. We can change our thought garments, but we can't go around naked, so to speak. In other words, one thought can be swapped for another, and when we do this, the previous thought automatically ceases.[24] It's impossible to think two thoughts at the same time.

One of our challenges is to obtain soulful calm and tranquility, a state free from worries in which we can concentrate, think clearly, and see a broad picture beyond the fears and passions that attract us. There is no experience of lacking while in this tranquil state. We feel a sense of completion that is deeply enjoyable. Obviously, this experience of completion is subjective and depends on the feeling that we are in what we believe to be the right place at the right time. In truth, wherever we currently find ourselves is the right place and time for us. And when we choose to think this way, we're less fatigued because we have won a battle. Furthermore, in this state, we are beyond the pull of undesirable

---

23. Talmud, *Yoma* 29a. See *Tanya*, *Likkutei Amarim*, ch. 11; and other sources.
24. The Lubavitcher Rebbe, *Igrot Kodesh*, vol. 13, 40.

thoughts. In the current moment, we choose not to focus on whatever may seem to be lacking or missing.[25]

There are several general methods to get a break from one's thoughts – in other words, from the exhausting battles being waged in the mind. The primary method is to focus our thoughts on something else. In such a state, intellect dominates over emotions, and the mind does not allow undesirable feelings such as stress or anxiety or undesirable tendencies to control us. This approach leaves us focused on what we're doing to such an extent that no thought can be expressed without guidance from the intellect. Our intellect pushes our thoughts and thereby directs their flow. However, when we fail to use our intellect to control and direct our thoughts, then the heart – the source of our emotional traits – navigates our thoughts into an involvement with mundane cravings and desires.[26] We want emotions, but those which are being led by the mind.

Another reason why focus and victory in our thoughts is so crucial to Rabbi Shneur Zalman is due to this teaching of the Baal Shem Tov: people are where their thoughts are. Thoughts are where soul revelation occurs. Focusing the mind on something causes it to become revealed in our thoughts – and then, on a spiritual level, we are also in that space. Focus enables us to redo ourselves and make decisions that impact our lives. We can visit a place without having to actually be there, since our minds remain with us. Conversely, we can sit in an office while thinking of the place where we want to be, and there, in a spiritual sense, be found. How about the person who goes on vacation but can't relax and get free from the torrent of work-related thoughts? According to the logic here, it's as if he never went on vacation. This is one of the reasons that Rabbi Shneur Zalman emphasizes to his readers that a person who thinks of doing something positive is considered as if he did it, even if he didn't yet actually do it.[27]

This power of focusing our thoughts and minds puts one of the

25. For more on this, see "Admor Ha'emtza'i," *Torat Chaim*, Shemot (Exodus), vol. 2, Parashat Vayakhel, 391d.
26. Our thoughts are constantly influenced by our emotions and our intellect. Due to the burden borne by our thoughts, they are often referred to as "Leah." For example, see "Inyan Ki Sanuah Leah," *Maamarei Admor Hazaken* (5572/1812), 100.
27. See Tanya, *Likkutei Amarim*, ch. 16.

most important models in the teachings of Chassidut at the core of our lives: that of being a *pnimi* (deep, interior-directed person). A *pnimi* is a person who is completely immersed in whatever he is doing at the moment, oblivious to worries about other things. In the teachings of Chassidut, the *pnimi* is held up as the ideal and proper model for living. An obvious example of what it looks like to be a *pnimi* in our daily lives comes from a conversation between the fifth Lubavitcher Rebbe, Rabbi Sholom DovBer, and his son, Rabbi Yosef Yitzchak. The Rebbe had entered the room to join a Chassidic gathering, called a *farbrengen*, with the students in his yeshiva, and asked them to sing a *niggun* (a wordless, soulful melody), the one typically said prior to the Rebbe's recitation of a Chassidic discourse, deep Torah teachings he had prepared to say, known as a *maamar*. The Chassidim sang, but the Rebbe could sense that the students weren't singing with concentration and intention. They weren't immersed in the *niggun*. They were singing, yet longing to hear the Torah teaching already.

> Nowadays, they sing out of strange obligation – forced and limited . . . all the while thinking about something else. They're unaware. Although they do the right action, they still think about something else. They preferred to already be done with the task at hand, despite being right in the middle, and were looking forward to moving on to what they found more interesting. It really should not be this way. People should be present where they are, and only after that, be in the next place. However, as long as this is what I'm currently doing, here is where I need to be. Naturally, if I'm elsewhere, that's where I am – since that's the truth of the matter. Truth is where I am. Wherever I am, there I truly am. The main thing is to truly be wherever you are, and not to already be running away.[28]

Focus helps move us toward positive thoughts, gives us some distance from negative ones, and points out the truth of the matter at hand. As we saw in the first chapter with the Arizal's question, the Baal Shem Tov teaches that the entire world is constantly being created every moment.

---

28. *Torat Shalom*, p. 39; a similar discussion can be found in the Lubavitcher Rebbe's *Torat Menachem*, vol. 2, 1951, part 1, 106.

The Creator speaks, and His words continually renew the entirety of creation. Anyone who does not take this concept into consideration might be considered a *chitzoni* (superficial person). The label *chitzoni* is applied to a person who is unaware of the inner pulse and vitality behind all of existence, and instead identifies only with external appearances. Such a person loses the ability to live in the moment and be in the present and is dragged by such thoughts into a life of things that aren't really there. According to this view, foreign thoughts are not necessarily negative ones, but any out-of-place thought is a foreign one, since it keeps a person away from living in the present reality.

Such focus is valuable since it frees a person from constant self-involvement. The Chassidic approach tells us that we can invite good into our lives by thinking focused and positive thoughts. Focus envelops the soul in a positive garment and greatly benefits us, as we are freed from worries and enjoy tranquility.

At the heart of non-positive thoughts is a person who is putting him- or herself at the center of everything. And anything that distances us from relating directly to our current reality requires repair and cure. Any thinking that lacks mental guidance and direction leads us into pleasure cravings, desires, and into seeking the actualization of our personal interests. Such thinking is also likely to eventually push us into unhealthy behaviors. "The eye sees and the heart desires."[29] Unfocused or indulgent thinking paves the way for action by giving us approval to manifest the subject of our thoughts.

Another way to calm our thoughts is by sleeping. While sleeping we have dreams, which arise from our thoughts. According to the teachings of Chassidut, dreams, like the thoughts themselves, clothe the soul and help it gain expression in a person. By their very nature, thoughts never stop flowing. Just as they continually flow when we're awake, so too they continue to work while we're asleep. However, for a significant portion of the time that we're awake, our intellect and emotion guides our thoughts.[30] This ends during sleep when our intellect stops directing us.

---

29. Rashi, Bamidbar 15:39, cited in Tanya, *Likkutei Amarim*, ch. 30.

30. An important principle in the Tanya, which will be addressed in greater detail here in chapter 8 ("Advice for Living"), is to get to a state of "mind ruling over the heart" even within our flow of thoughts. For example, see Tanya, *Likkutei Amarim*, ch. 7, 12,

We continue producing thoughts, but they no longer constitute a battle between the intellect and emotions. Waking up after a long break from being on a battleground, we feel alert and sharp. Throughout sleep, our thoughts continue to flow without any attempt by the souls' capacities to gain access and expression.[31]

According to this perspective, sleep means giving our thoughts a break from the battle they experience all day long. Sleep, like focus, is essential for a person who is looking to powerfully transform and employ the intellect during waking hours. Sleep also fulfills an additional role. During sleep, we are unable to control our thoughts. Therefore, dreams can provide us with a sense of things, with an indicator of where we are holding in life. The Tanya's author encourages his readers to get a picture of their spiritual state by contemplating their dreams:

> Let him further consider his dreams. For the most part, they are "vanity, and an affliction of the spirit," since his soul does not ascend heavenward [during his sleep].[32]

A dream can give us a glimpse into those things about ourselves that we've chosen to hide away. They reveal, among many things, the behaviors and drives that we've been pushing aside. If we spent the day involved in something negative and unhealthy, such as watching violent movies, this will likely have an influence on us in our sleep. Reserved, unemotional people are likely to have dreams through which those emotions, fears, and the like can be expressed – things pushed off and held at bay during waking hours. A review of our dreams typically demonstrates the extent to which we are connected to reality, or to our own feelings and opinions.

---

30 and more. The ideal state is when we use our intellect to direct our thoughts. In the words of the Lubavitcher Rebbe: "When we are awake, then (as long as we are fit for the title of *adam* [man], and 'man's advantage over the animals' is his intellect and logic) our intellect directs all of our affairs." See "Sichah of third day of Chol Hamoed Sukkot, 19 Tishrei, 5721," *Torat Menachem*, vol. 29, 1961, part 2, 54.

31. On the topic of dreams, see Rabbi Shneur Zalman's *Torah Ohr*, Mikeitz, 35c and 35d; "Sichah of Shabbat Parashat Shemini, Shabbat Mevorchim Iyar, 5716," *Torat Menachem*, vol. 16, 1956, part 2, 260; and Yehiel Harari, *Chalomot u'Mashma'utam* (Ashkelon: Hitbonenut Publishers, 2007).

32. Tanya, *Likkutei Amarim*, ch. 29.

Using our intellectual faculties to focus and control our emotions is challenging, but victory means preventing the animal soul from gaining power over our thoughts and directing them as it wishes. It's a challenge that fills our waking hours and our sleep.

2. Speech

The garment of speech is different from the garment of thought. Thought can't be silenced, because thoughts are always moving; speech on the other hand can easily fail or be silenced. Nevertheless, the topic of speech enjoys tremendous attention in Jewish teachings in general, and particularly in Chassidut. There's a story concerning Rabbi Shneur Zalman's daughter which illustrates the power of speech.

Devorah Leah, the daughter of Rabbi Shneur Zalman (who was named for his sister), passed away at the young age of twenty-six. According to Chabad tradition, she decreed her fate upon herself. In the year 1792, opposition to the Chassidic movement was at its peak, a large amount of which was directed at Rabbi Shneur Zalman and his Chassidim. Devorah Leah heard that her father was demoralized by the accusations against him, and his dedication to Chassidut in those days was so great that his life hung in the balance. As noted previously, it had been recognized that Rabbi Shneur Zalman's general approach was that occurrences in the physical world were generated by spiritual causes. There was battle being waged in the spiritual realms over the future of Chassidut and its revelation of the secrets found in *pnimiyut haTorah*, the Torah's inner dimension. The final decisions formulated down here in our world were to be a product of the decisions made on high.

This deeply impacted Devorah Leah. She deliberated for many days until she finally called upon three elder Chassidim. Her request was that they serve as judges on a special, impromptu rabbinical court that would be sworn to absolute secrecy. She had decided to sacrifice herself in place of her father, using her life to obtain atonement and remove the decree. As a result, her father would live a long life focused on one goal: to continue to further advance the spreading of the wellsprings of the Torah and the teachings of Chassidut.

On the first night of Rosh Hashanah, Rabbi Shneur Zalman was accustomed to refrain completely from speaking. As he teaches, a new light descends into the world on Rosh Hashanah which radiates for the entire year. Rosh Hashanah is the head of all the days of the year. Every moment during those forty-eight hours is of great significance and bears tremendous potential to influence the entire year to come. Accordingly, Rabbi Shneur Zalman would refrain then from unnecessary speech. That year, 1792, Rabbi Shneur Zalman deviated from his custom. He called his daughter to him in order to give her a blessing. But all he could say was "l'shanah..." – the beginning of a blessing for a good year – before she jumped in and wished him instead "l'shanah haba'ah tikasev v'tichasem" – may you be signed and sealed for good in the coming year. She had prevented him from giving her a blessing that promised she would be signed and sealed for a good year to come, and instead, turned that blessing back to him. In her eyes, a blessing spoken by a tzaddik possesses tremendous power, and she wanted to actualize her plan of self-sacrifice. Two days later, on the Fast of Gedaliah, she passed away.

Due to the unique circumstance surrounding Devorah Leah's unexpected passing, a heavy grief settled on her father and all of Liozna. Throughout the initial seven days of mourning, he led all three daily prayers. The day before Yom Kippur, he went to her grave along with her three-year-old son, Menachem Mendel. Through his sobs he called out to those present: "Just as righteous tzaddikim are greater after passing than they were while living, so, too, are their blessings greater than when they were alive in the world. Devorah Leah, the daughter of Shterna, today is Yom Kippur. Bless your orphaned only son, Menachem Mendel, that this young boy should grow to be great in the Torah's revealed and concealed dimensions, and in good deeds, while living a long and good life. Request mercy for me and for the congregation of Chassidim and for the teachings of the Baal Shem Tov."[33]

Devorah Leah's son, Menachem Mendel, grew up in Rabbi Shneur Zalman's home and merited great attention from him. Chassidic lore commonly features the following statement: "My dedication to her son is how I pay the debt I owe for her self-sacrifice." With time, this grandson would become the third Rebbe of Chabad.

The story of Devorah Leah's death illustrates the tremendous attention paid to the faculty of speech.[34] The tzaddik's words can bring

---

33. See Rabbi Yosef Yitzchak, "Torat Shmuel," *Sefer Hasichot 5753/1993*, 127.
34. An example of speech's tangible impact on reality, from a Jewish perspective, can

about a decree or salvation; however, his daughter's words in front of a rabbinical court influenced the world and impacted the future, via a decision rendered in the higher worlds concerning the decree.

According to Rabbi Shneur Zalman, speech's influence on reality makes it impossible, for example, to be satisfied with engaging in prayer, reciting the Shema, or saying blessings non-verbally in our minds and thoughts. Rabbi Shneur Zalman quotes the words of our sages that speech is considered an action.[35] Jewish law states that the commandments come to full actualization via the physical utterance of words. Moreover, verbalizing the words helps us pray with proper intention and concentration. According to Chassidic thought, Jewish law insists on verbalizing supplications because speech helps us contend with our animal souls and exerts an influence on our physical lives.

In addition, Rabbi Shneur Zalman encouraged his Chassidim to pray with volume and enthusiasm, despite the opposition at the time to such a style. In a letter he sent to one of his Chassidim in Shklov, he explained the importance of verbalizing the prayers for arousing our concentration and attention:

> The basis of the entire Torah is to know God...with a full knowledge that's solidified by the wisdom of the heart.... All of this occurs nowadays by reciting the words found in the prayers and blessings leading up to the Amidah prayer [the central part of the prayer service]...with full pronunciation and volume that inspired heartfelt intention.[36]

---

be seen in the recital of the Pitum Haketoret prayer prior at the beginning of prayer services. "We were taught: Rebbe Natan would say to those preparing the incense in the Temple: 'Grind it well, grind it well.' Because speech is good for the incense" (Talmud, *Keritot* 6b). Those responsible for preparing the incense were asked to speak out loud because of the positive influence their voices would have on the spices used and the spread of their fragrance. In fact, this was true to such an extent that in the times of the Temple, "Goats in Jericho would sneeze from the smell of the incense" and the women of Jerusalem had no need to perfume themselves (Talmud, *Yoma* 39b).
35. For "the movement of one's lips is considered as a deed" (Talmud, *Sanhedrin* 65a). This idea is featured several times in the Tanya. See *Likkutei Amarim*, ch. 37, 52; *Igrot Hakodesh* 29; *Kuntres Acharon*, ch. 2.
36. *Igrot Kodesh – Alter Rebbe*, letter 10, 34. The letter was written in approximately 1787.

The approach of the Tanya emphasizes the importance of speech as part of our spiritual efforts and our relationships with others. Speech forms a fundamental part of the connection between people. In certain situations, silence, in contrast to speaking, indicates seclusion, distance, and the absence of a connection. As we find with thought, the test of speech as a garment of the soul is whether it leads to separation and disconnect from others, or whether it inspires closeness and reveals our inner potential.

While speech seemingly lacks substance and quickly fades, nevertheless, its impact is tremendous. One good word can uplift another's soul and fill him with energy and joy. Alternatively, emotionless expression will likely cause damage and weakness, which is often imperceptible to both speaker and recipient.

Negative words also remain in the world long after they are uttered. A married couple might have a disagreement. Their fight could include painful words being flung at each other. Even after they are appeased and calm is restored, the harsh words said during the disagreement can resurface. The fact that such statements may not be forgotten attests to just how damaging and painful they can be. A spoken word may be fleeting, but the discord it causes is a wound that doesn't quickly heal.

Such words, spoken without respect and acceptance of the other, create a barrier. They highlight a person's weakness and push them away. To emphasize another person's lack is to have an incomplete outlook on life. Why? One reason is that human beings are multidimensional. Singling out what's lacking puts the spotlight on only one aspect of a person.

The first goal of proper speech is to create connection between people. While thought is specifically for our own self, speech and action form our communication with others. According to the teachings of Chassidut, all souls are interconnected in a very high spiritual plane. They only become detached after descending into the world and separating into physical bodies. The true reality is thus unity between people, not separation.

Speech that expresses disconnection and alienation derives from the animal soul. Such words flow from a person's seeing himself as distinct from others. This produces a barrier and is typically associated with conflict, critique, and an emphasis on other peoples' lacks.

Words that produce connection typically have the power to help us detach our minds from unhealthy thoughts and overcome fear, depression, and stress. Worry tends to squeeze us, impact our soul's strength, and oppose proper functioning. One way to deal with our fears is to discuss them.[37] By talking with friends, we can significantly reduce the level of difficulty and challenge we encounter in life. Our words prevent the worries from gaining strength inside ourselves. Talking to someone whose conduct is proper can be an experience of freedom, cutting off thoughts of strife that threaten upheaval to our inner state.[38] Moreover, a conversation that includes real listening can help us to not see ourselves as the center of everything and to be more sensitive to others, identify with them, and give them aid. Such a soulful maneuver, which embodies a movement away from self-absorption, naturally enables us to be less consumed by our particular concerns. Meanwhile, conversations that generate alienation and create barriers produce the very opposite effect: lack of trust, fear of others and strangers, isolation, and dread of baseless critique.

Rabbi Shneur Zalman highlights speech's lofty, high source, which attests to it being more than the plain and simple. It has the power to influence reality.[39] A discussion of speech and its spiritual power includes a complex Kabbalistic investigation that Rabbi Shneur Zalman presents at length in the Tanya. Here, we'll focus on one aspect relating to the technical detail in our speech.

There are three components in the process of speaking. The first is the content being spoken, meaning, the topics that are being shared, revealed from the soul's faculties of intellect and emotion. The second is the "material" from which actual speech is formed. Our expelled breath serves as the building block of speech. The third is the form and shape of the spoken letters, produced by the process that transforms the

---

37. This approach explains one aspect of King Solomon's words: "Worries in the heart, a person should speak them" (Mishlei [Proverbs] 12:25). In Hebrew, the word for speak can be vowelized to mean lower and bend, or discuss. For this reason, the sages present two commentaries: remove it from your mind, or talk it out with others. See Talmud, *Yoma* 8, 75; *Sanhedrin* 11, 100; *Sotah* 8, 42. Also discussed in *Hayom Yom*, 25 Sivan.

38. See "Shabbat Parashat Mikeitz, Zot Chanukah," *Torat Menachem*, vol. 7, 1953, part 1, 253.

39. In Tanya, *Sha'ar Yichud v'Ha'emunah*, ch. 4, concerning creative speech and the lofty source of the attribute of *gevurah*.

"material" of spoken words into letters as we recognize them. The shape of spoken words is formed by the interaction of our breath with one of the five organs of speech in the mouth: throat, palate, tongue, teeth, and lips. These organs shape the air into the form of letters. Without this interaction, our speech would merely be expelled air, and nothing would be understood.

One of the fascinating dimensions of speech described by Rabbi Shneur Zalman is the fact that we are unable to decide on the exact form the words and letters will take. Only the content we discuss is in our control, as well as the decision whether or not to speak. But the form of the words we speak is beyond our ability to shape or determine. The mechanism enabling a person to speak features each letter, deriving from the organ of speech it relates to. The letters start from the soul "hitting" the organ it relates to and forming an audible movement that expresses what was intended to be expressed.[40]

The process of forming spoken words is beyond our intellect and not inherently natural: that is, animals are physically capable of speaking, yet cannot, so it is clear the faculty of speech goes beyond nature. That is why, for example, we can't change how we purse our lips while we say the sound "o," or how we open them while we say the sound "ah."[41]

What's the lesson learned from the fact that we have no control over the physical structure of the way we pronounce words? According to Rabbi Shneur Zalman, this indicates that the form of the letters derives

---

40. The letters *aleph, heh, chet,* and *ayin* come from the throat. The letters *gimmel, yud, chaf,* and *kuf* derive from the palate. The letters *bet, vav, mem,* and *feh* from the lips. The letters *daled, tet, lamed, nun,* and *tav* come from the tongue. And, finally, *zayin, samech, tzaddik, reish,* and *shin* are produced by the teeth. Because of the way these five organs of speech work, they are also referred to as the five levels of *gevurah.* Tanya, *Sha'ar Hayichud v'Ha'emunah,* ch. 4. The five *gevurot* relate to five levels of contraction of God's creative speech. See *Likkutei Torah,* "u'Sefartem Lachem," Parashat Emor.

41. The Tanya mentions that, "As is empirically evident, the soul does not at all intend or know how to intend the change in the motions of the lips [which articulate] those distinctions [between the various letters]. This is even more evident with the pronunciation of the vowels. For when the soul wishes to utter the *kamatz* vowel, the lips spontaneously become compressed, and with the *patach* vowel the lips open [of their own accord], and not at all because of the will of the soul to compress or to open [them]. There is no need to go any further into a matter which is simple…" *Igrot Hakodesh,* 5.

from a very high place in the chain-like, descending structure of the soul's faculties. The mechanism that produces the structured forms in our speech, which express concepts and ideas, is not dependent on our preceding thoughts. We can't control the shapes made by the movement of our lips while we are speaking. The expression of letters comes from a far loftier source, which transcends our intellect. The process that forms letters does not go through the soul's faculties and garments. Rather, it bypasses them and comes directly from its higher source, far beyond what our minds can grasp.

For this reason, babies are unable to speak, even though they grasp the ideas being said to them, and even though they already possess all they physically require to produce speech. They grasps what's happening around them, but they have limits to the technical mechanism needed for speaking. Their core point of wisdom still needs to develop. It will develop as the baby continues to develop, but only later on, in the process of physical and spiritual growth.[42]

The garment of thought is designed to help us infuse positive and proper content into our lives. The purpose of our speech, however, goes in the opposite direction: to elevate life and reveal our godly soul's potential into the reality around us.[13] Forging a connection between the soul's inner dimensions and the world around us is possible by exercising care in the choice of our words so that our speech is fitting. Our goal is to create overlap between the hidden, exalted source of the shapes of the letters and the subject matter at hand. In this way, the spoken content expresses the deepest source of reality and existence.[44] For example, a person can say that two and two equals five, but such talk is surely absurd and does not reveal the depth of our understanding. Similarly, every spoken word that creates separation between people is hurtful to the revelation of our soul's inner dimension.

---

42. Regarding the example of the baby, see Tanya, *Iggeret Hakodesh*, siman 5.

43. Tanya, *Kuntres Acharon*, siman aleph.

44. Through the process of speech described until now, we can also understand the general form of the process of creation. The concept of the Creator's speech is explained in Tanya, *Likkutei Amarim*, ch. 20, 21. *Likkutei Torah*, Bamidbar 88c, Devarim 42a–c, and others. See Yehiel Harari, *L'Hakir et HaBorei*, 2nd ed. (Ashkelon: Hitbonenut, 2001), 150.

3. Action

In his first public discourse, delivered in 1951, the Lubavitcher Rebbe shared a well-known story about Rabbi Shneur Zalman which highlights the power of our actions.[45] According to the story, one Yom Kippur, Rabbi Shneur Zalman removed his *tallit* in the middle of prayers. He left the synagogue and walked to the edge of the town. The congregation was left wondering where their revered Rebbe had gone, and then were shocked to discover he had gone to help a woman who had just given birth. All of her family members had gone to pray and left her alone. On the holiest day of the year, Rabbi Shneur Zalman himself took the time to chop wood and cook soup for the recovering woman. How could he forego such an important prayer service like that? According to the lesson shared by the Lubavitcher Rebbe, such conduct highlights a fundamental principle of Rabbi Shneur Zalman's teachings, that actual deeds, such as helping a recovering person, are the most important element of man's duty in life

Our conduct is the soul's most external garment. Seemingly, our actions are disconnected from the soul once we complete the task at hand. However, the general principle established by Chassidut is that the lower the garment is, the greater the soul potential it expresses. By lower, what is meant is just how distant it is from the soul's essence. Our actions reveal deep faculties within us, and the potential that initially pushed us to act. Due to the importance of the garment of action, Judaism emphasizes that "action is the main thing."[46]

An additional story, which the Lubavitcher Rebbe frequently shared in his talks and letters, is called "the child's cry." Rabbi Shneur Zalman lived upstairs while his son, who would become his successor after his passing, lived with his wife and their children on the main floor. While Rabbi Shneur Zalman's son was deeply engrossed in his studies, Rabbi Shneur Zalman's grandson fell out of his cradle and burst into tears. But his father was so focused on his learning that he didn't hear a thing. However, the grandfather, Rabbi Shneur Zalman, who was also learning at the time, heard the cries from his room on the second floor. Quickly,

45. "10 Shevat, 5711," *Torat Menachem*, vol. 2, 1951, part 1, 199.
46. *Pirkei Avot* 1:17. See Rabbi Shneur Zalman's *Likkutei Torah*, Shir Hashirim 23a.

he put his books aside and went downstairs, returned the baby to the cradle, and calmed him. Once the baby was sleeping, he rebuked his son for inappropriate behavior.[47]

The Lubavitcher Rebbe's message was that even in a moment of deep concentration in learning, prayer, or connection to God, we have to remain sensitive to the cry of a child. We have to leave the spiritual world in order to have an impact on the physical world. We may be deeply engrossed in the loftiest spiritual matters, such as prayer on Yom Kippur, but we must remain alert to a cry, to what the other lacks, and be ready to take action in order to see to their needs.

The story comes to highlight that according to the depths of Chassidic teachings, there is no contradiction between one's spiritual connection with the Creator and efforts in the physical world. Even physicality can house godly connectivity, and even during moments of spirituality, we need to remain aware of the physical world.

In the Lubavitcher Rebbe's teachings, the baby or small child can also be a spiritual baby or child. A person can be in a state of having "fallen from the cradle," lacking stability and feeling lost and confused. Rabbi Shneur Zalman's action teaches us that everything happening in the physical world is likely to impact on us. The child's cry needs to reach us all. It should cause those listening to stop what they're doing and do all they can to help the child. All of us are tasked with influencing the world, taking action, and getting involved.

Deep contemplation, as important as it is, is not the main point. Helping others and getting out of ourselves are the most important products of our learning.

Rabbi Shneur Zalman's teachings differ from other teachings in placing action at the core of one's spiritual development. This invites us to ask ourselves questions about our self-awareness: *Who am I? What is the purpose of my life?* However, at the same time, it does not see the solution in internal dilemmas and self-definitions. Instead of trying to

---

47. See an example in "Sichah for Day Two of Shavuot, 5718," *Torat Menachem*, vol. 23, 1958, part 3, 44. Yehoshua Mondshine quotes several sources for the story and points out the connections and lessons learned from each one. See "Kol Yeled Bocheh," *Kfar Chabad*, vol. 991. The first time the story appears in a reviewed and checked talk by the Lubavitcher Rebbe was when he addressed donors to Yeshiva Tomchei Temimim on 4 Marcheshvan, 1963. See *Likkutei Sichot*, vol. 3, 802ff.

define oneself, a person has to go out and do. Rather than wondering if we're in the best place or not, or if we're doing it right or not, it would be better to fulfill our role in the moment and thereby give assistance to those around us. By getting out of ourselves, we come to find our truth and our happiness, no less than if we'd focused on achieving spiritual levels on our own, within ourselves. Such external actions save us from inner conflict and all kinds of questions and doubts about finding and discovering ourselves. In the majority of cases, the latter fail to produce personal growth and achievement.

In the life and thought of Rabbi Shneur Zalman, action is linked with our putting forth effort from our own potential, both spiritually and in financially supporting our families. An example of this can be found in the historical depictions of Rabbi Yosef Yitzchak, the sixth Lubavitcher Rebbe. Rabbi Yosef Yitzchak describes at length the life of Rabbi Baruch, the father of Rabbi Shneur Zalman. One of the main themes that he frequently repeats in his writing is Rabbi Baruch's lifelong stubborn insistence on making a living by his own hands and not relying on support from others. This was so much so that, in fact, "Rabbi Baruch even refused to stay somewhere on the afternoon before a holiday without paying for it." The stories present an appreciation for such an approach. And according to Rabbi Yosef Yitzchak's words, this insistence upon self-sufficiency passed down to his son, Rabbi Shneur Zalman.

Rabbi Baruch passed away in 1792, when Rabbi Shneur Zalman was forty-seven years old,[48] approximately six years after Rabbi Shneur Zalman accepted leadership of the Chassidic movement. As is told, Rabbi Shneur Zalman's father could not stand the idea of his son standing up for him out of respect, and so he moved to Hungary, where he later passed away.[49] Rabbi Yosef Yitzchak emphasizes that the description of the principles that guided Rabbi Baruch's life are not without significance. In his view, they had a direct impact not only on the father of the Chabad Chassidic movement, but also on the entire movement:

We should take some time to contemplate the events and life of young Baruch. For, as the father of the future founder of the Chabad

---

48. For a debate on the date of his death, see *Igrot Kodesh – Alter Rebbe* (1802), 9.
49. Glitzenstein, *Sefer Hatoldot*, vol. 4, 1187.

approach to Chassidut, he made a significant contribution to the approach by his personal righteousness and unique lifestyle.... Baruch especially arouses our wonder given the fact that he undertook his unique approach by himself, without any guidance or support. He completely rejected help from others and maintained a powerful trust that the Master of the universe would protect him from any danger, including hunger.[50]

Rabbi Yosef Yitzchak writes that Baruch's life seemingly focused on two different worlds: the world of Torah and the world of physical work. As he learned, Torah was alive: "He debated with the sages of the Talmud as if they were sitting next to him." And out in the marketplace, he was submerged in the world, "not as something secondary, but rather as a precious effort done wholeheartedly."

Rabbi Shneur Zalman's father achieved wholesomeness via his efforts on two fronts and by blending them together. Neglecting one side would have been a sign of lack. His physical activities were not disconnected from his studies and spiritual sensitivity. As expressed by Rabbi Yosef Yitzchak:

> A complete harmony was formed in Baruch between his spiritual life and his physical life, between the realm of the soul and the physical world, between the body and the soul, and between the heavens and the earth. For him, everything was one and whole – permeated with holiness and purity.[51]

Even within the garment of action we find the same core principle: victory is expressing our inner dimension to the world around us, rather than our natural soul's tendencies.

In 1969, Dr. Nissan Mindel's English-language biography of Rabbi Shneur Zalman was printed. In an unusual move, the Lubavitcher Rebbe wrote an introduction to the book. There, he writes that an ethical person is obligated to seek harmony between his daily conduct and the world of ethics and ideals. This is an extremely significant principle in the Jewish

---

50. Ibid., vol. 1, 35.
51. Ibid.

world, emphasized the Lubavitcher Rebbe, because actions are the most important outcome of knowledge in Judaism.

In the eyes of the Lubavitcher Rebbe, Chassidic thinking takes this concept a step further. Action is of prime importance, but the demand is that our actions be done with vitality and contemplation. In other words, actions themselves have a "soul." And when our efforts are done with passion and appreciation for their power and value, we express the "soul" of that action. In this way, we attain a harmony that is real, tangible, emotional, and intellectual, within our daily lives. It creates a harmony between the souls – the animal and the godly – and a harmony between ourselves and the world around us.

The harmony between Rabbi Shneur Zalman's philosophy and his daily conduct was outstanding, states the Lubavitcher Rebbe in his introduction to the biography of Rabbi Shneur Zalman. For this reason, Rabbi Shneur Zalman insisted on delving into the smallest of details in whatever area he was exploring. Dealing in details and the constant desire to learn and improve brought him, in the view of the Lubavitcher Rebbe, to such monumental achievements.

In Rabbi Shneur Zalman's thinking, actions are directly linked to his views on charity, giving, and the value of the commandments as part of daily Jewish life.

After Rabbi Shneur Zalman's description of the soul's capacities and its garments, he seeks to present the ideal state, the proper model of a person victorious in inner battles – the *beinoni*.

CHAPTER 6

The *Beinoni* – Pathways to Victory

*I*n the beginning of the previous century, the collective general ideologies, varieties of nationalism such as communism, fascism, and nazism, attracted the masses. They provided people with a sense of meaning and challenge, yet diminished the value of the individual in comparison to the country and its leader. In a response to those general outlooks, a philosophical approach was founded that placed the individual at the center. It was particularly attractive following the two world wars, with so many people tired of political approaches that limited people and denied them freedom.

This approach, known as existentialism, is an umbrella term that encompasses a wide range of ideas. In general, it is an ideology that deals with existence and the choices we make in every moment. According to its basic principles, categories and identities only limit a person. Given our free will, categorizations never apply to us. Through the practical decisions we can make, we avoid placing ourselves within randomly applied definitions and can carve our individual paths.[1] While we can't say that the modern existential view replaces the need to live a social and

---

1. See Ron Margolin, *Hadaat Hapnimit: Fenomenologia shel Chayei Hadaat Hapnimim*

moral life, the approach is distinct in that it views the inner dimension as being interchangeable with external reality. Modern existentialism restored man to the center of attention while rejecting general, all-encompassing ideologies of life and living. It sought to arm people with a focused perception through which to look at life and explain it. "Man is nothing else but that which he makes of himself," emphasizes Jean-Paul Sartre, one of the famed existentialist philosophers and writers.[2] In every situation, we have choice and freedom. Even someone walking to the gallows has a choice about what to think, what to say, and how to act. We're free not to be limited by the status symbols around us; we are free to choose who we are. This essential freedom applies even in a state of captivity: it is the freedom of the soul.

Early religious existentialism, that of the Danish philosopher Soren Kierkegaard, gave people the choice to live in whatever way they wanted and to give whatever meaning they wanted to their lives. Kierkegaard's harsh life pushed him to alienate himself, but his approach to existentialism restored his inner sense of choice. For him, making a personal choice didn't mean making a casual choice. Rather, it meant choosing for "oneself" via our inner potential. Such a choice expresses, first and foremost, liberation, and therefore one is free. When we choose our own path and make up our own mind, we assume full responsibility for our existence. The world around us is transformed from an environment that feels forced upon us into one that we can utilize according to our free will.[3]

In many ways, the questions that the existentialists grappled with had already weighed on Rabbi Shneur Zalman many years prior: What

---

v'Histakfutam b'Mekorot HaYahadut min HaMikra ad Chassidut (Ramat Gan: Bar Ilan University, 2012), 295–96.

2. Jean-Paul Sartre, Existentialism Is a Humanism, trans. Philip Mairet, in Existentialism from Dostoevsky to Sartre, ed. Walter Kaufmann (Cleveland: World Publishing Company, 1956).

3. Kierkegaard had a difficult childhood. "I never experienced the joy of childhood. The incredibly deep investigation I attempted robbed me of tranquility essential to childhood.... My lack of inner peace caused me to always be outside myself. However, sometimes, even often, it seems my childhood is returning anew." Quoted in Avraham Shagai's Kierkergaard: Daat V'Existatancia – HaMa'asa Shel Ha'Ani (Jerusalem: Mosad Bialik, 1991), 137–38, 141, 142.

inner choices does a Jew have to make regarding Judaism? What kind of freedom does a Jew even have, given the inner battle between the opposing forces that rage inside him?

Is there any similarity between the responses of Rabbi Shneur Zalman and those of the existentialist thinkers who came later? It's wrong to view Chassidic thinking as akin to existential philosophy. Events in the reality we experience have higher spiritual causes that are beyond the physical world, current existence, and any one person. The concept of divine providence is significant and speaks to the totality of creation. But divine providence can collide with choice, so that free will is still a clear component of our existence. However, despite those perceptions, according to Rabbi Shneur Zalman, every moment of our lives is fraught with conflict, and thus also with choice. We choose which soul capacities to identify with, which soul garments to wear, and what kind of meaning to infuse in our lives. To a certain degree, we have the ability to shake off limitations, labels, and status symbols that alienate us from our surroundings from birth. Out of that very same inner conflict comes the ability to develop, sanctify, and obtain meaning in our lives.

HERO OF THE TANYA

The freedom to choose is embodied in the hero of the Tanya. Rabbi Shneur Zalman did not call his book "Tanya." It was a nickname that stuck due to the book's first word.[4] Rather, the introductory page tells us that the first section, which deals with the structure of the soul, is called *The Book of the Beinoni*. In other words, the first section was designed for those people who could attain the level of *beinoni*. By contrast, Rebbe Elimelech of Lizhensk, one of the great leaders of Chassidut in Poland, wrote *The Book of the Tzaddikim* for those on a high spiritual level. Rabbi Shneur Zalman, however, focused on a different and broader audience.

---

4. In Hebrew, the letters of the word *Tanya* can also form the word *eitan* (strength), for learning Tanya arouses the soul's strength and capacity. See Rabbi Yosef Yitzchak's *Sefer Hasichot 5703/1943*, 95. An opposite explanation says that "Tanya" is the name of a *kelipah* that prevents people from learning the Torah's inner dimension (*Pnimiyut HaTorah*). The study of Tanya helps remove it. This is discussed in Heilman's *Beit Rebbe*, 106.

The *beinoni* is the ideal model, the hero of the Tanya, toward which Rabbi Shneur Zalman guides his readers. It's not an unreachable, impossible ideal. It can be attained by the majority of people. "The rank of *beinoni* is one that is attainable by everyone," emphasized Rabbi Shneur Zalman. "Each person should strive after it. For every person can, at any time or hour, be a *beinoni*."[5]

The rank of *beinoni* and the personal effort required to achieve that ideal lie at the heart of the Tanya. Rabbi Shneur Zalman's approach is built around it. As is easy to grasp, the *beinoni* is not yet a transcendent *tzaddik* with incredible abilities and talents and unbelievable spiritual genetics. Rather, a *beinoni* is a regular person, but one who has succeeded in vanquishing his inner battles. According to Rabbi Shneur Zalman, readers of the Tanya might see the *beinoni* as an existentialist. He's someone born out of the conflict between opposing inner forces. The *beinoni* makes the right choices and takes responsibility for his existence in each and every moment.

Rabbi Shneur Zalman's significant contribution, which arises from knowledge of the structure of the soul, is in defining the rank of the *beinoni*. Describing the battle between the souls was a necessary preparatory step for describing and outlining the category of *beinoni*. On the one hand, the *beinoni* doesn't succumb to the seductions of the natural tendency, the *yetzer hara*. The animal soul's interests rumble inside, but the *beinoni* never allows them control of the soul garments of thought, action, or words. The *beinoni* doesn't gossip, judge others, wallow in unhealthy thoughts, or allow worries to conquer the mind. The *beinoni* avoids anger and keeps a distance from depression, while at the same time working to create a pleasure and excitement in every action.

Generally speaking, we would have likely thought a *beinoni* is half meritorious and half guilty, not a *tzaddik* (perfectly righteous person) but also not a *rasha* (wicked person). But Rabbi Shneur Zalman keeps the Tanya's hero far from such categorization. The first principle he describes in his teachings is that a person is constantly in the midst of a battle between two souls. The stage for this battle is in the soul's garments: thoughts, speech, and actions. It is the interaction between

---

5. Tanya, *Likkutei Amarim*, ch. 14.

the souls on the level of their capacities, expressed during the course of battle in the garments of the soul, that indicate a person's rank.

Each soul fights for total and complete victory. Each wants full control over the garments so that all of one's thoughts, words, and actions become vehicles for its expression. The animal soul seeks to put itself at the center of everything, while the godly soul wants its thirst for the Creator to take center stage as it focuses on the world outside the self.

The *beinoni* is a person whose godly soul dominates his animal soul in the three garments of thought, speech, and action. It always wins the battles and harnesses his animalistic nature for holy purposes. But, despite the godly soul's victories, the animal soul never weakens and never stops fighting back. The *beinoni's* victories are hard-fought, demanding great effort each and every time.[6] The animal soul never wins, but it never eases up.

To a certain extent, a *beinoni* is an existentialist because he chooses his path and his true identity in every moment. He decides to connect to his being, inheritance, insight, and faith with every thought, word, and deed. He exercises total control over all his garments. He's not in the middle ground between a *tzaddik* and a *rasha*. Rather, his is a precise title that indicates the present, a title used by our sages to express the moment between the past and the future. The *beinoni* lives in the present, and he constantly needs to win the battle in each moment he faces. He's defined by his deeds in the here and now, and not by anything external.

A *beinoni* also can't relax and take pleasure in his past accomplishments. It's specifically those achievements that will make future battles more difficult. When he does a good deed, such as encouraging and supporting something positive or pushing away depressing thoughts, in the very next moment, he'll likely encounter a push to loosen up the reins. Successes are dangerous for him, quietly possessing the promise of more difficult battles to come. A feeling of self-satisfaction presents a threat to future progress.

Yehoshua Fishel Schneerson, author of *Chaim Gravitzer: Story of the Fallen*, presents a gripping dialogue between his protagonist and

---

6. There are a few times, such as in prayer, in which the godly soul acts without any opposition. See Tanya, *Likkutei Amarim*, ch. 12.

another man. Chaim Gravitzer is a Chabad Chassid full of vitality who seeks to fully live a life of connection with God. Laizer, a different type of Chassid, is a big Torah scholar who tries to cool his passions. Laizer encourages Gravitzer to pursue some humility, simple joy, and fear of heaven, not self-nullification and deadening of the soul via drinking and rowdy conduct. Gravitzer is quite far from the level of a *beinoni* (he drinks, shouts, and so on), but he is described as someone who really gets the main point about working on the self. We see Gravitzer respond to Laizer with a vision of the *beinoni* model before his eyes:

> "Let the wild ones drink alcohol," said Chaim. "Otherwise, you are likely to soon become smug and satisfied with yourselves. Like ragged Mitnagdim. And you, Laizer, need to get others to drink properly in order to quickly sober them up from their self-satisfied drunkenness.... Don't you know that being drunk on alcohol is among the most superficial things, lasting no more than a short while? But folly and complacency, that a person is satisfied with himself, is an inner level of being drunk that blocks up the mind and heart for life."

And he concludes:

> "It's better for a person to lose his head, as long as he doesn't spend his life carrying a donkey's head on his shoulders."[7]

Gravitzer, as mentioned, isn't presented as a model of a *beinoni*, but he's well versed in the challenge depicted by Rabbi Shneur Zalman. Obviously, a *beinoni* isn't a drinker, but he is well aware of the battles at hand, and works to avoid complacency.

THE TEST OF THIS MOMENT

How can a *beinoni* be complete? How can he never fall even once, as all regular people do? On one hand, a *beinoni* is defined as a person who never sinned and never will sin. His inner evil never overcomes the good. At the same time, his qualifying test is always the test he faces

---

7. Yehoshua Fishel Schneerson, *Chaim Gravitzer: Story of the Fallen*, translated to Hebrew from the Yiddish by Avraham Shlonsky (reprint, Tel Aviv: Yediot Seforim, 2003), 60.

right now in the present, an existential test. He's not defined by the past. Had that been the case, he could have looked into his past, made repairs, and any instance in which he fell would no longer be considered a sin for him. The title of *beinoni* can be regarded as a temporary title. Just one moment of preparation and revealing your inner core point, and it's yours. But one fall, and it's all gone. However, the *beinoni* never falls. Given his sensitivity and determination, slipping is impossible. That unique moment in which he wins is the moment in which he actualizes his life's purpose. That instant of victory over his drives is beyond threat from the past or future.

One of the reasons for revealing the teachings of Kabbalah and Chassidut is to enable a person to contend with the negative traits generated by his animal soul: anger, lust, jealousy, depression, fears, and the like. At the moment of controlling thoughts, words, and actions despite the wars raging inside, the *beinoni* actualizes the exalted purpose for which he or she was created. Egocentric feelings strengthen our selfish sense of independence and prevent us from seeing anything besides ourselves. In contrast, the power to overcome negative traits derives not from seeing only one's own small and limited set of personal interests in the world, but rather from revealing meaning and order in the world as whole.

It should be emphasized that Rabbi Shneur Zalman was quite aware that not all people are alike in their inclinations and in the intensity of their inner battles. Some have burning desires and impulses that are difficult to control. That is why they need greater mental powers to help them overcome them. On the other hand, some are cool by nature. Their inherent attraction to bodily pleasures is less powerful.[8] They may also be less prone to acting out or having anxieties. Each person has unique struggles that are part of the rectification suited to each personality.

In addition to the different natures we all have, the environment to which we are exposed directly influences the intensity of our struggles. As Rabbi Shneur Zalman says in the Tanya:

> Don't judge your fellow man until you have stood in his place. For it is his "place" that causes him to sin, since his livelihood requires

---

8. See Tanya, *Likkutei Amarim*, ch. 15.

him to go about the marketplace all day, and he is of those who sit at the street corners. His eyes see all sorts of temptation, and "what the eyes see, the heart desires." Additionally, his nature burns like a baker's fiery oven.... It is different, however, with him who goes about but little in the marketplace, and most of the day he is at home. Even if he does go about the marketplace all day, yet it may be that he is not so passionate by nature. For the natural impulse is not the same in everyone...[9]

Despite all this, each of us can overcome crises and temptations and achieve a life of meaning. The greater our ability to cope, the greater the powers we wield to help us toward victory in those struggles.[10]

In order to illustrate the potential we all have to reach the level of *beinoni*, Rabbi Shneur Zalman points to an analogy from the *Zohar*.[11] It describes a great king who hired a harlot to test his son. The king's intention was to assess whether his son would follow his temptations or control them, as befitting a prince. The hired woman, for her part, knew that she was hired by the king and that her job was to seduce the prince. On the other hand, it was clear to her that the king's true desire was for the prince to overcome the test. The lesson is that our tendency to fulfill the *yetzer hara* instinct (desires of the natural inclination) and to view it as existing independently of the Creator was also created by the Creator. However, the purpose of this inclination is to give us an opportunity to overcome it and turn it from a temporary desire into a meaningful force.

Rabbi Shneur Zalman teaches that ideas of the inclinations of the animal soul and the godly soul are both rooted in holiness, the commandments of the King, the Creator. The animal soul doesn't necessarily

9. Tanya, *Likkutei Amarim*, ch. 30.
10. The Tanya states that "An oath was administered: be righteous and don't be wicked." *Likkutei Amarim*, ch. 1. This is typically explained by pointing out the connection between *masbi'im* (an oath was administered) and *sovaya* (empowered with ability). We were given the power to be victorious. See an example of this from Rabbi Sholom DovBer Schneerson: "This is also the simple meaning of the oath – when we take an oath to do something, even if there are challenges and difficulties, they are inconsequential since we have to succeed. Meaning, our hidden inner powers rise up," "Kuntres u'Mayon," ch. 1, maamar 14.
11. In Tanya, *Likkutei Amarim*, ch. 9, 29; *Zohar* 2:163a.

contradict the forces of holiness. While our natural inclination draws us downward toward material things, our spiritual roots want and long for us to withstand the test, as in the analogy of the harlot whose desire was to be beloved by the king.[12] Therefore, though she knows in her heart that the king will be happy if the son overcomes the test and pained if she succeeds in tempting him, she nevertheless must undertake her mission.

For Rabbi Shneur Zalman, the message here is directed at the person in the midst of battle: don't be intimidated by the power of temptation, by the forces that distract you from focus. Not only can they be defeated, but they are only there and working and grappling so that you vanquish them. The doubts, inner confusion, instability, and lack of faith are intended for us, to use them in order to discover our true capacity. They feature great power, and with proper guidance, they can be part of the process of realizing our potential. The *beinoni*'s high level is rooted in his ability to harness the powers of the animal soul to fulfill the will of the godly soul.[13]

As Rabbi Shneur Zalman expresses in the Tanya:

> Furthermore, the Sitra Achra [the side opposing holiness] itself has no doubts at all concerning faith. It has merely been granted permission to confuse us with false and deceitful words, in order that a person may be more richly rewarded for mastering it. It is similar to the harlot who attempts to seduce the king's son through falsehood and deceit, with the king's approval, as in the parable stated in the *Zohar*.[14]

The conclusion that Rabbi Shneur Zalman expresses is that we are not meant to be animals. The seductive forces that appeal to us are powerful, but controllable. They are imposed on the person from the outside for

---

12. An additional expression of this is: "The Satan [accusing angel] and Penina both acted with holy intentions," Talmud, *Bava Batra* 16a. This is also quoted in Rabbi Shneur Zalman, *Likkutei Torah*, Parashat Chukat 62a.

13. "A *beinoni* manifests the concept of 'much produce is generated by the power of the ox,'" Mishlei 14:4. *Torat Menachem*, vol. 5, 1952, part 2, 166. This means that the ox, the physical world around us, also has a spark of godliness that is revealed through our efforts.

14. Tanya, *Likkutei Amarim*, ch. 9, 29.

the sole purpose of interfering with our trek down the straight path. And if we are drawn to the animal side, we can go to war. It's a battle in which victory means rescue from that abyss, even if we already fell into it. For the *beinoni* at war, the next moment also presents a new opportunity.

"THE WORLD WAS CREATED FOR ME"

One of the core principles that should help us in our struggle is recognition of our uniqueness. The approach of Chassidut emphasizes that man is the center of creation. Rabbi Shneur Zalman develops the Baal Shem Tov's view which highlights how each individual must say to himself, at every moment, "For me the world was created."[15] This statement has several meanings, but none of them include that we should be egocentric, placing ourselves at the center of everything. Rather, in every situation and in every event that we are aware of, we have to try to discover the unique message it carries for us.

Every person is a unique and original entity in the eyes of the Tanya. No one is a copy of anyone else. Because of this, each person has a unique task in life and is created with the intention and role most appropriate to that task.

The very fact that we were created is a declaration of our importance. In this light, a meaningful life is one in which we know we are needed by someone or something. We are responsible for the created world by virtue of having been created.

Self-realization in life is meant to be expressed as victories over our inner struggles. In this respect, even the challenges, concealment, and skepticism we experience were created for us, to refine and purify us when we overcome them.[16] Adopting the attitude that the world was created for us in order to contend with it fills us with strength and pushes us to never surrender in battle.[17] The awareness that we are essential and necessary for the world helps us on the path to victory.[18]

---

15. "For a person is obligated to say: The world was created for me." Mentioned in Tanya, *Likkutei Amarim*, ch. 41. Quoted in Talmud, *Sanhedrin* 37a.
16. *Torat Menachem*, vol. 11, 1954, part 2, 9.
17. *Torat Menachem*, vol. 10, 1954, part 1, 59.
18. The Lubavitcher Rebbe, *Sichot Kodesh*, 1981, vol. 3, 752–53.

Achieving mastery over our emotional traits is difficult, but possible. The *beinoni* is on a very high level, but one that every person can aspire to. As mentioned above, we can all reach the level of the *beinoni*. Almost everyone is engaged in a similar struggle and has the ability to control thoughts, words, and actions. It takes constant awareness, maintaining a tension that accompanies our every thought and movement. Only at very special times does the tension ease. Rabbi Shneur Zalman tells his readers of these challenges, and only once in the Tanya does he acknowledge that it is not an easy struggle: "Truly, it is a great, fierce struggle to break one's nature, which burns like a fiery flame…"[19] Aside from this, he offers no empathy while continuing to call for our engagement in the struggle. The main way to win the battle is by being aware and alert. The Tanya's strategy for victory is to have the mind control the heart, so that intellectual contemplation overcomes and directs the emotional attributes. The *beinoni* is one who is aware of the struggle raging within, recognizes its value and uniqueness, and is constantly on guard for the dangers that lie ahead. Through struggle and tension, we reveal ourselves, as well as our potential to transcend the material world.

ARCHETYPES IN THE TANYA

The Tanya's featured character is the *beinoni* – or more accurately the average person who is endowed with the potential to become a *beinoni* –but Rabbi Shneur Zalman does not suffice with this description. He presents an outline of the entire spectrum of personality structures, working to define four additional archetypes through which one can both understand the human experience as well as appreciate the challenge of the *beinoni*. These four additional types are the complete and incomplete *tzaddik*, and the complete and incomplete *rasha*, defined below. To a large extent, the definition of the *beinoni* is incomplete if not accompanied by descriptions of the other existing personality patterns. Who are these other personalities? These archetypes comprise the continuum between the absolute *tzaddik* (righteous person) and the complete *rasha* (evil person).

---

19. Tanya, *Likkutei Amarim*, ch. 30.

Tzaddik

As described, one of the most effective tools used by Rabbi Shneur Zalman to disseminate his teachings was to attract outstanding students. He gathered young men who displayed knowledge and devotion and promoted them in their studies and spiritual work. As a young man, even before the age of eighteen, he was surrounded by a group of Torah students who studied books of ethics and Kabbalah together. In 1771, at the age of twenty-six, he was known for spreading the teachings of the Baal Shem Tov, and for his tremendous influence on young gifted scholars. Already at that time he had a number of young and talented students who were connected to him and who viewed him as their rabbi.[20]

His cultivation of scholars can be seen as a way in which he influenced the environment. As far as he was concerned, investing in outstanding students paid dividends, and he toiled to produce as many models of eminent scholars and refined men as possible. The young men who invested their time and energy in Torah study under his guidance, along with his brothers, spearheaded the effort to spread Chassidut.

Externally, many of these students appeared to be *tzaddikim*. Seen from the outside, there is no difference between the *beinoni* and the *tzaddik*. But Rabbi Shneur Zalman's teachings distinguish between the *beinoni* and the *tzaddik*, the *tzaddik* being the personality pattern unattainable for most people.

Who is a *tzaddik*? What was the difference between such a person and those senior students who were not *tzaddikim*? The *beinoni* is not sinful and never slips but is still not a *tzaddik*. The *beinoni* manages not to fall not for lack of attraction to the natural world and negative traits, but rather for seeing the world as a series of battles that must be faced nearly every moment and won every time. The *beinoni* has to continually win every moment of life. This is not done through molding character traits; the *beinoni*'s traits remain constant. The work focuses instead on the three garments of the soul. The *beinoni* vanquishes the natural inclination in thought, speech, and action. In contrast, there is the rank of the complete *tzaddik*: a unique individual who manages not only

20. Glitzenstein, *Sefer Hatoldot*, vol. 1, 181.

to overcome the seduction of the animal soul's faculties, but also to transform its strength into total good. A *tzaddik* will not experience lust, being instead completely focused on the Creator, almost totally devoid of any sense of self. The *tzaddik* seeks devoted connection, holiness, and eternity, and not that which is temporary and transitory.

A story attributed to Rabbi Shneur Zalman presents a detailed description of the *tzaddik's* virtues. According to the story, Rabbi Shneur Zalman once went to the house of one of the rabbis who was opposed to Chassidut. The rabbi asked him about the book *Noam Elimelech*, referred to as the Book of the Righteous, and its author, Rabbi Elimelech of Lizhensk. Rabbi Shneur Zalman recognized that the rabbi likely disparaged Rabbi Elimelech, since he had placed the book under the bench on which he sat. Rabbi Shneur Zalman said:

> Imagine the author was standing here before you. Even if you put the author himself under the bench, he would remain silent and say nothing, being humble and lowly.

Although a *tzaddik* has no temptation for the natural inclination, he too is required to work on himself. He is repulsed by the pleasures of the world, yet remains free to choose and even make mistakes in his choices.

There is an additional figure between the *tzaddik* and the *beinoni*: the incomplete *tzaddik*. While there is only one level of complete *tzaddik*, there are tens of thousands of levels of being an incomplete *tzaddik*. He is on a very high level and has struggled with his inner nature and expelled it, but has yet to transform the evil into total good. The incomplete *tzaddik* is a *tzaddik* who retains a tiny attraction to evil. Although this evil is subordinated and nullified to the good, it still has a certain connection to the *tzaddik's* life. He does not completely hate evil, but a trace of love and pleasure in the material things remains.

On the surface, it's nearly impossible to distinguish between a *tzaddik*, with all his variety of levels, and the *beinoni*. These three archetypes represent many ranks and variations of the internal struggle, yet appear similar in their external behavior. Their differences are internal, and understandable given how much strength the animal soul puts forth in battling against the godly soul.

The *beinoni's* greatest virtue is that despite not being perfect and still having his battles, he wins every one, explains Rabbi Shneur Zalman. The exalted image of the *tzaddik* lacks the quality of the battle's victories experienced by the *beinoni*. The *tzaddik's* evil is nullified by the light, good, and positive he possesses. He does not have to battle and defeat it.

To clarify the advantage of the *beinoni*, Rabbi Shneur Zalman employs an image from the culinary world: "Just as with material food, there are two kinds of delicacies. One sweet and luscious, the other sharp or sour, but well spiced and prepared so that they become delicacies that revive the soul."[21]

One food is a sweet and delicious delicacy that needs no seasoning. The second food is sharp or sour, not palatable as is, but just as tasty as the first delicacy once seasoned. The *tzaddik* embodies the first delicacy: sweet and savory without inner struggle. The *beinoni* is the worked-on delicacy. Its virtue is that it becomes very tasty because of the spices, the achievements accomplished by the *beinoni's* own efforts and work.

In Rabbi Shneur Zalman's eyes, the two delicacies, the two figures, *tzaddik* and *beinoni* – are also two kinds of contentment that we give to the Creator. Each has its own uniqueness.

Rasha

The average contemporary reader will find it hard to identify with the *tzaddik*. If he looks at himself honestly, he will find that the image of the *rasha* is quite often representative of what is going on inside him.

A *rasha* is someone who does slip up in the three garments of his soul. He'll think problematic thoughts, allow himself to wallow in forbidden schemes, gossip, waste his time in vain, engage in mockery or act in opposition to the Jewish code of law. He has good within, but he fails and loses battles because his godly soul's goodness is subjugated and nullified to the evil he possesses. The incomplete *rasha* doesn't want to get pulled into all of that, but he submits when the actual moment comes. Most people want good, but find it hard to keep away from anger or overcome sadness. They want to believe and stay optimistic, but in the vast majority of cases, the anxieties seep in and take control.

As we see with *tzaddikim*, the rank of *rasha* is diverse. Generally

---

21. Tanya, *Likkutei Amarim*, ch. 27.

speaking, there are two kinds of *rasha,* encompassing many levels and degrees. Below the *beinoni,* there is the incomplete *rasha,* and under that is the complete *rasha.* Between the two exist tens of thousands of degrees of incomplete *rasha.* What all those ranks have in common is that evil does not totally rule over good. It does have moments in which it successfully invests itself into one of the soul's garments of thought, speech, and action. But after that, it is very possible that the good prevails, the person feels regret, and he takes steps to ensure his repentance is accepted. As soon as he wins and overcomes, he immediately transcends his level.

The complete *rasha,* in contrast to the incomplete *rasha,* is one whose evil grows. He loses all the battles that take place in the soul garments of thought, speech, and action, and there's no balance between good and evil. He has a godly soul, but struggles to express it, and even when he understands he's under the control of his animal soul and that he behaved poorly, he does not regret it. His inner state is one in which the godly soul is so covered that it lacks sufficient strength to overcome and defeat the egocentric tendencies.

FREE CHOICE

In his masterpiece of Jewish law, the *Mishneh Torah,* Maimonides states that one of the foundations of the Torah is that every person has been blessed with free choice:

> Free will is granted to all men. If one desires to turn himself to the path of good and be righteous, the choice is his. Should he desire to turn to the path of evil and be wicked, the choice is his.

Maimonides points out that it's up to us to pave our way. We can do either good or evil and will be defined by our choices.

> A person should not entertain the thesis held by the fools among the nations and the majority of the undeveloped among Israel that, at the time of a man's creation, God decrees whether he will be righteous or wicked. This is untrue. Each person is fit to be righteous like Moses, our teacher, or wicked, like Jeroboam. [Similarly,] he may be wise or foolish, merciful or cruel, miserly or generous, or [acquire] any other

character traits. There is no one who compels him, sentences him, or leads him toward either of these two paths. Rather, he, on his own initiative and decision, tends to the path he chooses.... Accordingly, it is the sinner, himself, who causes his own loss.

This principle is a fundamental concept and a pillar [on which rests the totality] of the Torah and mitzvot as stated: "Behold, I have set before you today life [and good, death and evil]." [22] Similarly, it states, "Behold, I have set before you today [the blessing and the curse],"[23] implying that the choice is in your hands. Any one behavior that a person desires to do, he may, whether good or evil.... From this, we can infer that the Creator does not compel or decree that people should do either good or bad. Rather, everything is left to their [own choice].[24]

Maimonides finds evidence of freedom of choice from the fact that the Creator commands the Jewish people via the prophets to do and not do things. If there were no freedom of choice, Maimonides asks, why did the Creator have to command? Man's freedom of choice is what the Creator desires and therefore permits. Maimonides also emphasizes that the right to choose is accompanied by punishment, meaning the person who chooses the evil path self-inflicts punishment.

Contrary to what one might think, the division of personalities presented by Rabbi Shneur Zalman does not put limits on our choices generally and on the *beinoni* in particular. His description of the personality patterns does indeed teach us about our emotional potential, but it still allows for taking responsibility for our lives.

Rabbi Shneur Zalman also separates external behavior from the inner structure of the human psyche. The great sage Maimonides writes that a regular, average person can choose at any moment to avoid sin, and in this way resembles the *tzaddik*. Rabbi Shneur Zalman affirms that Maimonides is correct: there is no difference between the essence of the *tzaddik*'s godly soul and that of the *rasha*. At their core, they are equal. However, Rabbi Shneur Zalman identifies a distinction: the

---

22. Devarim 30:15.
23. Devarim 11:26.
24. Maimonides, *Mishneh Torah*, Hilchot Teshuvah, ch. 5.

difference lies in the extent to which the godly soul is revealed. The *tzaddik* experiences the revelation so strongly that choosing good is no longer the inner battle found in the *beinoni*. Accordingly, one might think that the right to choose is less pronounced in the *tzaddik* than in an ordinary person, while the gap between the essence of the *tzaddik's* soul and its external manifestation is far smaller.

From the descriptions of the *tzaddik*, *beinoni*, and *rasha*, we see that the difference between them is not in their essences. In every person, regardless of spiritual rank, is a godly soul. The difference between the different personalities is in the extent to which this godly soul expresses its authority in us.

If we were to give an analysis, we would likely place the structure of the common psyche in the category of incomplete *rasha*. Typically, our best energies are devoted to the fulfillment of physical needs and not to their restriction. It is possible that a person will be attracted to holiness, giving, tenderness, and gentleness, but in most instances it will be short-lived. One may wrap oneself in these for a while, but eventually the animal soul will take control again and return the person to a previous, lower state. Although hidden traces of the experiences of the godly soul will remain, they will not have sufficient force to impact and direct the person's life.

Despite all this, what can help us change? How can we win battles more frequently and not fall into our natural tendencies?

From a theoretical and practical point of view, the battle between the souls and the image of the *beinoni* leave the reader with an unresolved question: Who chooses? Who determines the victor in the battle between the souls? How do we choose which side to identify with and why?

Based on the way the Tanya is written, we can say that an average person is not inherently a godly soul. The godly soul is something additional to the person. Does that mean a person is inherently the animal soul? The sum total of the natural inclinations? The animal soul does indeed animate us, but the life force is unable to make the choice between the animal and godly souls.

It is correct to define our identity as a struggle and not as the victory of one of the souls. The struggle – and of course the victory – is also what the Creator most wants from us. But the definition of a person as being in constant struggle still lacks the element of agency over the decision. It doesn't account for what, exactly, pushes us to choose one way or the other.

Rabbi Shneur Zalman does not answer this question as clearly as he outlines the two souls and their fight. The existence of a third soul, the intellectual soul, appears in a relatively small number of references in his writings.[25] The intellectual soul expresses a repetitive idea in the Tanya. The regulation of human life is rooted primarily in our intellectual-rational dimension. We are primarily intellectual creations. Both the animal soul and the godly soul turn to the intellect and try to influence it, and the intellectual soul decides which one to follow.

Choice, according to the Tanya's categorizations, belongs to the intellect. The animal side, prone to emotion, cannot choose freely. Its choices are limited to the alternatives that fulfill its interests. On the other hand, the consciousness of the godly soul is the experience of nullification, also characterized as divine connection, and therefore does not have the ability to choose between alternatives. The choice therefore stems from the intellectual soul, which originally does belong to the natural soul,[26] but has the power to choose whether to allow the godly soul to shine and radiate through it.[27]

---

25. Tanya, *Iggeret Hakodesh*, siman 6. See *Torah Ohr*, Mikeitz, 39d; *Likkutei Torah*, Parashat Matot, 82d.

26. "The intellectual soul comes from *kelipat nogah*, whose source is in the World of Tohu," *Torah Ohr*, Parashat Mikeitz, 39d. The same can be deduced from the Lubavitcher Rebbe's words: "Just as plants have something more than inanimate matter, animals have something more than plants, and humans have something more than animals – i.e., the intellectual soul – so, too, do the Jewish people have something more than the intellectual soul (the level of man); namely, the godly soul…" *Torat Menachem*, vol. 8, 1953, part 2, 45.

27. The intellect is not the soul's essence, but rather one of its garments. Some garments are completely separate from the wearer, while others are united with him. Thought, speech, and action are garments of the separated type, not bound up with the soul's essence. The proof that intellect is only a garment for the soul comes from the many changes it undergoes. The intellectual soul causes the essence of the soul to unite with the intellect. This bond is what gives us the capacity to win our battles. Therefore, according to the Tanya, the true power needed for victory in our battles comes from the intellect's advantage over the emotions. See "Second Day of Sukkot, 5716," *Torat Menachem*, vol. 15, 1956, part 1, 42.

The principle outlined by Rabbi Shneur Zalman is that man has the freedom to choose: neither the drive to cling to the Creator nor our physical needs can force us into a certain way of life. Only the intellectual soul has the power to decide how to shape our inner image, the principles with which we identify, the ideals to which we aspire, and the extent to which these principles will be realized in our lives.

As will be explained in the next chapter, because the ability to choose comes from the intellect, it occupies a significant role in the system of guidance offered by the Tanya for mental and spiritual distress.

Up to this point, we've described the battle between the souls, detailed the inner faculties of the soul, and clarified the ideal of the *beinoni* who struggles to win every moment of his life. In the next stage, the Tanya teaches us how to attain that ideal.

CHAPTER 7

Contemplation

War between the souls is the reality of life for most people. From the vantage point presented by Rabbi Shneur Zalman, man is doomed to constant soul struggles. The flow of thoughts, the worries, the sense of imperfection, the bitterness, the solitude, and the fluctuation in the soul never cease for nearly everyone: rich or poor, wise or simple. We have a variety of desires related to, among other things, success, financial well-being, physical health, and a healthy family life. Desires express lack, but the structure of the soul is such that even when we fulfill one aspiration, another immediately emerges to replace it, and the sense of calm is fleeting.

Is it possible to overcome our sense of lack? Rabbi Shneur Zalman's message is that most people will not succeed in winning a crushing victory over the flow of thought running off into undesirable channels, unfocused contemplations, internal resentments, tendency toward depression, anxieties about the future, or feelings of pride and independent existence. The victories are always temporary. The feelings of joy, completeness, and harmony between our inner and outer dimensions can be achieved only by small victories, every moment anew. This is because of the value in the internal struggle. In fact, we were created for the sake of that struggle. Every moment of life is so important because it embodies the struggle of that moment, and our life's mission is to win – in every present moment.

The image of the *beinoni*, the victorious person, presents us with our challenge and the desired image we must aspire to reach. It's not an unattainable ideal situation, but one that, though it sounds unrealistic, is attainable for nearly everyone.

From the personality of the *beinoni* we get a sense that the soul, in spite of the forces it grapples with, is full of optimism. No matter what happened a moment ago, we always have the present moment in which to win. Spiritual rewards are the product of constant inner work. On the one hand, we can never rest on laurels and bask in the victories of yesterday. On the other hand, the reward, the payoff for overcoming problematic traits and tendencies, is directly proportional to the level of awareness and effort.

The third part of the Tanya's therapeutic method includes the path to that desired state, *beinoni*. It involves training and effort on the part of the student. For many, Rabbi Shneur Zalman's guidance on how to reach that ideal state is a significant contribution and an important practical aspect that can be derived from his comprehensive teaching.

INSPIRATION

The method of the Tanya, which grew out of the teachings and writings of Kabbalah, avoids signs, miracles, and charms, and distances itself from any form of self-torture and fasting. In one of his testimonies, Rabbi Shneur Zalman writes:

> However, there is something else that some people call "Kabbalah" – administering oaths to angels so that they perform signs and wonders. However, I have never seen this mentioned in any book...[1]

Rabbi Shneur Zalman once said that "[in the presence of] the Maggid of Mezeritch there were miracles everywhere, but we had no time to pick them up.... We were fully immersed in learning the Torah's inner dimension."[2]

---

1. Quoted in *Igrot Kodesh – Alter Rebbe*, letter 58, 223.
2. Rabbi Yosef Yitzchak, *Igrot Kodesh*, vol. 2, 94.

Rabbi Shneur Zalman viewed awe over miracles as being of marginal importance. In contrast to other methods in the world of Chassidut, the Tanya's approach is that we all need to do our own work. The *tzaddik* does not spare the Chassid from doing his own work. Stories of miracles may be of help to someone who does not yet believe, but they are a means and not an end.[3] According to Rabbi Shneur Zalman, humanity's job is to influence our traits through intellectual activity. The believer does not need a miracle, he needs only to contemplate so that his faith crystallizes and becomes internalized and attained.[4]

Awakening ourselves and being willing to question our actions and life's purpose is for Rabbi Shneur Zalman the first step in his system of working on ourselves. Without honest contemplation, we can't implement the path outlined in the Tanya. The story commonly told among Chassidim about Rabbi Shneur Zalman during his first incarceration emphasizes the importance of this awakening as a precondition for our spiritual work.

When Rabbi Shneur Zalman was arrested, he was held in Petersburg in advance of his interrogation. On one occasion, one of the senior investigators entered his cell and began a conversation. That investigator, who is referred to as a government minister in the story, asked the rabbi a seemingly provocative question. He noted that he had read the Bible and did not understand what is written in Bereishit (Genesis). "How can it be that the Almighty, Who knows everything, asks Adam, 'Where are you?'"

Rabbi Shneur Zalman responded: "Do you believe that the Torah is eternal and speaks to every person at any time in any generation?"

The minister replied that he did.

"If so," said Rabbi Shneur Zalman, "this is what God asks every person in every moment: 'Where are you?' Where are you holding in your life? Such-and-such number of days and years have already passed by in your allotment of life, and how far along have you gotten in your mission? Do you not know the reason for which you were created, and what you are expected to accomplish? For example, God is calling out

3. The Lubavitcher Rebbe, *Torat Menachem*, vol. 1, 1950, 43.
4. *Torat Menachem*, vol. 11, 1954, part 2, 70. See also *Torat Menachem*, vol. 13, 1955, part 1, 99.

and asking: You've already lived forty-six years, and how far along are you on your life's path?"

When the minister heard the number of years expressed by Rabbi Shneur Zalman, he was startled and put his hand on Rabbi Shneur Zalman's shoulder, saying, "A son of valor," but his heart was quivering inside.[5]

Martin Buber, who analyzes the story, points out that the minister's questions seem to be similar to those already asked in the Talmud, when a Roman or other gentile asks one of the Talmudic sages about the meaning of a biblical verse in an attempt to find a contradiction in the words of the Torah. The sage does his part and demonstrates how the question has no contradiction. Sometimes, the responding rabbi includes a moral rebuke for the questioner in his answer.

But the story here doesn't answer the minister's question. Rabbi Shneur Zalman offers no answer to the minister's question. Instead, he raises the questioner to another realm. But there's no reconciliation of the contradiction: Why does the Creator, who is everywhere, need to ask where a person is?[6]

In his response, Rabbi Shneur Zalman turns the spotlight on the human condition. God's question wasn't intended to reveal where a person is geographically. Instead, it gets us to move spiritually, awaken, and perform an accounting of ourselves.

Man naturally hides among the trees of the garden. He shirks responsibility for his life, and the more he hides, the more entangled he becomes in the depths of his delusions and stubbornness. The question "Where are you?" is meant to confront the person with himself and shake him up.

The reason we need to be willing to deal with the big, essential life questions is that it gets us to transcend the small worries and anxieties of everyday life. We come to see ourselves and our lives from a much broader and deeper perspective. Knowing that we come from God's vast

5. There are several sources for this story, such as "19 Kislev, 5718," *Torat Menachem*, vol. 21, 1958, part 1, 206.
6. Mordechai Martin Buber, *Darko shel Adam al Pi Torat Hachassidut* (Jerusalem: Mosad Bialik, 1957), 7–13.

infiniteness beyond creation, which is a very lofty source, inspires us to refuse involvement with insignificant issues and helps us not to get angry at small things or to fear life's occasional challenges.

However, self-examination is likely to invite a focus on deprivation and a sense of dissatisfaction, resentment, and seclusion. The person doing the asking may not be satisfied with his condition and may therefore fall into depression. In his analysis, Buber asks how to ensure that the self-examination goes in a positive and productive direction rather than a paralyzing one.

To answer this, Buber points out that the minister's heart fluttered in response to Rabbi Shneur Zalman's words. It quivers when something new is discovered, when things become relevant, when they touch the person's core; otherwise, the person doesn't get excited.

The minister's heart quakes because he knows deep down that the time has come for him to change and progress in life. From Rabbi Shneur Zalman's response, Buber concludes that this applies regardless of the success a person has had in life, whether rich or poor, successful or a miserable failure. Even age doesn't matter.

As long as a person continues to hide, he's unwilling to boldly ask himself "Where are you?" and he won't find his true, authentic way. He is not on his life's path. "Where are you?" is a question that arouses a desire for repentance and a sense of commitment to see it through. Truly asked, "Where are you?" generates movement as well as awareness of the route the questioner needs to walk. The very willingness of a person to accept this question, and ultimately to answer it, is the beginning of his true path.

The question "Where are you?" is the one that the Creator expects each person to ask himself. This is a precondition for man's success in implementing the Tanya's approach. It is intended to give a person the desire to discover the right way of life.

CONTEMPLATION TECHNIQUE

This awakening is only the beginning of the road. What is the main tool that needs to accompany a person in the therapeutic process, the tool intended to help him overcome loneliness, sadness, anxiety, and negative thoughts? "This is the aspect of awe and love that are born in the heart due to intellectual contemplation."[7]

Unlike several trends in the world of psychology, and especially psychoanalysis, the Tanya does not emphasize a focus on inner distress and scars of the past, but rather a focus on conditions of the present.

Rabbi Shneur Zalman's approach does not value obsessive preoccupation with previous wounds, but rather, with changing thinking patterns. The history of the emotional problem or its cause is less relevant than the perceptual distortions that allow the emotional problem to continue. A person who has experienced trauma as a child suffers as an adult from resulting embedded perceptions and views, not from the trauma. They hold back his liberation from the trauma he experienced. It is those perceptions that the Tanya's method seeks to address.

The main challenge is to create intellectual processes that will affect emotions. The intellect is the main force we wield, and it has the potential to produce real inner change. The first task facing the person who diagnoses his state and condition is to identify the views and perceptions that lead him to emotional problems. He needs to understand that they are caused by external forces that disconnect him from his inner self. Then he has to replace the problematic perceptions, while implementing the Tanya's advice for the problems he has discovered.

Along with these intellectual exercises, the Tanya encourages taking action and facing things. Since victory occurs in the garments of the soul, the therapeutic idea is to create a framework that facilitates their change. For example, one might avoid people who speak in an unacceptable style, or one may escape from situations that evoke unwanted thoughts. Carefully creating a suitable space for the exchange of soul garments is a way to support the spiritual healing process.

The Tanya describes two ways of making a change. One is short-term and immediate. The other is long-term and thorough. The first requires revealing one's inner core point. Typically, this comes as the result of a crisis, an extraordinary event, or a moment of pressure. In such cases, the person encounters previously unimagined forces of change, and the powers of the godly soul to shape behavior are revealed with great force.

---

7. "Shema Yisrael," *Maamarei Admor Hazaken* (5567/1806), vol. 1, 62.

Rabbi Shneur Zalman calls this power that breaks out at special times *ahavah mesuteret* (hidden love). It's a level of natural, deep, inner love that we possess, but it is typically hidden. It takes an effort or extreme state to be expressed. In essence, *ahavah mesuteret* expresses the soul's desire to return to a state of oneness with the Creator. In moments of distress and crisis, it becomes revealed and stimulates the person to make a change.[8] The disadvantage of this path is that it's uncommon in daily life. The power of *ahavah mesuteret* gets covered over by daily hassles. Without external pressure to force its revelation and point out the passing nature of things in the world, and the Creator's presence in them, a person will likely continue previous ways and habits.

The other method – the Tanya's primary approach for dealing with our sense of self and independence and for winning the internal struggle – is through contemplation. Contemplation is the primary means a person has for self-awakening and creating an internal, deep, and stable change.

What is contemplation? When the Tanya mentions contemplation, it doesn't refer to using one's intellect to understand something. Rather, contemplation is a more advanced stage. It is continued involvement with an already understood concept, yet from different angles. The mind, which directs and controls emotions, doesn't naturally feel disgruntled. Mental issues arise from the disorganized expression of feelings. Often, they also express a feeling of lacking. A person wants something or complains about a plan that never came together. The guidance of the intellect is intended to get a person away from seeing lack and deprivation and instead to form a picture of completion. The role of the intellect, when properly directed, is, among other things, to describe reality in detail. An in-depth understanding of reality can change a person's perception and perspective, and through this process, facilitate change. The mind can be used to create healthy balance by preventing our feelings, anxieties,

---

8. *Ahavah mesuteret* is primarily aroused when confronted with issues of faith. It is mentioned in several places in the Tanya. See Tanya, *Likkutei Amarim*, ch. 12, 14, 15, 16, 19, and others. This love is unlike regular love, which expresses expansion and emphasizes the "I" of the one feeling love. *Ahavah mesuteret* includes a feeling of awe, a desire for self-nullification and inclusion. See *Torat Menachem*, vol. 16, 1956, part 2, 178.

and sorrows from detaching from reality. The inner sense of lack, which also holds us back in life, is thus restrained.

For the sake of illustration, using the mind to direct emotions can be compared, in a limited sense, to a well-known method of quitting smoking. This method is able to achieve impressive results without hypnosis, patches, or crystals. It is based on six hours of conversation, during which the smoker is invited to observe the illusion of the cigarette's role. The smoker is invited to ask whether smoking really pays off in different everyday situations and the extent to which one could live a full and happy life without them. Contemplation in which the smoker imagines smoking after a meal or when drinking coffee leads to the conclusion that cigarettes are unnecessary. Cigarettes don't add to the enjoyment of the moment. The conclusion from the contemplation is that pleasure is disconnected from the act of smoking. The urge to smoke is provoked by feelings of deprivation, and the smoker seeks to satisfy some perceived lack. However, in practice, the cigarette increases the sense of deprivation, because we're unable to enjoy the current moment without it.

The Tanya details many types and levels of contemplation.[9] In general, the goal of all contemplation techniques and levels is the same: to arouse the intellect and direct the emotions. Meditating on an idea allows it to become significant in one's life and to influence one's feelings. Contemplation is intended to awaken our intellectual faculty of *daat* (knowledge). *Daat* can direct our emotional traits in appropriate directions and not in pursuit of the superficial and fleeting. In this way, contemplation can calm anger, push off depression, avoid arrogance, and limit economic insecurity or fear of public opinion.

Deep contemplation transforms a person into a *pnimi*, an inner-minded, focused person. In chapter 5, which dealt with the soul's

---

9. One can differentiate between general contemplation and detailed contemplation. See Tanya, "Chanoch l'Naar," *Shaar Hayichud v'Ha'emunah*. General contemplation is the contemplation of the structure of life which leads to a recognition of the Creator. Detailed contemplation is an attempt to understand God's connection to our life, and not just His existence. It's contemplating specific phenomena while deeply absorbing the messages emanating from them. This way is called *derech prat* because it reveals the Creator to the person who searches for God in the framework of personal experiences. For further details, see "Shabbat Parashat Devarim," *Hemshech Ayin-Bet*, vol. 1, 332.

garments, *pnimi* was categorized as a fundamental concept in Chassidut. A *pnimi* is a person who is completely absorbed in the present and is not preoccupied with other things that are irrelevant to that moment. The *pnimi* lives the moment, focused on what's happening now. Ambient noise does not interfere. When the *pnimi* is with his or her children, worries about work aren't relevant. Such a moment is a connection to the inner self, the deep essential point that connects to the faculties of the soul. The contemplator goes outside the self, forgets about "I," and concentrates on the moment. *Pnimi* in the language of Chassidut indicates the superiority of seeking out the essence in any matter, the central point and not the external aspects. A *pnimi* lives with the wholesomeness of being and not lack and deprivation. A *pnimi* is, in many ways, a description of the *beinoni* – the person who wins every moment anew.

Rabbi Shneur Zalman's method of contemplation can be clarified and focused when contrasted with the technique of seclusion promoted by Rabbi Nachman of Breslov. Like Rabbi Shneur Zalman, Rabbi Nachman insists that the only way to overcome the feeling of being far from the Creator is to nullify our sense of self and independent existence.

According to Rabbi Nachman, the way to become nullified is by seclusion. While alone and secluded, a person can nullify lusts and negative traits. By the end of the process, which includes isolation techniques, one is able to nullify physicality, integrate into spiritual roots, and cling to the Creator. Seclusion primarily occurs at night when a person is free from the trivial matters of this world that interfere with recognition of the oneness of the Creator.

This implies that isolation is the first prerequisite to contemplation and our ability to be a *pnimi*. According to Rabbi Nachman, seclusion, which is an important and central element in serving God, needs to occur in a special place, far from the city, without the likely distraction from people. What should a person do during seclusion? Pray and speak to the Creator. This gradually dispels one lust after another.[10] We are free to fulfill the will of the Creator once our desires, needs, and cravings are negated, according to the approach of Rabbi Nachman.

In the Israeli cult film *Ushpizin*, there is a powerful scene close to the

---

10. "Haniur ba'Lailah," *Likkutei Moharan*, 52.

beginning in which a Breslov Chassid, Moshe, played by Shuli Rand, returns to his home, and the dire poverty is evident. He tells his wife: "Today I heard a beautiful teaching from Rabbi Natan: Wherever I see deficiency, I know that either I didn't pray about it at all or I didn't pray about it enough." Hearing his Torah thought, his wife urges him: "Then maybe you should go pray." Moshe tries to get away, looking for the bed. His troubles have left him fatigued. She insists: "Why are you bringing me teachings from Rabbi Natan? This is as if saying, we have nothing with which to fulfill the commandments of the upcoming holiday, and you tell me Torah teachings. Go pray." So, Moshe goes to pray, secluding himself in a playground overlooking Jerusalem to talk with his Creator. Solitude and prayer yield immediate results. A charitable contribution to help observe the holiday comes to him in a miraculous way. In prayer, Moshe is careful to not ask for his needs. Instead, he seeks help in fulfilling the commandments, observing the holiday, and to be a kosher Jew so as not to upset his wife. He does not need money for his wants; he needs it in order to use it for holy purposes and elevate the physical world.

For Rabbi Shneur Zalman, contemplation does not necessarily require physical isolation. A person doesn't have to distance himself from the city and go to a place where his daily troubles won't interfere with his self-nullification before his Creator. Although prayer is the main time for contemplation, the goal is for it to help a person develop awareness all day long. Contemplation is supposed to guide him in every step he takes and develop his awareness of every detail in his life. But it's not about stopping life to do soul-searching in order to nullify desires and cravings. They can't be annulled unless a person is a *tzaddik*, but they can be beaten in the moment. Contemplation is a tool for working with reality, in the midst of the noise and commotion of daily life, says Rabbi Shneur Zalman.

Rabbi Shneur Zalman doesn't shy away from describing a world of *kelipah* and Sitra Achra, hardship and torment, where evil and wickedness prevail.[11] He does not conceal the bad in the world. His description is not intended to weaken a person or cause despair. Yet, the dominance

---

11. "That is why this world with all it contains is called the world of *kelipah* and Sitra Achra. This is also why all affairs of this world are severe and evil, and the wicked

of the animal soul is also not intended to justify our spiritual slips and falls. His exploration of the ideal situation, the existing situation, and the difficulty in overcoming our independent sense over time is intended to ward off our sadness upon encountering evil, difficulty, agony, challenge, and concealment of God's presence in the world. We're taught about the battle between the souls in order to be aware of the war and know we can win battles. "Why did the Creator make a world of difficulty and suffering?" is an important and significant question, but we should not delay the treatment until we obtain the answer. In fact, the existential questions sometimes interfere, because the challenges are likely to confuse us and prevent focus and achievement.

Contemplation, as a practical technique, is designed to help a person peel away layers of worry, anxiety, and deprivation that conceal at any moment. It's meant to bring about internalization of the fact that, according to the framework of creation, experiencing lack is impossible. In order to permeate our lives with this insight, we must be willing to change our perspective and stop making ourselves the focus of everything. Rabbi Shneur Zalman aspires to have contemplation become our primary mental effort throughout the day.[12] For, if the battle is constant, then effort is required constantly.

HAPPINESS AND OUR GOAL

At this point, one wonders about Rabbi Shneur Zalman's practical contribution to the treatment of emotional distress today. How effective is contemplation, and how does Rabbi Shneur Zalman's theoretical structure of the soul translate into practical advice in the lives of all kinds of people everywhere?

As mentioned above, the psychological infrastructure that the Tanya contributed to our understanding of the human psyche and its treatment has made it a fundamental book in popular therapeutic training today. Its

---

prevail in it," as is written in *Etz Chayim*, shaar 42, end of ch. 4. See also Tanya, *Likkutei Amarim*, ch. 6 at the end.

12. See Tanya, *Likkutei Amarim*, ch. 42, as well as *Torah Ohr*, Parashat Chayei Sarah 16b, "And then a desire will be aroused in the heart to be connected to this contemplation all day long."

contribution to therapy can be better appreciated by comparing general coaching and Jewish coaching.

In the not too distant past, emotional distress, not fulfilling one's potential, or a sense of lacking, suffocation, or missing vitality would lead to one or many sessions on the psychologist's couch or to having an encouraging talk with the local rabbi.

Today, a common approach is personal coaching. The principles of coaching are basically similar. All the necessary desire, skills, and knowledge are already found deep within the client. They only need to learn how to act on them. The coaching is typically highly focused and yields large, measurable results.

But there is a fundamental difference between the coaching trend and what has developed in Jewish training based on the Tanya. Jewish values and traditions are not an essential part of Jewish coaching. Rather, what's unique about Jewish coaching is how the Creator is brought into the conversation between the coach and trainee.

In typical training, an athlete's self, ambitions, and yearnings are at the center: the coach assists with overcoming fears and obstacles on the way to self-realization. Jewish training that is in the spirit of the Tanya guides a person to act in the opposite way. The only way to strengthen self-confidence, improve relationships, find fulfillment in work, or cope with financial changes is by removing yourself, not by making "I" the central focus. Self-nullification is the negation of our sense of "I," the perception of self as an independent entity that is detached from its source. This nullification, according to Rabbi Shneur Zalman, comes from contemplating the inner, deeper source for the world and those alive in it. Awareness of this nullification needs to be made a part of the framework of a person's emotional, moral, and, of course, intellectual life.

Our own sense of self is a primary motivator. It causes us to believe that we'll only find happiness if we gain more publicity, are beloved by others, or have more success in business and our endeavors. According to the teachings of Rabbi Shneur Zalman, this assessment is an illusion. As a motivating force, our sense of self is very important, but only when it is cleansed of the emotional problems it provokes. Happiness resulting from self-gratification is always temporary, deceptive, and followed by a spiritual fall.

Through contemplation, Rabbi Shneur Zalman's approach directs a person to recognize that happiness cannot be sustained if the animal soul is allowed to assume control. Long-term happiness is not possible for a person who is troubled over other people's opinions or who obsesses over receiving enough or deserving more, and other such destructive thoughts. To be fundamentally happy, we have to focus on activities in which our being is not of prime importance.

When we're released from an obsession with the self and our contemplations connect us with the true reality – that of the Creator's power, which fills and animates all of Creation – then, in the natural course of things, all the problems that were bothering us take on a completely different meaning, and our unhealthy tendencies self-correct.

Self-nullification is not intended to produce bitterness or constriction when it seemingly contradicts the natural sense of reality. According to Rabbi Shneur Zalman, the opposite is true. The nullification does not negate our reality. Instead, it shows us that we were not created to be small and insignificant. Rabbi Shneur Zalman intends to elevate our value and demonstrate that our reality is an expression of the Creator's image. Therefore, we are not merely limited physical creatures. As a result, we have a significant role in the world: to have our lives reflect our connection with the Creator.[13] The wording used by Rabbi Tzadok of Lublin in his book *Tzidkat Hatzaddik* effectively expresses this idea of the Tanya: "Just as one must believe in God, so, too, must he then believe in himself... believing just that his soul comes from the source of life."[14]

TANYAX

An interesting example of viewing the Tanya as a source of self-help as well as a path of serving the Creator can be seen in a video recently distributed by actor Gili Shushan and former basketball player Doron Sheffer called *Tanyax*. In the video, Gili Shushan is the patient and Doron Sheffer is the therapist. The patient suffers from anxiety. His surroundings lead him to envy, hatred, and stress, but when he succeeds, he loves

---

13. See this discussed in detail by Rabbi Yosef Yitzchak, *Igrot Kodesh*, vol. 4, 524ff.
14. Rabbi Tzadok Hakohen of Lublin, *Tzidkat Hatzaddik* (Lublin, 1803), 26.

everyone. When he doesn't, he is jealous, angry, short-sighted, and full of hatred, a painful hatred that consumes every good part of his soul.

The student knows that he needs treatment. The therapist, inspired by the film *The Matrix*, gives the patient a pill. Not a blue or red pill, but a "Tanyax." The pill allows the patient to see the true reality, the infinity that creates the world in every moment and constitutes its inner vitality. The patient becomes addicted to the pill. The only way to achieve happiness in life is to discover the point of oneness and give up the sense of "I," give up material and temporal interests and stick to infinity. Without the pill, the patient is lost. Or thinks he's lost. Reality is shaky. The battles are difficult. The neighbors are annoying. He wants to live in the true reality all the time, a reality of infinite potential that is not limited by the finite.

After the patient has been using the drug for a while, the therapist tries to convince the patient that he can do it without the pill. On his own he can achieve true happiness, learn to love and give, and stand on his own two feet.

What is interesting in Shushan and Sheffer's film is that contemplation of the Creator's power in creation, based on the Tanya, is presented as a remedy for mental health problems. In some Torah works, several answers are proposed to the question of why we should strive to recognize the Creator. None of them have anything to do with practicality. Some say the Creator must be recognized in a deeper way and learned about in order to awaken our emotions of love and fear for Him, or to strengthen our faith. Others suggest that recognizing the Creator's existence in everything is an essential logical deduction if we accept the basic premise of Jewish thought, that the world has a Creator Who cannot be changed or increased.

In the film, in the spirit of postmodern culture, we are introduced to a new motivation. Paraphrasing John F. Kennedy's famous words, "Do not ask what you can do for infinity; ask what infinity can do for you." According to the actors, remembering infinity can do a lot, especially in terms of granting us happiness. Awareness of the Creator pushes aside worry and anxiety, which are the products of falsity. It invites the connection between the godly soul and the state in which our sense of self ceases to be a factor that can shake us.

Is this also the view that Rabbi Shneur Zalman offered to thousands of his followers 220 years ago?

Rabbi Shneur Zalman believed that knowing the Creator is a positive commandment. Maimonides rules that "the foundation of all foundations and the pillar of wisdom is to know that there is a Primary Being Who brought into being all of existence."[15] According to Rabbi Shneur Zalman, the use of the word *know* is not accidental. It points to the value of the knowledge that emerges out of study and contemplation. Knowing the Creator is the primary goal of the believing person. The first commandment is intellectual: to know that there is a Creator "Who brought into being all existence." And this knowledge calls for active learning efforts on the part of the believer. In other words, besides simple faith, the believer must take faith in the Creator to a level of knowledge and understanding.

In chapter 3 of the Tanya, on which the video of Shushan and Sheffer is based, Rabbi Shneur Zalman teaches that unless we constantly, tenaciously contemplate the infinite force of the Creator that constitutes creation in every moment, we will suffer from delusion and false perceptions. We will be taken up by all those trivial hassles, worries, and paralyzing desires.

For Rabbi Shneur Zalman, utilitarianism and individualism are not a natural part of the world of ideas. But he certainly teaches that, paradoxically, devotion to God and self-negation are of greater value than personal benefit. They are the only prescription available for achieving happiness. This is the paradox presented by the Tanya. Anyone who wants happiness has to give up personal benefits, which are momentarily fleeting. It is only through a sense of nullification that we can enjoy the greatest benefit we can hope for: happiness. Now, this may not be the primary motivation for serving God in the approach of Rabbi Shneur Zalman, but according to the video *Tanyax*, this is the result, and it is crucial to the emotional experience of today's students of Tanya.

Happiness, according to the Tanya, stems from discovering the inner part of the heart within reality. This revelation, it turns out, does not come from the fulfillment of self-interest, but from the revelation of our connection with the Creator.

---

15. Rambam, *Mishneh Torah*, Hilchot Yesodei HaTorah.

Rabbi Shneur Zalman sees himself as a meditation instructor who teaches about the benefits of contemplation. His advice for dealing with mental imbalance and obtaining victories in the soul is scattered throughout this book. These ideas were elaborated, expanded, and explained by the leaders of Chassidut, that is, those who succeeded him. The purpose of the advice he gives in the Tanya is not to instruct his readers to do this or that. Instead, he wants to lead them to a significant change. He wants to help them change their perspective: to change the way they understand life, how they deal with difficult events and challenging news. At the end of that process, the nature of their character traits will also change, in the sense that there will be victory of the godly soul's faculties over the tendencies of the natural soul.

CHAPTER 8

Advice for Living

*I*n the town of Liozna, where the Tanya was written, Rabbi Shneur Zalman lived in a two-story building called the Heichal. It stood at the center of a large courtyard with rows of trees, a vegetable garden, and other buildings. The other buildings belonged to Chassidim and included a synagogue and study rooms. Together, the complex served as the center of Chassidic activity.

The length of the hall was about twelve and a half meters long and only six meters wide. There were a total of seventy-two square meters on the lower floor. This floor was divided into two apartments. The apartment on the right served as the private residence of Rabbi Shneur Zalman. On the left was a small synagogue that the Chassidim called Gan Eden Hatachton (the Lower Paradise).[1]

Visitors would wait in Gan Eden Hatachton for their one-on-one *yechidut* meeting with the rebbe. The second floor also had two rooms, and there was a corridor separating them. One room served as a study and seclusion room for Rabbi Shneur Zalman. The second room was where he received visitors for *yechidut*. The Chassidim called that room Gan Eden Ha'elyon (the Higher Paradise).

The terms Gan Eden Hatachton and Gan Eden Ha'elyon come from

---

1. See Rabbi Yosef Yitzchak, *Reshimot – Divrei Yemei Chayei Admor Hazaken*, 4.

the world of Kabbalah and describe stations occupied by the soul. They
were adapted by the Chassidim to describe the rooms in which they were
privileged to meet with the rebbe, that is, any one of the seven Chabad
rebbes. These terms remained in use from the times of Rabbi Shneur
Zalman until meetings with the last rebbe, the Lubavitcher Rebbe. For
comparison, in the Lubavitcher Rebbe's famous study hall at 770 Eastern
Parkway in Brooklyn, New York, the waiting room for *yechidut* was called
Gan Eden Hatachton by the Chassidim. The Lubavitcher Rebbe's room,
which served as his office where he stayed most of the day and received
those who turned to him for meetings was called Gan Eden Ha'elyon.

In Liozna, the Chassidim pushed to be able to meet with Rabbi
Shneur Zalman so he could guide them in their soul work as well as in
their daily struggles. Crowds would gather at his door, pleading with
secretaries to be allowed to enter.[2] As described in the introduction, the
thirst for trustworthy leadership that offered clear explanation for real,
actual occurrences in life was great. However, as noted, Rabbi Shneur
Zalman gave his audience more than that. They came away not only with
pleasure and meaning in life, and in Torah and mitzvot, but also specific,
precise direction. The advice was based on a profound theoretical
philosophy, yet remained entirely practical, which was exactly what the
audience wanted to hear.

Rabbi Shneur Zalman knew that he would not be able to meet with
everyone who sought him.[3] At first, he tried to convince his followers
that they could easily overcome their need to meet with him. On their
own, they could find what they were looking for in the subject matter
and classes he was teaching. As mentioned, later on he established the
Liozna Regulations, a series of policies designed to regulate the number
of arrivals to the town. These may have succeeded in repelling the crowd
at his door, but they failed to meet the demand of the community.
Ultimately, there was no choice but to write down the specific advice
he would give. This made up the Tanya.

In the Tanya's introduction, Rabbi Shneur Zalman explains the

2. Etkes notes the overseers of the Rabbi Shneur Zalman's courtyard. See the chapter
"Irgun U'Minahel" in *Rabbi Shneur Zalman of Liadi*, 89–98.
3. Ibid., 70–71.

need to write the book. During the first period of Chassidut, it was not customary to write down Chassidic ideas that were based on Kabbalistic thought, because it was considered too esoteric for the masses. But from Rabbi Shneur Zalman's perspective, the times demanded such a book. It was the only proper way to convey his approach to a large audience. This would help preserve his method. Furthermore, he emphasized that those studying the Tanya would find answers to all their questions and advice for every spiritual challenge. As he writes in the introduction:

> All of them are answers to many questions posed continually by members of the Chassidic brotherhood in our country seeking advice, each according to his stature so as to receive guidance for themselves in the service of God.
>
> Because time no longer permits [me] to reply to everyone individually on particular queries, and also because forgetfulness is common, I have therefore recorded *all the replies to all the questions* [emphasis added], to be preserved as a sign and to serve as a reminder in everyone's mind. No longer will one need to press for a private audience, for in it one will find tranquility for his soul and true counsel on everything that he finds difficult.

After much preparation, the Chassidim would enter to talk to Rabbi Shneur Zalman regarding the many questions, difficulties, and anxieties they faced. In the Tanya, Rabbi Shneur Zalman successfully summarized all of these personal questions and formulated ways of dealing with them. He precisely characterized the common problems among the general public and among Chassidim who turned to him, in particular: laziness, heaviness, fatigue, sadness, insensitivity, selfish interests, arrogance, vanity, excessive satisfaction, coolness, anxiety, tension, unfocused thoughts, anger, lust, passions, weakness of faith, and insecurity.

According to his approach, although environmental, cultural, political, and economic conditions are constantly changing, the structure of the soul has not changed substantially since man's creation. Due to the similar structure of the psyche found among humans, almost everyone should be able to identify with Rabbi Shneur Zalman's description of emotional and spiritual issues.

It's true that everyone approaching him had specific, personal, sometimes intimate problems. Everyone is unique and has specific problems and particular circumstances. But similar principles for handling issues apply to most people. For every hardship, Rabbi Shneur Zalman found a singular source that he sought to treat. The source of all emotional and spiritual problems stems from the animal soul's tendency to place the "I," itself, its being, at the center of perceived existence. In other words, this self-focus is the main cause of our spiritual suffering.

TREAT THE PERSON, NOT THE SICKNESS

As mentioned, Rabbi Shneur Zalman promises in the introduction that the Tanya will present "all the replies to all the questions." After such a promise, we would expect to see a detailing of the problems and their solutions. However, the book only contains a small amount of advice for some specific problems, which is to be employed sparingly. Where are the answers to all the questions? In the majority of cases, Rabbi Shneur Zalman avoids dealing with a person's negative aspects and, instead, offers him a new method of treatment. The method is designed to disconnect the person from the negative traits that handcuff him and connect him to the essence of his lofty soul. If there is one cause for most mental struggles, Rabbi Shneur Zalman's primary method is to treat that cause at the root of all problems, and not each individual mental struggle. In personal spiritual work, there is no division of illnesses into categories. Why? Because spiritual illnesses are cured automatically when one treats the person.

A metaphor that effectively describes the Tanya's method of treatment is that of a fly trapped in a bottle. The fly is trying to get out. He goes up and up in an attempt to go free. Since the bottle neck narrows toward the opening, the fly collides with it, and the direction of his flight is altered. He goes back down, but gets stuck in the liquid. So he goes up and down, moving left and right, takes another hit and another, and he can't get out of his prison. If someone aimed him toward the bottle's opening, he would avoid the blows he gets from the inside.

According to Rabbi Shneur Zalman, as long as we're stuck in our personal reality, we will rise a bit only to receive a new blow. We change direction but get stuck again in the liquid. And it repeats over and over again. In other words, the least effective approach to treatment is to explore those same blows and how to avoid them. The easier and better way is to ask to be shown the way up.

Another analogy is that of a small child making noise when his parents want to rest.[4] Rebuke typically fails to help and may scar the child. The child will find it hard to maintain restraint. The easier way to deal with the situation is to give the child an intriguing game. He'll become absorbed in the game, lost in another world, and the parents will rest.

According to Rabbi Shneur Zalman, as one rises to a different world, a world connected to the inner dimension in which the Creator's presence is more revealed, the disturbing and bothersome elements of the lower world cease to be heard. The mental health issues caused by our self-focus are automatically resolved.

In other words, dealing with the root of the problem, our obsession with self, also uproots diseases. It is not necessary to explain to a person the reason anger, depression, pride, or arrogance are serious issues. It is enough to let him realize that he has no reason to be angry or depressed or arrogant and rude.

Hitbonenut (contemplation) takes us out of our position and connects us to a completely different view of reality. It makes it unnecessary to probe emotional wounds and gain familiarity with our egocentricity. Rather, it presents us with the sublime alternative we already possess, which naturally elevates us from our situation. In most cases, Rabbi Shneur Zalman wants to move people away from such questions as "Am I feeling fulfilled?" and "Do I really love what I do?" to questions such as "What is my role in the present moment, which is truly an infinite moment of eternal significance?"

Rabbi Shneur Zalman pushes us to use the tool of contemplation to seek out the unity in reality and not the multiplicity and separation. Contemplation can help us as an effective tool for relieving anxieties and stress. It prevents us from worrying about the uncertainty of the future, about losing our material wealth, or about social insecurity.

In this chapter we will examine how to apply Rabbi Shneur Zalman's

---

4. Both analogies appear in an interview with Rabbi Mendel Vechter featured in *Maayanotecha* 44 (April 2005).

method in cases of mental struggle, and how to derive accurate direction from it.

DEALING WITH STRUGGLE

One of the most significant challenges facing Rabbi Shneur Zalman, much like anyone in the helping professions, is teaching how to cope with difficult situations such as suffering, loss, bereavement, and physical or mental anguish. Generally speaking, there are three approaches and perspectives that he proposes for dealing with such situations. Each approach is meant to fit with a different situation, but all three approaches have the same goal: to lead the student to change his or her relationship with reality.

A. *The Good within the Bad*

The first approach calls for the person to recognize that behind the challenges and suffering is only absolute good. However, this good is hidden, and as a result, suffering is perceived, though in our eyes only. If we could adopt a different broader perspective, then over time we would realize that suffering is not really a bad thing.

The basis for this approach comes from the Baal Shem Tov's commentary on the verse "And I have placed [*shiviti*] God before me always."[5] *Shiviti* is related to the word *shavyon* (equality). One of the highest spiritual levels one can attain is to equalize our relationship to every moment of our day and every event we experience. We are to develop a sense of spiritual equanimity in times in which we are put down and in times in which we are praised, in times of failure and times of success.[6] The reason our attitude to reality should be devoid of preference is because everything has its source in the Creator. There is nothing that happens in the world that is not a result of the Creator's power bringing it into existence. The Creator is not limited to being found in the events we perceive as good. In truth, everything is good. Therefore, this equanimity needs to be present constantly, in every moment of the world's ongoing creation.

---

5. Tehillim 16:8.
6. The Baal Shem Tov, *Keter Shem Tov*, vol. 1, 220–21.

According to the Baal Shem Tov's explanation, the Creator is the source of reality. The foundation of his faith is that there is nothing that is free from the presence of the Creator. Another concept is that it is impossible for the Creator to create anything bad or painful. Therefore, explains Rabbi Shneur Zalman, even if we suffer, through proper contemplation we can see that the challenges are complete good in their source, and we should, therefore, be happy with them.[7]

Joy, according to this approach, is one of the central elements of Judaism. True, inner joy is evidence that a person has successfully overcome personal struggles. If anger, sadness, and anxiety indicate victory for the animal soul, then joy indicates victory for the godly soul. Why? Joy expresses overcoming the sense of self and of arrogant independence, of reliance on oneself alone. An unhappy person, writes Rabbi Shneur Zalman to his Chassidim, shows a lack of faith, at least when complaining about suffering.[8] Walking around in a dark and gloomy state is akin to denying the entire structure of creation.

Rabbi Shneur Zalman's advice is that dealing with difficulties and suffering requires the acquisition of a faith-based theoretical outlook that is broad and full of awareness. A person who falls into anxiety and sadness demonstrates a lack of belief that the world is created anew in every moment and that the Creator is the inner vitality that brings us to life out of nothingness. Logically, those who accept Chassidut's view of the Creator are seemingly unable to see bad, suffering, or difficulty in the world. The true believer, according to Rabbi Shneur Zalman, will not feel suffering due to anything in the world. Mourning one's fate shows

---

7. In this context, the sages say that "Just as one blesses on the good, so should one bless the bad" (Mishnah, *Berachot* 46b). One should literally bless things that are bad news, just as one blesses on things that are obviously good. The reason for such an acceptance is that "no evil descends from heaven" (*Bereishit Rabbah* 51:3) and that "it is the nature of the Good to do good." See Rabbi Naftali Hertz, *Emek Hamelech*, ch. 1, sha'ar 1: Sha'ar Sha'ashuei Hamelech. See also Tanya, *Shaar Hayichud v'Ha'emunah*, ch. 4. And evil, even if it is difficult to accept at present, possesses hidden good from the highest of levels, since according to the principle established by Rabbi Shneur Zalman, everything down here in our physical lives has a higher source in the chain-like descent of worlds in the upper realms, which is good. See *Torat Menachem*, vol. 14, 1955, part 2, 174.
8. See Tanya, *Iggeret Hakodesh*, siman 11.

that a person puts personal interests and the self above faith. According to Rabbi Shneur Zalman, it is impossible to actually lack anything. All our needs are satisfied. With proper contemplation, we realize that even what seemed bad actually comes from a higher level of good.[9]

Of course, this idea is interesting from a theoretical point of view, but difficult to implement. To adopt this view and be able to overcome one's emotions, it is helpful to learn the logic of creation according to Jewish mysticism. The purpose of this study is to help the mind to direct one's feelings. Chaim Gravitzer – the hero of Yehoshua Fishel Schneerson's book who was mentioned in the previous chapter – offers an extreme example of this kind of *bitachon* (confidence in God). Gravitzer spends time with the Chassidim. When he returns home radiant and exalted, he finds his wife broken and crying. She informs him that their only son, Yossi, is dead. As she faints, Gravitzer's response astonishes everyone around him. He does not recognize the difference between life and death. It's all equal in his eyes.

> Chaim raised his hands toward her with great love. Those gathered there stopped singing and listened with bated breath.
>
> "Leahla! What is there to cry about? Along with Yossele, we'll bury death. For death is literally like life, included and subsumed in godliness..."
>
> Everyone shuddered, and with blazing joy he called out loudly: "There is nothing but Him, there is nothing but Him!"
>
> ...And again there was a singing voice of thousands of souls.
>
> Chaim's face lit up, radiating the melody, and very close to his deceased son he began to dance a passionate dance.[10]

The continuation of the story follows Gravitzer's fall. When he realizes that his son is truly dead, he deteriorates mentally. In this respect, Gravitzer doesn't exemplify the encompassing view that Rabbi Shneur Zalman asks his followers to adopt. The intellectual understanding that everything in the world is equal, life and death, has an impact at first, until it's shattered with a painful awakening. Another example that emphasizes

---

9. Ibid.
10. Schneerson, *Chaim Gravitzer*, 88–89.

the value of Rabbi Shneur Zalman's approach is that of two fathers who each lost a son. The first one falls into a sense of victimization and deteriorates mentally, which then affects his physical health. The other, however, adopts the approach of the Tanya and transforms his loss and bereavement into a recipe for growth and maturity. He honors his son's memory in ways that contribute to his surroundings as well.

Coping, according to Rabbi Shneur Zalman, is a result of trust and belief in the existence of the Creator. In less extreme situations, confidence gives a person a sense of calm, allows him to function better, and even brings him success. The power of *hitbonenut* and of leaving our suffering behind is demonstrated when, according to Rabbi Shneur Zalman, we contemplate how the only true reality is the Creator's reality. Worries distance a person from seeing the Creator in the world and cause constriction of the mind and heart to the point of being unable to see or discover anything other than oneself or the extent to which one is a "victim" of reality.[11]

B. Cleansing

One method, which according to popular opinion is common in religious thought, is completely absent from the Tanya: that of reward and punishment. Suffering is not described in the Tanya as punishment imposed upon a person by the Creator because of the offenses he committed. According to the second approach presented by Rabbi Shneur Zalman, suffering is not the result of punishment, but of the Creator's love. It expresses a form of cleaning and polishing.

"Whom He loves, He rebukes,"[12] says King Solomon. Rabbi Shneur Zalman compares suffering to a father cleaning his child. It's not pleasant for the child, but stems from the father's great love and constitutes part of his role as a parent.

In a similar way, the Creator purifies our souls through suffering. A person who went far from himself and the Creator through his unhealthy behaviors can return and seek closeness. However, after the act, he has

---

11. Rabbi Yosef Yitzchak, "Shabbat Parashat Toldot," *Sefer Hamaamarim* 5712 (1942), 151.
12. Mishlei 3:12, cited in Tanya, *Iggeret Hateshuvah*, ch. 1.

to undergo a type of cleansing from the memory of his former behavior. Like a gift given to someone who already forgave you for hurting him, the relationship is still not the same as before. The purpose of the gift is to strengthen the relationship and raise it to an even higher level.

According to Rabbi Shneur Zalman, there is a purpose to seeing suffering as a form of renewal of the connection between humanity and the Creator. By recognizing that suffering, like good things, also stems from the Creator's great love for us, we acknowledge His presence in our lives, strengthen our bond, and ask the Creator to make our cleansing and purification easier, without as much suffering.

C. Refinement and Tests

Based on the third approach presented by the Tanya, suffering is a test placed before a person by the Creator. Rabbi Shneur Zalman's message for his Chassidim during his first incarceration sharpens this idea. During Rabbi Shneur Zalman's arrest, the Chassidim intensely waited for any sign or message from their revered rebbe. How would he direct them to act? What was the meaning of the imprisonment?

He was aware of their concerns. After being taken to Petersburg, they found a note he had left, in his handwriting. It quoted a number of psalms: "Princes pursued me for nothing, but my heart feared Your word."[13] With this verse he summarized the main message he wished to convey to his Chassidim during one of the most difficult times they had experienced. It expressed the essence of his approach to handling difficulties.

Anyone familiar with Rabbi Shneur Zalman's teachings could guess at the deeper meaning he intended. The message featured two parts.[14] In the words he quoted, Rabbi Shneur Zalman intimated that a Jew is not under the control of the czar or landowner. They are not the ones who decide his future, and he is not enslaved to them. Therefore, according

---

13. Tehillim 119:161.
14. The Lubavitcher Rebbe explains the two possible explanations of the verse regarding the imprisonment and how the two possibilities are really one. See "Sichah of 19 Kislev," *Torat Menachem*, vol. 2, 1951, part 1, 118; "10–19 Kislev 2002," *Sha'arei Hamo'adim*, 142; and "19 Kislev 1964," *Sichot Kodesh*, paragraph 2.

to the first part of the message, although imprisonment is likely life threatening, his supporters should not be frightened by it. The government that arrested him is only "an ax in the hand of the woodchopper." Decisions about his life, the life of the Chassidim, and the future of the Jews and Judaism are not really in the hands of the czar.

The second part of the message relates to working on our emotional traits. Each person can choose a path, actions, words to say, and thoughts to think. It's a choice that arises from a struggle between inner opposites that needs to be repeated constantly. Success in this battle removes the suffering and sets us free from challenges.

In a message he sent moments before going to prison, Rabbi Shneur Zalman wanted to instruct his supporters who feared for his fate that when people win the inner battle, when they decide between the tendencies of the souls and succeed in living in the moment, they transcend nature. It can no longer control them. With such an eternal choice, they have no reason to fear or be troubled. Suffering is only meant to push them to pray, do inner soul-searching, and work on their character traits. Once they recognize this and do what is required of them, they save themselves from having to undergo the test.

The purpose of a test is to elevate us. By withstanding it, we climb to a higher level.[15] Coping, difficulties, and suffering bring us to handle the situation, and thus, to grow. Therefore, the very act of handling a test pushes away the suffering.

According to Chassidic thought, the entirety of existence is comprised of tests that invite two kinds of general challenges. In the language of Chassidut, these struggles are called *avodat habirurim* (the work of refining and clarification) and *avodat hanisyonot* (experiencing tests). *Avodat habirurim* is a fundamental Kabbalistic concept. In practical terms, it means that we have to deal with reality, distinguish between the good and bad parts, and separate out the good from evil and real from false. In this way, the world is repaired and transformed into a dwelling place for the Creator, a place where the Creator is tangibly present. The other

15. *Nisayon* (test) is related to the word *nes* (elevation). Also, "For God is testing/ elevating [*menaseh*] you" (Devarim 13:4). See the Lubavitcher Rebbe, "Shabbat Parashat Matot-Masai," Mevarchim Chodesh Menachem Av 1959.

method of dealing with the world is *avodat hanisyonot*. This necessitates a deeper, more internal strength.

In *avodat habirurim*, the one doing the refining works with the material that needs to be refined. There is a real problem, be it psychological or physical, that needs to be addressed. In general, this work is usually related to a person's needs. Those who suffer from nutrition-related problems need to do *avodat habirurim*. They choose what to eat, when and how much, from the range of food available.

In many ways, this is also true of the challenges in earning a living. As mentioned above, a person struggling with financial worries has to construct two plans. One is practical, a plan that helps him to overcome the struggle and grow from it. The other is spiritual, to help him develop his trust and confidence in the Creator (i.e., that He supports and sustains everything, and that there is no need for concern).

Avodat habirurim, whether it encourages action or inspires withholding from a reaction and practicing control over desires and anxieties, demonstrates that there is a connection between the person and the material situation that is being refined. There is a real entity that has to be dealt with. Ignoring it will only exacerbate the situation. *Avodat habirurim* does require dealing with an external, practical problem, but also with the individual.

Dealing with *avodat habirurim* usually involves effort, struggle, and overcoming. The refiner has to contemplate the root of the conflict, the root of the matter needing refinement, and identify the source of the problem. For example, a violent child's problem could be a lack of attention. Digestive disorders may result from insecurity or fear of public opinion, lack of confidence and self-esteem. *Avodat habirurim* often demands control of our instincts, overcoming urges, and fighting with lusts. It's a struggle that demands vigilance and involves a reliance on approaches and techniques that help a person to identify the point of goodness as well as the problematic situation that needs resolution.

In contrast to *avodat habirurim*, *avodat hanisyonot* calls not for trying to cope, but rather for disregarding the distressing situation. Underlying *avodat hanisyonot* is the assumption that there isn't really anything inhibitory, humiliating, or harmful in the world around us. It's all just a test. And withstanding the test immediately gives birth to a miracle that eliminates the threats. On the other hand, if we debate the issue and try to negotiate with external reality – especially with the fear of what others will think – the test grows stronger. It clouds our minds and makes it harder to escape. A connection forms between us and the distressing reality we are perceiving, which makes it difficult to withstand the test.

After we withstand the test and ignore the background noise, we see that from the outset the test wasn't truly real. Then the hold-ups and difficulties cease to cause pain.

A test is a situation in which the Creator is so hidden in creation that He cannot be identified. According to the teachings of Chassidut, in this type of test, the only way to recognize that there is no place absent from the presence of the Creator and that the Creator is the force that sustains us is via stubborn insistence that transcends logic and reason. We become insistent and determined to preserve the covenant and loyalty that we previously pledged. We stop continually questioning its usefulness.

The teachings of Chassidut cite the Akeidah (the Binding of Isaac) as an example. There was no question at all whether Abraham would agree to sacrifice his son. He withstood the test via the haste with which he set out to fulfill the mission of the Creator. In other words, Abraham's true test is not that he went to sacrifice his son, but that he hastened to do so. The Midrash relates that on the way, the Satan (the accusing angel) tried to dissuade Abraham and Isaac. He disguised himself as an old man, approached Abraham, and asked him where he was going. When Abraham rejected him, he intensified his challenge until his true mission was revealed. The Satan was trying to disturb him in his mission. So he turned himself into a great river of water that blocked their path. But Abraham did not flinch and continued walking in the water until it reached his neck. He called out to the Creator: "You told me to sacrifice my son as a burnt offering, but how will Your name be sanctified in the world if we drown?" Immediately, God rebuked the Satan, the river dried up, and the two continued on their way.[16]

The moment Abraham passed the test, the command was canceled. The message is that when we decide that we can overcome the difficulties

---

16. *Midrash Tanchuma*, Vayeira 22.

and realize that what we perceive as reality only hides the light of the Creator, then the frightening reality is changed to a positive one. The willingness to self-sacrifice nullifies the *nisayon*. The test becomes a miracle.

During the test, the spark of the Creator is hidden in Creation. The purpose of *avodat hanisyonot* is not to discover that there is a world and a Creator, and that the Creator governs the world, but that the world and the Creator are one. The goal of *avodat hanisyonot* is to disallow the thought that there is any reality other than that of the Creator. Serving the Creator involves a strong rejection of even the thought of *shituf*, the idea that the Creator has partners in creation. If the general public believes that the world has a Creator, and they pray three times a day, give charity, and believe in divine providence over everything, but they still worry about what the rich local landowner is doing, then they've committed the sin of *shituf*, which is akin to idolatry. The landowner has no freedom of choice that removes the Creator from the equation.

There's a well-known Chassidic story that can help clarify the difference between *avodat habirurim* and *avodat hanisyonot*. The following version of the story was told by Shabtai Slavatitsky, the Chabad emissary in Antwerp:

> Rabbi Mendel Futerfas, the famous Chassidic mentor, was arrested for all his "crimes" against the Communist regime and sent to prison. So, what does a Chassidic Jew do in such a situation? He reviewed all the chapters of Tanya and Chassidic discourses he knew by heart. They placed him in a cell, and he found a corner and began to review. He reviewed constantly. A guard entered with a meal for him, but seeing Mendel absorbed in his thoughts and oblivious to his presence, muttered to himself: "Well, here's another one who constantly speaks to himself." Reb Mendel understood these words and they inspired him. He immediately realized that there was another Chassid in the jail. He began to converse regularly with the guard, who developed a liking for him. When an opportune moment presented itself, Mendel asked him, "Please do me a favor. Tell the other prisoner who talks to himself to meet me at five o'clock this afternoon by the hole in his cell's bathroom."[17]

As far as Reb Mendel was concerned, the Soviet regime, the arrest, the restrictions – they were all merely tests. If he were to concentrate on the inner reality, the external test would disappear without his having to deal with it or give it weight or attention. He would simply continue on. A test is a shell, a meaningless exterior that needs to be disregarded, not clarified. The existence of the Soviet regime was intended to hide the reality of the Creator. Reb Mendel sought to remove the concealment. But with the slight hint from the guard that there was another Jew in the jail who might need his help, the experience switched to *avodat habirurim*. Now he had to go out of himself and be there for someone else who needed his help, as became clear in the continuation of the story.

Avodat hanisyonot, to a large extent, is a person's inner belief that he's on the right track. It's a spiritual move to ignore the background noise. This produces a sense of security completely motivated by firm belief. A trusting person does not entertain internal or external discussions with the environment while undergoing a test. Ultimately, any such discussion only brings a person down from his level and drags him into doubt about his path and faith.

What is the purpose of a test? To enable a person to discover the essential deep point to which he or she connects and is thereby elevated. Overcoming a test is akin to overcoming the seduction of the evil tendencies and revealing one's highest levels.

If *avodat habirurim* collects fragments and reconnects them, *avodat hanisyonot* is aimed at determining what is real and what is false, choosing between good and bad, and using free will to make decisions. From the perspective of Chassidic conduct, *avodat hanisyonot* is meant to reveal a person's backbone. The discovery itself is evidence of trust, which in any case ultimately attracts positive regard and appreciation to the person. Retreat, anxiety, and a lack of faith leave the darkness intact and grant legitimacy to the false reality.[18]

The message that emerges from these three approaches to dealing and coping is that the presence of agony and loss in the world is for the purpose of exposing another reality, cleansing and elevating a person

---

18. See the *maamar* of the Lubavitcher Rebbe, "Shabbat Parashat Chukat-Balak," *Natata l'Rei'echa Nes l'Hitnoses*, 12 Tammuz 1966.

188 · WINNING EVERY MOMENT

above daily routine and involvement with issues that are of secondary importance.

According to the Tanya, a person who experiences suffering needs to contemplate. If we turn our backs on suffering, it will repeat itself until the lesson emerging from it is learned. On the other hand, being open to change and willing to learn of our own free will, while simultaneously self-nullifying and growing, may even help prevent suffering. Struggles have no inherent meaning, and they become revealed as meaningless once the person knows the reason for them. Therefore, according to the teachings of the Tanya, self-awakening and arousal can prevent suffering.[19]

THE VALUE OF EFFORT

Another accompanying principle of this kind of contemplation is that change isn't easy. For a person seeking development, overcoming challenges takes coping and effort. The harder a person tries, the greater the chances of success. According to Chassidut, there is a direct connection between effort and result. Rabbi Shneur Zalman presents two examples from the Talmud that clearly emphasize the additional effort a person has to invest in order to achieve self-development.[20] The first example is that of a student who reviews his studies merely as part of his daily routine and is, therefore, referred to as someone "who does not serve." In other words, this is a person who has success without having to invest more than the typical amount of effort. On the other hand, a student who reviews his learning even one time more than the amount to which he is accustomed is called "a servant of God." The original example in the Talmud speaks of the period preceding the writing of the Oral Torah. To precisely recall every detail of the material, students would review every chapter a hundred times. Although one hundred repetitions of

---

19. "One chastisement in the heart of man is better than many lashes," Talmud, *Berachot* 7b. See *Torah Ohr*, Miketz 31c.

20. Tanya, *Likkutei Amarim*, ch. 15. It is pointed out that the *beinoni* "who does not serve" is not a person who falls or sins. This is because his *yetzer hara* is generally easy to vanquish. He's a person who naturally wants to learn and isn't attracted to worldly pleasures.

one's studies today appears monumental, in the days of the sages of the Talmud this appears to have been a routine occupation that did not require special attention. However, one who went beyond his custom and gave a little more of himself in order to internalize his learning, even one more round of study, was considered, according to the Tanya, to infuse new vitality throughout the previous hundred times. Because of his sacrifice, he is called "a servant of God." In this case, one additional round of review has the equivalent amount of investment as the hundred previous times. It enriches the learning with an appreciation and understanding that could not be accumulated from the habitual conduct.

The second analogy comes from the business of the donkey drivers in the marketplace. The usual price for renting donkeys to carry a load is one *zuz* (silver coin) in order to travel ten *parsa'ot* (one *parsah* is about two and a half miles). However, carrying freight for eleven miles costs two *zuz*. The small addition in the distance of a mere *parsah* is beyond what the donkey is accustomed to. Therefore, the price does not go up incrementally, but rather multiplies.

With these examples, Rabbi Shneur Zalman seeks to emphasize that the secret of success, for most people, is perseverance and investment time after time, and doing a little bit more than what's customary. Investing more than the customary amount and going out of our comfort zone, the safe path and sense of satisfaction, reveals our point of inner strength. Effort helps us overcome the unconsciousness of daily life, even if the routine is positive and successful.

DEPRESSION, FEARS, AND GOOD THOUGHTS

A lot of the Tanya is dedicated to the treatment of sadness and its causes. It can be said that although depression is an experience in modern society, Judaism has never accepted depression as a desirable internal state. Rabbi Shneur Zalman sees it as part of man's constant struggle. Depression, which is a naturally occurring phenomenon, constricts us and prevents our progress.

Sadness is a result of lack and dissatisfaction. Things didn't work out as expected, so the person is sad. Depression prevents a person from seeing beyond the self and strengthens insensitivity toward one's environment. It's typically derived from one's surroundings, and the feeling that one has not received what's due. It is not a result of real content and ideas. The danger of depression lies at the door of someone who is convinced of his or her abilities and skills, yet in the process of handling struggle fails to meet self-imposed standards. The Tanya states that excessive self-esteem and lack of recognition of the naturalness of having internal battles contribute to the coarse insensitivity of the soul.[21] A person's crass lack of feeling is evident in the lack of self-acceptance with all one's weaknesses and shortcomings. The result is depression and sadness. Even pessimism, to a certain extent, is an aspect of depression. It stems from a lack of confidence that things will work out well.

Rabbi Shneur Zalman uses the image of battle to explain the effects of depression. A person afflicted with depression and anxiety will likely fail. For example, in a boxing ring with two fighters, if one is full of sadness, which leads to laziness, he is likely to fall and be easily beat, even if in fact he is stronger and favored.

A condition for success, emphasizes Rabbi Shneur Zalman, is to embark on every task with zest and passion. Zest is a product of the joy we feel toward the task. A person who wakes up happy quickly and enthusiastically gets to work, while one who gets up sad moves slowly. Joy opens the heart and removes heavy, burdensome worries. A person in high spirits with a good attitude toward work has a greater chance of success than one who starts off with a tendency for pessimism and a gloomy attitude. Meanwhile, the person soaked in worry feels like a heavy weight is tied to his or her feet, restricting every step.[22] Depression also affects our surroundings. People prefer business associates, friends, and marital partners who are happy and not those who tend toward melancholy. Sadness testifies that we have succumbed to our natural tendencies. It generally fails to attract others or arouse an interest in taking action.

---

21. "On the contrary, such sadness is due to conceit. For he does not know his place, and that is why he is distressed because he has not attained the level of a *tzaddik*." Tanya, *Likkutei Amarim*, ch. 27.

22. For the example of two fighters, see Tanya, *Likkutei Amarim*, ch. 26. Rabbi Shneur Zalman excludes a certain kind of bitterness from which a positive benefit can be derived. Concerning bitterness that leads to a broken heart, and then to growth, King Solomon teaches in Mishlei 14:23, "in every sadness there will be profit."

A classic joke about anxiety has an old man saying, "My life was full of terrible disasters, most of which never happened." Researchers point to several factors that lead to longevity and robust health. These factors are familiar to everyone: healthy diet, community bond and belonging to supportive community structures, physical activity, peace of mind, and reduced pressure and anxiety about the future.

It is just as well known what kind of impact poor nutrition and inactivity have. Moreover, stress is one of the leading causes of death. The inability to find peace of mind, the constant racing, the feeling of alienation, the need to live up to expectations, feeling a lack of belonging, and sensing no control over events, all of this along with the modern pace of life and cost of living, lead to huge stressors. Stress invites disease and premature aging and interferes with having focus in life, as well as meaning and purpose.

Anxiety and stress are typically the result of thoughts flowing without control and direction. Fears thrive in the dark, with ambiguity and confusion. Mental clarity generally suppresses anxieties, or at least prevents them from intensifying. Stress, as an expression of mental and physical distress, is not necessarily the result of anxiety. According to the teachings of Chassidut, it often also depends on a person's state of consciousness. Clarity and a sense of purpose also have the power to prevent or reduce the intensity of our distress.

How Do We Deal With It?

How do we handle the pressure, depression, sadness, and fear?

Understandably, each person has unique characteristics and, therefore, each person's methods of coping are different. Still, the teachings of Chassidut present several general suggestions that can be useful at any time. These approaches require practice, contemplation, and refinement so that they remain fresh and relevant. They are part of a larger and more complete structure which emerges from the general view offered by the Tanya.

1. Free choice is completely in our hands. The first step in dealing with sadness, anxiety, and pressure is the recognition that these issues are subject to our choices and within our control. We have the tools and abilities to defeat fear and choose to live with peace of mind, to conquer sadness, and to live joyfully. Many people believe that stress-free living is not a choice. They are confident that such a life can't be theirs, nor can they imagine being free of pressure. The most important barrier that the Tanya seeks to remove is the illusion that this choice isn't entirely in our hands.

In order to sharpen and clarify the choices that we have, Rabbi Shneur Zalman's grandson, the Tzemach Tzedek, compares dealing with fears to a soldier preparing for battle.[23] His challenge is to vanquish cowardice. Just as a fighter entering the ring increases his chances of losing if he's sad, similarly, going off to war with fears about being injured and defeated makes it more likely he'll be defeated. In fact, he'll lose before he ever gets to the battlefield. Rejecting fear and preventing it from settling in the heart is, thus, an obligation and a condition for success.

The teachings of Chassidut identify the first step toward overcoming anxieties: we must recognize that we were born to be warriors. We are warriors fighting at every moment against the natural soul's inclination to recoil within itself, which stems from skepticism and lack of faith. We're also endowed with all the tools necessary to win the battle against our fears in the present moment.

2. Deal with legitimate worries by designating time for confession and soul-searching. Rabbi Shneur Zalman identifies several kinds of sadness, worry, and despondency. One type has a cause that is true. For example, this could be someone who committed a misdemeanor, or even a misbehaving business owner. He's made a mistake in a particular law or is awaiting a review from the authorities. The examination gives him anxiety. In other words, there is a very real factor that stimulates his anxiety and sadness. On the other hand, there are worries and anxieties that surround a person for no reason whatsoever. These are thoughts of "that's just how it is" running around his head and generating gloom that cannot be solved.

The Tanya's advice for dealing with the first type is to devote time to self-examination.[24] As he does that, the worries and anxieties need to be

---

23. *Igrot Kodesh Admor Hatzemach Tzedek*, 322–26.
24. See the note in brackets in the Tanya, *Likkutei Amarim*, ch. 31.

shut out. This is the stage during which all thinking about the problem should take place. Self-examination allows us to observe reality and detail it through the power of the intellect. Getting into the details helps reduce the magnitude of the problem and enables our perspective to change. A relevant application of this advice is, for example, if a person is concerned about a financial debt. There is no use to thinking about the debts all day long. Instead, the reasons for the debt need to be calmly analyzed and a plan of action formulated to change the economic situation. Any preoccupation with the matter beyond the time allotted for soul-searching will only lead to unnecessary grief. Addressing and adjusting our economic anxieties in a well-defined period of time with a calm rational approach enables us to function properly throughout the day. According to Rabbi Shneur Zalman's approach, stress and anxiety offer no contribution to our mental health and our achievements. Encouraging them is an ineffective and fundamentally irrational choice.

3. *Do not deal directly with illegitimate worries.* In order to deal with the second type of sadness and anxiety, the kind that does not stem from a particular cause, we have to learn to not think about it and instead stay busy and focused. Dealing directly with such a negative thought leads us to wallow in its misery. Moreover, anyone who tries to deal with worrisome thoughts with logical arguments and debates will eventually fail. It's time wasted on futile struggles in unnecessary arenas. When depression, for example, is not due to any changeable factor in reality, then it cannot be defeated and we can't rise up over it as long as we try to relate to it and work with it. Negative scenarios in the mind can't be addressed with the hope of emerging victorious.

The reason for this is that these negative tendencies feed on our preoccupation with them in our minds. Our challenge is to win our thoughts, to change the soul's garments. The way to win over those tendencies is to not allow them to settle in our minds. When fear and depression are denied expression in our thoughts, they will fade. Feelings of fear are nourished by our preoccupation with the object of the fear. Without our involvement in the subject, the force stimulating those feelings is weakened.

According to Rabbi Shneur Zalman, only by becoming deaf to those negative and fearful thoughts can we fulfill the statement: "Answer not a fool according to his folly, lest you too become like him."[25] Responding to a fool leads a person to the fool's low place. The idea is that "for he who wrestles with a filthy person is bound to become soiled himself."[26] The person struggling with negative thoughts becomes filthy because he brings himself to low places instead of focusing on thoughts filled with content and meaning.

In the "Liozna Decrees," Rabbi Shneur Zalman uses strong words to describe his difficulty having conversations with people who insist on focusing on their troubles, instead of looking for positive ways to overcome them.

> And I bear the burden, in writing, of the great distress that literally embitters my life: those who come themselves and share their grief, in broad explanation, in order to instill deep sorrow in their hearts.[27]

From this letter we learn that those who insist on delving into their suffering not only fool themselves but also harm their surroundings and those who lend them a sympathetic ear. In this way, they are also not available to receive real help, but continue to stay stuck in their own preoccupation.

4. *Fake it till you make it.* One of the suggestions offered by Rabbi Shneur Zalman's grandson is to look outwardly while filled with joy.[28] The guidance is to smile, even if we don't feel that way inside, for the joy is external and seemingly artificial, yet it ultimately penetrates inward: "Their hearts are drawn after their actions."[29] This advice stems from the fact that, as noted, the three garments of the soul (thought, speech, and action) are external to the soul and influenced by it, but they also influence the soul.

Joy is the result of spiritual work. Our natural inclination is not to be joyful, but the very insistence of a person to be happy, even if forced,

25. Mishlei 26:4. Quoted in Tanya, *Likkutei Amarim*, ch. 28.
26. See Tanya, *Likkutei Amarim*, ch. 28.
27. *Igrot Kodesh – Alter Rebbe*, letter 35 (1793), 113.
28. *Igrot Kodesh Admor Hatzemach Tzedek*, 322–26.
29. *Sefer Hachinuch*, positive command 16.

holds anxiety at bay. Moreover, as a person expresses himself, so, too, does he invite others' attitudes toward him. A person who radiates anxieties will invite an anxious conversation while pushing away people who seek emotional strength. Conversely, a person who practices joy will attract happy and joyful behavior.

Additional advice that has already been discussed includes using contemplation to create a state of consciousness that rejects sadness and anxiety, strengthens faith, and deepens ties with friends. Another suggestion (which will be expanded upon later, among other things) that helps release emotional tensions is thinking positive thoughts and learning to give to others. But even before that, the Tanya accentuates another aspect of the bitterness in the psyche that hinders spiritual growth and offers unique advice to deal with it.

Feel Unconditional Joy

"The lofty soul is very sick with bitterness and negativity,"[30] writes Rabbi Shneur Zalman in a letter he sent to a relative by marriage, Yitzchak Yaffe of Kapust, in which he explains the inherent difficulties in our efforts to grow spiritually.

In his letters, Rabbi Shneur Zalman not only guided and directed the communal life of the Chassidim, but he gave advice on spiritual matters. In this special letter, which he sent before 1792 when he was in Liozna, he explains why it is so difficult for people to be happy and what technique they should use in order to achieve great joy that is true and expansive, a joy that's independent and unconditional.

It stands to reason that *marah schorah* (misplaced bitterness) is a prominent Jewish feature. "A Jew is a *marah schorahnik* [full of melancholy]…"[31] Such melancholy is an unwillingness to heal, rise, and rejoice. And it's designed in such a way that only when it comes to the fulfillment of material lust does the soul manage to rejoice, and even then, only for a short while. However, when it comes to spiritual efforts, the melancholy strikes. It is as if a dehydrated person is offered water to quench his thirst, yet rejects the offer because he does not feel thirsty.

---

30. *Igrot Kodesh – Alter Rebbe*, letter 19, 64–66.
31. *Torat Menachem*, vol. 12, 1954, part 3, 36.

Of course, he needs to drink, but he only agrees to drink when he's in a normal state. He has actually promoted his own dehydration.[32]

Melancholy is an exaggerated self-judgment and evaluation of evil. It's then followed by a sense of not being entitled to happiness. The melancholy takes control of the person and pushes him or her to reject joy using all kinds of claims, allegedly related to a lack of personality integrity or defective spiritual work.

The soul's problem is that it sets high expectations for itself, sometimes unfulfillable ones. Its tendency toward melancholy is one of the evil inclination's tricks. When people come to the moment when they should choose joy, they begin to judge themselves for past actions and blame themselves for their shortcomings.

For these reasons, *marah sc.horah*, or melancholy, is characteristic of people of high spiritual rank who cannot accept their daily reality.[33] Because of the virtues of those suffering from melancholy, it is not easy to lift them from their condition. "Therefore," says Rabbi Shneur Zalman, "the Baal Shem Tov greatly distanced those with melancholy from him, since their spiritual source was very high and they fell, etc., and it's very difficult to lift them up."[34]

As mentioned, the ideal and correct situation according to the Tanya is joy. Happiness rejects foreign and negative thoughts.

> But this is suggested advice: to pray with infinite joy, and then, naturally, all the foreign thoughts will be dispersed. For even if they rise, they will fall and descend immediately.[35]

The happiness described by Rabbi Shneur Zalman is not joy in one particular thing. Joy derived from something specific will always be limited and measured. We are motivated by a yearning to achieve something new that we do not possess. At the same time, if we examine ourselves in such a light, we'll have very few happy days.

---

32. Compare this to, for example, the melancholy described in *Torat Menachem*, vol. 10, 1954, part 1, 133.

33. On the concept of melancholy, see the analysis of Netanel Lederberg concerning the personage of the Maggid of Mezeritch in *The Gateway to Infinity: Rabbi Dov Bear, the Magid Meisharim of Mezhirich* [Hebrew] (Jerusalem: Rubin Mass, 2011), 21–38.

34. *Maamarei Admor Hazaken Haketzarim*, 488.

35. *Igrot Kodesh – Alter Rebbe*, letter 19, 64–66.

The Tanya speaks of a sublime joy born out of gratitude for the very essence of creation and the greatness of the Creator. It's not a joy that depends on anything in particular, and it's accompanied by great pleasure. It's a joy in which one is allowed to be and allowed to accept oneself as one is. This joy, which involves rising above our worries and anxieties, stems from a connection to the inner point of the soul, a level on which we do not perceive ourselves as defective. Rather, it's a point of wholesome perfection that doesn't allow the faculties of the natural soul to interfere with its connection to the inner dimension.

Based on this, and on the recognition of our perfection, we can succeed in changing our nature. With this inner joy, which is independent of achievement, we can change our natural traits. For example, Rabbi Shneur Zalman points out that a person who is stingy by nature will be transformed into a benevolent and exalted person due to the experience of great joy.[36] The tremendous power of happiness to create change stems from the fact that it can penetrate the soul more effectively than can the soul's conscious faculties.[37]

How do we overcome melancholy? How do we connect to our soul's essence and wholesomeness, which transcends its revealed potential? Rabbi Shneur Zalman offers a suggestion that seems unusual at first glance: use the disease of melancholy itself in order to escape it and get to joy.

> However, you first need to remove all traces of sorrow, sighing, and depression from your heart. The way to do this is to submerge your heart in sorrow and sighing before prayer, and be brokenhearted over the sins of your youth.[38]

In order to rejoice, the melancholy, sadness, and grief must be removed. Since melancholy is a natural expression, a disease of the soul, it is best to give it room for expression until it has exhausted itself. Rabbi Shneur Zalman's advice is practical. We must devote a period of time to weeping and expressing grief over our sins, agony over our imperfection, and

---

36. See Tanya, *Likkutei Amarim*, ch. 14, 15, and others.
37. The Lubavitcher Rebbe, *Maamarim Melukatim*, vol. 4, Shabbat Parashat Ki Tetzei, 13 Elul, 1981.
38. *Igrot Kodesh – Alter Rebbe*, letter 19, 64–66.

regret for our spiritual state. When we are finished, we can feel satisfied. We made a confession and wept at our lowly state. Now, we're free to stand before our Creator, distanced from the melancholy. We can connect to our inner being and be ourselves without feeling deficiency. Once we have recognized our shortcomings and accepted them, they become less meaningful to us.

Think Good and It Will Be Good

"For without any doubt, all of his sins are forgiven him at that time," Rabbi Shneur Zalman encourages his readers.[39] The very act of breaking oneself down invites cleansing and advancement. Since the joy to which we aspire is not dependent upon anything, it also does not depend on not falling from this level in the future. "And even if he slips back to the old way and then again asks for forgiveness, even a thousand times, he's forgiven every time in that moment."[40]

The moment in which a person firmly resolves to get rid of melancholy is loaded with tremendous power. It doesn't depend on any other moment. It releases a person to ascend without establishing conditions for the future.[41] It's a moment of contemplating teshuvah (repentance), return to the true inner self, holiness, and the "I" that is part of the spark of the Creator embedded within us.

Now, having finished with the stage of grief and heartfelt sighing, after regretting our sins and cleansing our grief, we can put together a proper contemplation on joy that is not dependent on anything. Not only are we independent of our physical condition, but also of achievements in our efforts at self-refinement. Naturally, this spiritual movement of joy is also the expression of spiritual growth.

The spiritual experience of melancholy demonstrates how our challenges are quite often not the result of something external, but rather of inner suffering, of submission to thoughts that drag us down. The expulsion of negative, foreign thoughts and their replacement with positive thinking is one of the beinoni's most significant tasks. But using

---

39. Ibid.
40. Ibid.
41. See Tanya, Likkutei Amarim, ch. 25.

melancholy against itself is not the only technique presented by Rabbi Shneur Zalman, and it's also not suitable for all situations. In some cases, there is a real danger that a person will become "addicted" to melancholy and not succeed in escaping it.

One hundred fifty years ago, long before the publication of the self-help book *The Secret* by Rhonda Byrne, the Tzemach Tzedek, the grandson of Rabbi Shneur Zalman, uttered the saying "Think good and it will be good." It's a statement that flows from the logic of the Tanya. According to his well-known commentary on the statement, the Tzemach Tzedek wanted to teach that positive thinking, the very thought and trust that things will be good, is what actually attracts the good, in a real and tangible way.

This fundamental principle in Chassidic thought is based on the core assumptions described in the previous chapters. One assumption concerns thought as a revelation of the soul. Just as we can dress in one way or another, so too the mind can be focused and productive or flow in destructive directions. Our thoughts never rest and are never neutral. According to Rabbi Shneur Zalman, in the framework of the struggle between the godly soul and the animal soul, there is never a vacuum. For, immediately, an inclination, desire, constriction, or lust will perceive the available space created by the repression of a drive that just occurred. If we don't focus our thoughts productively, they can rapidly slip into problematic, immoral places that waste time and energy.

From this we conclude that ignoring anxieties and causes of sadness is not enough. We have to aim for positive thinking. What is the solution to the constant flow of thoughts? As mentioned, it never stops. However, we can change their content. Our challenge is to exchange one thought for another and thereby reject thoughts that reflect the victory for the animal soul.

The only way to beat fear is not just to ignore it, but to insist on positive, uplifting, and happy thoughts that indicate mental health and our potential.

According to the teachings of Chassidut, reality at its core is not bad. Only the natural tendencies of our animal soul can present it as seemingly being bad. We see that reality, in fact, is always a positive picture. Good thoughts, therefore, are not illusion, but a manifestation of the true reality. Conversely, thoughts about catastrophes usually cause great spiritual damage. They weigh on a person and take away all motivation. Negative thoughts indicate a low spiritual state, because, in essence, they show that a person does not trust that things will work out in the future. Anxiety and insecurity are caused by insufficient faith.[42]

Positive thinking also usually tends to be focused thought.[43] When we think in a positive state, it is so significant. Rabbi Shneur Zalman emphasizes that it transforms into a pillar of light for us. We go to bed and wake up with those thoughts. Our positive thinking and optimism attract spiritual abundance. Meanwhile, negative thoughts produce a negative and corrosive atmosphere.[44]

Another element that lies at the basis for recommending good thinking is the belief that it is insufficient to only say that the Creator might rescue a person from distress. Rather, the believer fully trusts that God will do so in practice. Positive thinking embodies peace and tranquility. The inner calm stems from the certainty that the Creator will act for the believer in the best and most appropriate way for him in the current situation.[45] A trusting person gets to the point that despite the hassles in which he finds himself, he manages to reject any concern.

Trust does not mean that the person will receive the Creator's graces without having to work and strive on his own. Rather, trust is knowing that work on the self will produce results. By relying on the Creator while working and striving, we ask the Creator to behave with us in a similar manner and to grant us benefit even if we are not fully deserving of it. Rabbi Shneur Zalman encourages his readers from the words of the sages that "a good thought, the Creator connects it to the deed."[46]

---

42. *Maamarim Melukatim*, vol. 1, Motzaei Shabbat Parashat Noach, 1968, 246.

43. This is one of the explanations of the idea "The attribute of goodness is greater than that of suffering." Talmud, *Yoma* 76a, *Sotah* 11a. See Tanya, *Kuntres Acharon*, 1.

44. *Likkutei Sichot*, vol. 38, Parashat Korach, sichah 1, 63; Tanya, *Iggeret Hakodesh*, siman 22.

45. See the introduction to "Sha'ar Habitachon" in *Chovat Halevavot*, the section beginning, "But the advantage of trust." Also: "The essence of trust/bitachon is calm and tranquility of the one who trusts; and that his heart relies on the one he trusts to do what's good and right for him regarding the issue entrusted to him," Sha'ar Habitachon, ch. 1. See the Lubavitcher Rebbe, *Likkutei Sichot*, vol. 36, Parashat Shemot, sichah 1.

46. Talmud, *Kiddushin* 40a, cited in Tanya, *Likkutei Amarim*, ch. 16, 44.

One of the fundamental principles in the teachings of Kabbalah and Chassidut, which is threaded throughout the ideas of the Tanya, is that there is an awakening and inspiration that comes from above from the higher to the lower realms. This effect is known as *isarusa d'l'eila*, arousal from above. This influence is a measure of kindness that the Creator gives to the world. On the other hand, there is an influence that goes from the bottom up, *isarusa d'l'tata*, arousal from below.[47] A person feels inspired and influences the higher realms. Through his efforts in this world, he encourages the upper worlds to send abundance and blessing to the lower world. The arousal from below leads to an arousal from above. Both in thought and in action, the arousal from below – when a person pushes himself to think in positive directions – creates an arousal from above. By going in a positive direction, we merit tremendous assistance from on high.[48]

With this advice, Rabbi Shneur Zalman turns to a person contending with the helplessness and heaviness produced by troublesome thoughts and promises that if one will only get up and try to direct one's thoughts in positive directions, one will discover new doors opening. One's range of opportunity is greater than one thinks, and so are one's chances of vanquishing individual tendencies in every moment.

NEUTRALIZING ANGER AND EMOTIONAL BLOCKAGES

Another problematic trait that requires significant attention according to Rabbi Shneur Zalman is anger (particularly fury and outbursts of rage). Rabbi Shneur Zalman points out that different expressions of anger frequently appear in our daily lives and cause harm.[49] What is

---

47. "By accustoming ourselves to delight in the Creator by meditating on his greatness, our arousal from below brings an arousal from above ..." Tanya, *Likkutei Amarim*, ch. 14, and other sources.

48. For example, see Tanya, *Likkutei Amarim*, ch. 14, 27, 29, and other sources.

49. Some are naturally prone to excitation. Others are less passionate. On the verse "From an ox and from a sheep you will bring a sacrifice," Rabbi Shneur Zalman comments: some people are naturally angry and need to sacrifice their inner angry animal, and some are naturally dispassionate and incline more toward lust. See Rabbi Shneur Zalman's *Likkutei Torah*, Vayikra (Leviticus) 2:4. Even Moses, the most beloved of the Prophets, who was totally self-nullified to the extent that "the

this experience of anger during which one loses the ability to control emotions with the mind? Why is it that during such anger fits, we are compared to a "flaming fire" that threatens to destroy everything and interferes with our being calm and collected? What happens to a person who is angry, and how can one handle anger?

Anger is usually the product of injury. As a result, the anger expresses a tendency or desire to negate aspects of the offender's being.

The angry person is being controlled by the power of self-destruction and thereby loses wisdom. The same force that acts to negate another person acts on the angry one as well. Anger is like a temporary declaration because in the moment of anger, one allows one's emotions to take control and use the intellect to direct one's character and behavior.[50] At that moment of anger, the person doesn't believe that every occurrence is the result of a renewed creation that is personally meaningful. During moments of anger, faith is lacking, and does not return until the mind regains control of the emotions.[51]

As in a state of depression, when one is angry, one expresses dissatisfaction with the surrounding reality. It's not going precisely as expected. A sense of helplessness causes one to go wild. Rage causes the ego to take the place of faith.

Anger, as explained in the Tanya, comes from the element of fire. Like fire, anger seeks to rise up and burn anything in its path. Under the influence of anger, a person ignores prohibitions and safeguards. It spreads inside from the heart outward in all directions. Anger also rises to the mind and generates rationalizations for actions. This is how it intellectually convinces the person to remain in a state of anger, until it grabs hold to the point of making release feel impossible. An angry person is caught up in *kelipah*, in external elements that sap the strength

---

Shechinah [Divine Presence] spoke directly from his throat," it is said that when he "was angry he became susceptible to mistakes." See Sifri and the commentary of Rashi on Matot 31:21. Furthermore, it is said that anger can cause a person to forget Torah laws. See the Lubavitcher Rebbe, "Sichat Shabbat Parashat Vayeira, Mevarchim Chodesh Shevat," *Torat Menachem*, vol. 1, 1951, 18.

50. Our sages emphasize that "being angry is akin to idolatrous practices," Talmud, *Shabbat* 105b, cited in Tanya, *Iggeret Hateshuvah*, ch. 7, 25. See *Likkutei Sichot* 17:20n33.

51. Tanya, *Iggeret Hakodesh*, siman 25.

ADVICE FOR LIVING · 203

and drag the person into unnecessary confrontations. But anger allows the person to be convinced that his or her actions are justified. It's like a cloud is obscuring the ability to be focused and to minimize the importance of the events that initially caused anger. Getting agitated only exacerbates the importance of the triggering event.

The source of anger is limited insight. A person with *mochin d'gadlut* (expansive consciousness) is directed toward a goal and doesn't waste energy on marginal things.[52] Thus, a small child immediately becomes angry when thwarted in getting what he or she wants. A settled, thoughtful, capable person can tolerate contradictions. The degree of love that a person can feel and demonstrate is in accordance with the power of the mind, the intellectual faculty of *daat*.[53] A thoughtful person is not hurt or stressed by contradictory ideas and doesn't get mad when "hit" by them. Instead, such a person is able to remain focused on the main point: a goal to which he or she aspires without wasting energy on minor things along the way.[54] Therefore, anger expresses "the external forces syphoning off energy." Unreal and nonessential aspects only steal attention and drag us into a lack of focus.[55]

A simple example is when someone is hurrying to a meeting and is delayed by a slow-driving car. Squandering energy fighting with that driver may prevent the person from arriving at the meeting at all, in addition to provoking high levels of tension and anger, which could even lead to physical violence. But accepting the problem and seeking alternative ways to get to the meeting may lead to success both in the meeting and in the sense of accomplishment from having dealt with the test and challenge.

Anger is a natural trait. Helplessness, disrespect, and dissatisfaction with events can lead to anger. The inner test is how quickly the anger expands past its natural levels and boundaries.

We find that our trait of anger can be overcome through recognition

---

52. Such a person attracts a greater radiation of the light of the godly soul within, due to a broader spiritual capacity. For example, see *Maamarei Admor Hazaken* (5573/1812), 206.

53. See Tanya, *Shaar Hayichud v'Ha'emunah*, ch. 8. See also *Likkutei Amarim*, ch. 6.

54. See the Lubavitcher Rebbe, *Maamarim Melukatim*, vol. 1, 13 Tishrei, 129.

55. See "Mayim Rabim," *Maamarei Admor Hazaken* (5570/1809), 35.

and contemplation. It is important to contemplate that we are not the sole ruler over creation, and also that not everything that appears to be bad really is bad. As is customarily said: "We connect meritorious things to worthy days, and unworthy ones to deserving days."[56] Even if a certain person who has free choice between good and evil chooses to curse, strike, or harm a superior, his choice of evil was, at least from the injured party's perspective, already decided. Simply put, the damage was predetermined. Once again, we see the concept of "there is no place devoid of Him."[57] There is no space that's free of the Creator's presence. The notion that a person who is causing harm is not fulfilling the will of the Creator removes the presence of the Creator from the moment in which harm was inflicted. This deviation is a denial of faith and, therefore, is compared to idolatry. If something happens to a person, it might be meant as a sign for him. Precisely by discovering that sign, he can grow.

Dealing with anger requires control over all three garments of the soul: thought, speech, and action. Anger gains momentum in the garments. That is, it is expressed in the same ways in which the soul is revealed and not via our intellectual or emotional faculties. As stated, due to our nature, anger can appear without our being able to control it. It's natural to be angry. The extent to which we ignore it and stay focused on our primary mission is our main test in the world.[58]

The role of contemplation in calming anger is to identify the situation's true nature with proper and proportional perspective. Our effort to answer questions such as "What is life? What am I living for? What is my purpose?" softens anger. Such thoughts remind us of the Creator's presence and reduce our dissatisfaction with life. A contemplating person can't be angry with reality or be sad about it – he can rejoice at the opportunity he has been given to choose. Instead of being angry when things don't work out, he tries to pause for a moment, contemplate, and grasp what he has to learn from the annoying situation and how to turn the darkness of that moment into light.

---

56. Talmud, *Taanit* 11b.

57. *Tikkunei Zohar*, tikkun 457, 91a.

58. "Shabbat Parashat Tetzaveh, Parashat Zachor, 9 Adar, 5718," *Torat Menachem*, vol. 22, 1958, part 2, 96.

Contemplation is part of the process aimed at anticipating anger and handling it until events pass. When anger increases, first aid, so to speak, is needed to stop its intensity and destructive pull. The approach needs to prevent raising a fist or one's voice, and even stop thoughts generated by the anger. The problem with thoughts is that they can't turn themselves off. Since our thoughts are very close to the soul, they enflame the anger. The first step in handling this, as in the case of depression, is by distraction. We need to immediately find purer things to engage our minds in and think about in order to halt further aggravation of our rising anger.

Alongside distraction, the Tanya also offers a technique to convert negative anger into positive anger, or positive rebuke. Rabbi Shneur Zalman mentions the verse in Tehillim: "Be angry and do not sin."[59] In other words, anger can save a person from sin. How? Isn't anger destructive? The Tanya proposes redirecting the anger to beneficial channels.

Positive anger is a person's anger at his own attitude toward insignificant things, so that things are categorized as external or *kelipah*. With positive anger, instead of getting angry at those who cut us off on the road or who cause us financial loss, we are furious with ourselves: "How can I get angry at such nonsense?" Such redirected anger is helpful because it helps us to eliminate the *kelipah* that is represented by daring to be angry over such meaningless things.[60]

Congested Emotions

As discussed, the natural soul is not bad, but it may evoke wicked traits. This is because evil and bad stem from being sealed and insensitive, unable to see others. A person who is exclusively self-focused is unaware of the suffering he or she causes others. For this reason, Rabbi Shneur Zalman teaches that the animal soul is the source of human evil. And there are degrees of evil: the more one focuses on the self, the more likely one is to hurt others, act inconsiderately, or, in cases of severe evil, not to see humanity in others.

Timtum (dullness), in the teachings of Tanya, derives from the same source as this. Like evil, dullness is an emotional blockage, a kind

---

59. Tehillim 4:5.
60. Tanya, *Likkutei Amarim*, ch. 29.

of sealing. However, this imperviousness is not toward another, but toward the self. Wickedness may be caused by dullness, and it's generally directed toward others, while dullness is when a person is sealed off from the self.

A person suffering from *timtum*, as described in Chassidut, is someone very likely to become a bad person. That is to say, one who tends to grant free range to impulses without identifying with others or recognizing their needs, desires, difficulties, or weaknesses.

There are two types of dullness that Rabbi Shneur Zalman seeks to uproot from his audience. There is a dullness of the heart and a dullness of the mind. Dullness of the heart is the inability to feel, connect, or get excited. The feelings are all dull. The person can't wake up, lacks vitality and enthusiasm, and sees everything as being of secondary importance. It's a safe bet that a person who suffers from dullness of the heart and an inability to feel won't be able to be sensitive to others.

The sealed-off person is not moved by family, children, or surroundings. In the context of the Tanya, such a person also fails to develop invigorated feelings toward the Creator. The person suffers from an emotional numbness to everything sacred and to anything that does not express the natural will of the self. The heart is like stone: there is a wall that prevents ideas from penetrating. When it comes to worldly affairs, the sealed-off person understands them well and finds them interesting, exciting, and stimulating. However, when it comes to matters of the spirit, to the revelation of the soul and character improvement, the blockage is revealed. Things are stopped and do not penetrate into the heart.

Dullness of the heart creates sadness and heaviness. When enthusiasm is lacking, we lose motivation to act; thus our chances of succeeding are lessened. A person who acts without feeling lacks a connection to what he or she does and moves without passion, like a child who cleans his room with obvious reluctance, only because his parents demand it from him.

Rabbi Shneur Zalman says that emotional barriers invite suffering. The person undergoing difficulty, having to cope and face tests, has something within opened up and gradually has a chance to be sensitive toward others. Anyone who experiences personal trauma may also be able, through painful experience, to recognize the feelings of others. The suffering that accompanies emotional blockage is a form of invitation to a person to change. In this sense, the purpose of suffering is to move us off the point where we're standing, release our emotional blockages, open us up, help us recognize our limitations, and break us out of our bonds.

The effective way to deal with the dullness of the heart and avoid superficial torments is to eradicate self-satisfaction and the wall formed by our independent, arrogant sense of self by "crushing" ourselves. Rabbi Shneur Zalman quotes the head of the yeshiva in the Garden of Eden, who says in the *Zohar*: "A tree trunk that isn't catching fire should be splintered and smashed into small pieces for it to quickly ignite."[61] Similarly, a person who is not being ignited by the soul's light – the fire, passion, and vitality – needs to experience self-abasement. One must see one's lowest dimensions and expose one's lowliness until one is heartbroken about one's condition. This crushing is supposed to open the heart to connect the self, and thereby perceive others. It removes our crudeness and releases us from being the primary focus.

If a person does not overcome obstacles through self-initiative, suffering awaits to help the person wake up and feel. In the view of the Tanya, if we recognize the changes we have to make, we'll be spared the suffering.

The Slingshot

Sometimes worldly suffering fails to help a person remove dullness of the heart. This happens when the faculty of *daat* is inactive. As discussed, *daat* is the key to the emotions. If it's not working properly, feelings cannot be generated. And without contemplation, the heart will remain locked and sealed.

This situation is part of what the Tanya calls *timtum hamoach* (dullness of the mind). In contrast to *timtum halev* (dullness of the heart), dullness of the mind is usually an inability to cope intellectually with spiritual issues. We're too physically oriented and coarse to be able to grasp ideas and values. A person can be blessed with a brilliant, sharp, and wise mind and have an impressive grasp of business or mathematical principles, yet remain completely sealed when it comes to spirituality

---

61. *Zohar*, Parashat Shelach, 3:168a, cited in Tanya, *Likkutei Amarim*, ch. 29.

and the movement of the soul. Such a person is deprived of understanding in the spiritual sphere due to excessive immersion in a world
of physicality and desire. According to Rabbi Shneur Zalman, intense
physical preoccupation dulls the mind.

The treatment for dullness of the brain is called *kaf hakela* (the
slingshot), a form of rectification in life for indifference and numbness.
It's a state of spiritual fluctuation. The soul oscillates between the real
and the imagined, between the true and the false. The wavering causes
it suffering, disharmony, and lack of perfection.

Kaf hakela is a Kabbalistic concept involving a spiritual consequence
for disconnected spirituality: the soul, after death, is flung from one end
of the universe to the other as if from a slingshot, to allow the soul to
see and understand the person's spiritual deficiencies (and their consequences). Unlike purgatory of the grave, which describes a process of
cleansing and purifying the body, the slingshot is a process of purifying
the soul of idle things. Although the term traditionally refers to a certain
connection between man's conduct during his life and what awaits him
after death, the teachings of Chassidut show that one can get a sense of
this or experience some of the meaning of this concept already in this
physical world [62]

In everyday life, this concept describes a state in which the soul is
blocked and unable to function. The mind is trapped between what is
real and what it should seek to express, and a life of mundane emptiness

---

62. The source of the term *slingshot* comes from Avigayil's words to King David in the
Book of Samuel: "And the soul of my Lord was bound in a bound of life with God,
and the soul of your enemies will be slung out as from the hollow of a slingshot [*kaf
hakela*]" (1 Samuel 25:29). The Talmud, in tractate *Shabbat*, comments concerning
the souls of the wicked, "They are fettered – two angels are at opposite ends of the
world, and they repeatedly sling the soul to each other." Since the soul does not
have permission to connect, to get back to its source, the origin of all souls, when it
is damaged, it must undergo a purification process that is akin to shaking off dust:
it removes the idle things it was involved with during life in the physical world. The
soul separates from the mundane things it was accompanied by while in a body in
order to move toward higher spiritual levels. Experiencing the sling is like breaking
away from the experiences of this world while entering a process of refinement. See
Torat Menachem, vol. 16, 1956, part 2, 247; Tanya, *Likkutei Amarim*, ch. 8 and in other
places.

and pointless physical desires. Just as we toss a stone from place to place, so too is the soul moved from place to place. One moment, it's allowed to be enveloped in a sense of spiritual pleasure, and in the next, it's thrown into cravings for physical pleasures. And this continues on and on.

The oscillation between sublime spiritual aspiration for the truth and the thirsting for material lusts causes the soul great sorrow over its inability to be in one place. But the sorrow itself is not punishment; it's a catalyst for self-correction and a life of more focused choices.[63] Excessive desires cause a person to lose the ability to function in an orderly fashion.

As an illustration, we can use the example of a student tempted to go out with friends on the night before an important test. Instead of preparing for the exam with diligent studying, our student goes to hang out. But while there, it's likely he or she will feel uncomfortable about not learning and, naturally, find it difficult to spend time with friends. In those moments, the person experiences a form of slingshot rectification. The soul aspires to be purified through the distress it experiences and the lack of harmony in which it finds itself.

The slingshot is a rectification and healing process designed to extract a person from a state of dullness of the mind. It helps illuminate the direction in which to walk. The way to escape dullness of the mind and avoid the slingshot is by shaking "the dust of worldly things from the mind," as Rabbi Shneur Zalman said in a talk he delivered in the summer of 1796.[64] And how do we shake the dust off the mind? Through acts involving dedication and commitment, such as the giving of charity and assisting others. According to the Tanya, self-nullification – that is, placing the idea or mission above one's own concerns – leads to a transformation of the mind into a tool for refined spirituality. A person who goes out of the self to focus on others develops an appropriate spiritual focus.

63. See the Lubavitcher Rebbe, "Shabbat Parashat Shemini, Mevarchim Chodesh Iyar, 5716," *Torat Menachem*, vol. 16, 1956, part 2, 246–47.
64. "The common advice given is to purify oneself by immersion in the mikveh and learning *Zohar*...and also giving tzedakah; as stated in the Talmud: 'Rabbi Elazar would give a coin to a poor person and then go pray.'" See *Maamarei Admor Hazaken Haketzarim*, Drashat Shabat Elul 1796, 486.

CHAPTER 9

Others Are Our Mirrors

One of the most significant aspects of Rabbi Shneur Zalman's philosophy is the emphasis on the special bond and mutual responsibility between all people. This connection emerges directly from his description of the godly soul and its complete structure, which extols *ahavat Yisrael* (love of one's fellow Jew), the unity among all the souls, and the virtue of every soul. And it is this unity that obligates us to a nonjudgmental acceptance of others and transcendence over personal interests.

Before describing the conceptual elements that bring Rabbi Shneur Zalman to emphasize the value of unity of all the Jewish people, it should be noted that for him these were not merely theoretical ideas that stayed on an intellectual level. He strove to actualize them in his life, despite the difficult battles he was pulled into.

The first step Rabbi Shneur Zalman took after being released from his first imprisonment was to moderate the Chassidim and prevent them from retaliating against the Mitnagdim (opponents of Chassidut). He asked them to be careful "with the utmost care to the greatest degree" to not retaliate in any way. In his mind, the worst thing that could happen among the Jewish people is disagreement and baseless hatred. "I will also demand this," Rabbi Shneur Zalman stressed, "to accustom your hearts to love every Jew ... and judge them favorably."[1]

Rabbi Shneur Zalman's warning to avoid disputes and revenge after his release did not stem solely from a fear that it would be perceived as a victory and therefore fuel the struggle. Even before the incarceration, when the Vilna Gaon passed away, Rabbi Shneur Zalman made a point of mentioning in a letter sent to the Chassidim that they should not say a word of reproach "following the death of the Torah scholar." Now, after his release, he reinforced his words. He warned his followers not to fall in speech or action, be it small or large, against the Mitnagdim, even if members of the group mocked, raised arguments, and acted against Chassidim. According to Rabbi Shneur Zalman, the way he himself behaved in his heart, he demanded of the Chassidim. He judged every Jew favorably. "For, in truth, all Jews are literally like brothers, and regarding all of them it is said, 'You are the sons of God.'"[2]

After three decades of persecution at the hands of the Mitnagdim, who even damaged the livelihood of the Chassidim, Rabbi Shneur Zalman still insisted on restraining the Chassidim. Time and again he prevented them from responding. And from the Chassidim who clashed with the Mitnagdim in Vilna, he demanded, also during the lifetime of the Vilna Gaon, restraint and silence in the face of the lies and deceit disseminated against them.[3]

To the Chassidim in a certain small town, he wrote, probably before the year 1790, "Please work with all your heart and soul to insert love of a fellow Jew into the other's heart, and do not think about his evil in your heart; as it is written: 'Do not ever consider it.'"[4]

Ahavat Yisrael, being nonjudgmental, avoiding condescension, and seeking out unity stand out as common threads of his thinking on the

---

1. See Rabbi Shneur Zalman's letter from 1799, quoted in Glitzenstein, *Sefer Hatoldot*, vol. 3, 723–25.

2. Wilansky, *Chassidim v'Mitnagdim*, vol. 1, 305–6; Haim Meir Heilman, *Igrot Baal Hatanya*, 116–17; Etkes, *Rabbi Shneur Zalman of Liadi*, 283.

3. See Mondshine, *Kerem Chabad* 4, no. 1 (5752): 111–13. See also *Igrot Kodesh* 2, 18–21; the letter seems to have been written in 1797. See Etkes, *Rabbi Shneur Zalman of Liadi*, 247. And see *Igrot Kodesh*, 183–84; Heilman, *Igrot Baal Hatanya*, 231.

4. *Igrot Kodesh – Alter Rebbe*, letter 14, 50.

way to achieving the ideal personality, the path to becoming a *beinoni*. His calls were not just to prevent conflict. They were a part of the self-refinement demanded of his followers. They were conditions on their path to spiritual elevation and treating the distress of the soul.

ONE SOURCE

What is the source of such unity among all people? What are its conceptual roots? Rabbi Shneur Zalman gives these questions a detailed explanation in his approach.

To explain the unity, the Tanya emphasizes the idea presented in the teachings of Kabbalah that every godly soul is connected at one source. They derive from the same root and thus are intertwined.[5] What can be learned from the fact that in their source, all souls comprise a collective whole, which Kabbalah compares to the way limbs form a whole body, with each soul being a limb?[6]

The first insight derived from this view of the connection between souls is that all Jews are spiritual siblings. They are all interconnected with a deep, soulful bond. The more one can spiritually transcend the bonds of the body and draw close to the root of the soul, the more this connection becomes apparent.

The second insight is that every soul plays a different role in the world, just as each organ has a different role in the body. The unique mission of each soul is expressed via the potential of the godly soul which it

---

5. See Tanya, *Likkutei Amarim*, ch. 32. Regarding the connection between the souls, see also *Likkutei Sichot* 34:222; "Sichat Yom Gimel, Parashat Va'eira, 24 Tevet, 5712," *Torat Menachem*, vol. 4, 1952, part 1, 251.

6. According to the teachings of Kabbalah, the soul of Adam, the first man, comprises 248 limbs and 365 sinews (see also the Lubavitcher Rebbe's letter on reincarnation, *Igrot Kodesh*, vol. 2, 200), which parallels the number of mitzvot in the Torah and limbs in the body ("Rabbi Simlai explained: 613 mitzvot were told to Moses; 365 prohibitions corresponding to the number of days in the year on the solar calendar, and 248 positive commandments corresponding to the limbs in the body...," Talmud, *Makkot* 23b). The souls, overall, are subdivided into 613 roots or general sections, corresponding to the limbs in Adam, i.e., the all-inclusive soul that breaks down into sections and additional souls. In the same way, an individual soul is an individual spark from Adam's soul; see for example in Tanya, *Iggeret Hakodesh*, siman 7.

reveals in the world. Thus, there are souls whose level can be compared to that of a heel. In other words, these souls have a lower radiation of the Creator's life force, that is, of the ability to discover the presence of the Creator in reality. They need more external support in order to achieve self-nullification and victory over the natural soul. Still, they are essential to the body because they hold up the entire body. On the other hand, there are very high souls on the level of the head. These souls are revealed, according to the Tanya, in the *tzaddikim* and leaders of the Jewish people who are tasked to strengthen the faith among the other souls.

Heel-level souls and head-level souls all have a point of similarity and of difference. The similarity is that they are all equal in a certain aspect, in that potential is found equally among all organs and in every soul. At the same time, the souls may differ in their missions.[7]

The similarity between the souls and the idea of mutual responsibility may be compared to business. A strong, financially solid business may serve as a guarantor for a smaller business; it is unlikely that the smaller one will ever be a guarantor for the larger one. But all of this works differently when it comes to the connection between the Jewish people. The general rule states, "All Jews are guarantors for each other."[8] Each Jew serves as a guarantor for the other, because every Jew has individual virtue, without which the entire body cannot function properly. Returning to the example of souls as limbs of the body, each organ has an advantage over the other. The legs, for example, have an advantage over the head. In the same way, a Jew far from the Creator has an advantage over another Jew who seems to be closer. Thanks to his unique aspect, he is considered a rich business owner, and able to be a guarantor for his friend.

---

7. This potential is determined by the location of the soul within the "body of souls." Each individual soul has its own uniqueness and at the same time, all souls come from the same source and all are part of the same body structure. To clarify the idea, the Tanya uses the metaphor of a father and son. The root of all the son's limbs derives from the father's brain. All of the son's limbs, both the more important ones (e.g., the brain) and the less important (e.g., the fingernails) have one source: the father. Tanya, *Likkutei Amarim*, ch. 2.

8. Talmud, *Shevuot* 39a; *Sanhedrin* 27b.

THE TZADDIK CONCEPT

The process by which the godly soul descends from its divine source is one of the fundamental principles of Chassidic thought, and from it developed the concept of the *tzaddik*. The *tzaddik* is a central topic in the teachings of Chassidut. The soul of the *tzaddik* is supposed to be the head of the soul collective. Therefore, the Creator's influence is more pronounced in them. The *tzaddik*, or the rebbe, is not necessarily the greatest scholar, but rather the one whose soul is on the level of the head for all souls. The people who connect to the *tzaddik* have souls rooted in other limbs and require vitality from the *tzaddik* in order to strengthen the discovery of their spiritual potential.

The *tzaddik*, whose soul is the head of the limbs, is supposed to sense every limb and unite them together. If one limb hurts, if one Jew suffers physically or spiritually, the head should feel it. And anyone who disconnects from the heads of the Jewish people, the *tzaddikim*, will be denied spiritual connection from the innermost level of the soul, according to the teachings of Rabbi Shneur Zalman. In this respect, the spiritual support the rebbe gives to his Chassidim is part of his role in the world. He feels their pain and distress, as if they were parts of him. This feeling he obtains by virtue of his ability to connect to a high spiritual level.

An example of this can be seen in Rabbi Shneur Zalman's efforts to assist thirty Jews who were arrested by the authorities for an unknown reason in 1791. Their trial lasted about three years, and the liberation efforts involved unusually large sums of money. Rabbi Shneur Zalman wrote several letters using very strong language. He could not bear the idea that some people would spend money on fine clothes for their families while there was a chance it could mean that even one soul would be lost.

> A tear will see my eyes.. and my stomach will rage and my body will tremble...that every man honors his wife and children with more than he has, employing all kinds of means to obtain clothes that glorify and honor those who don them, while causing the loss of another's life. How can a single Jewish soul not be precious in your eyes? It's like a whole world; like the clothes of his wife and children.

This is shameful, and there is nowhere to hide if we cause the loss of one Jewish soul because of this, God forbid.[9]

In his letter, he demands that the community go out of its way and contribute more than it can. He calls on them to refrain from "excuses," as he puts it, all of which are the schemes of the evil inclination. "Pour out the silver and the gold without limit; for a man would give all he has to redeem a soul."

The foundation of the *tzaddik* concept, which Rabbi Shneur Zalman presents in the second chapter of the Tanya, is also the foundation of *ahavat Yisrael*. At their root and core, the Jewish people are intertwined and interdependent, because their souls descend from the same source, even though the body and soul remain distinct. A defect in one soul is like a flaw in the entire collective body of souls and causes the entire structure to feel pain.

THE MITZVAH OF LOVING OTHERS

In chapter 32 of the Tanya, which is considered the "heart of the Tanya" in the eyes of the Chassidim, Rabbi Shneur Zalman deals at length with the commandment to love others, a mitzvah (commandment) he sees as the core of the entire Torah.

In general, the commandments can be divided into two categories: *mitzvot bein adam l'chavero* (commandments that apply to behavior between one person and another), and *mitzvot bein adam la'Makom* (commandments referring to the behavior of people toward the Creator). At first glance, it is possible to understand how the mitzvah of *ahavat Yisrael* serves as the root and foundation of the mitzvot between people. But what does a mitzvah that relates to the relationship between two people have to do with a person's service of the Creator or efforts at spiritual refinement and growth? How is love for others the basis for the mitzvah of tefillin, for example? Rabbi Shneur Zalman explains that the demanding spiritual work of fulfilling the commandment of loving others enhances one's relationship with the Creator as well. As a result of the relationship with another, a person can assess his or her spiritual state and analyze the direction needed for self-improvement.

---

9. *Igrot Kodesh – Alter Rebbe*, letter 24 (summer 1791), 81–84.

In the eyes of Rabbi Shneur Zalman, deep self-improvement is a basic condition for our relations with others. How do we know that we're growing and heading toward self-healing? When we succeed in getting closer to others, without developing contempt, resentment, and anger. In order to attain true love of others, we are tasked with making our souls primary and our bodies secondary. As physical needs and the physical world around us become less significant in our daily lives, we become better able to connect to and love others.

Love that is connected to the material world does not facilitate true love of others. From the body's perspective, relationships are based on enjoyment, benefits, and gains. A love based on the body will always be dependent on something. We hold ourselves in high regard and love ourselves very much. Therefore, we also love people who praise us, serve us, or provide benefit. Material expediency places a boundary of cause and effect on love. And when the material reason is canceled, the interest will disappear and the love will fade away. A person who primarily thinks of personal interests will certainly cherish those who help him or her to achieve material needs, as opposed to those who impair their fulfillment.

On the other hand, those whose personal interests are not the central focus of their lives, who give their souls top billing and see their bodies as secondary, lay the foundations for sincere and deep love. These strong foundations ensure that even if their interests are eliminated – and with them, all the calculations of being worthwhile, profitable, and convenient – their love will withstand the test.

Based on the explanation that all Jewish souls have the same source, it is understandable why *ahavat Yisrael* is so profoundly fundamental to Judaism. In order to truly love the other, you have to learn to overcome your animal soul and stop putting your personal interest and "I" at the center of everything.

Given this common root, it's understandable how one can love another as one loves oneself. Self-love is natural. True love for others is seemingly not natural, and is created by contact, personal impressions, and emotional connections. Of course, a strong connection is a bond that gradually crystallizes and is acquired. Discovering the common source of all Jewish souls creates the potential for making the love of others a natural and strong love, rather than a love born of self-interest.

Being Nonjudgmental

In a letter in 1801, Rabbi Shneur Zalman strongly rebuked one of the Chassidic communities. As the letter indicates, he had heard about cases in which young people were behaving disrespectfully, ridiculing members of other communities. After hearing such reports, Rabbi Shneur Zalman quickly sent a strong letter to the members of that community, condemning the youths' arrogance and any possible thinking that their one community could be better or more chosen than others.

> The reports that I have heard are not good...that the young among the flock raise their voices and act in jest.... Their tongues walk through the country, pouring out contempt and disgrace.... For the whole entire congregation is holy...why do you exalt yourselves?[10]

Rabbi Shneur Zalman's teachings describe the root of rejecting others and feelings of arrogance. When one does not feel at peace with or does not accept oneself, one cannot be at peace with one's environment. In this state, one's soul cannot be integrated with other souls. In order for a soul to connect with its roots, it must be healthy. What is mental health in this context? Here it means that one avoids hatred, being exacting of others, and feeling jealousy. A person can only connect with the source when at peace with the self and with one's surroundings, free of bitterness and recognizing that each person's way of coping is unique.

Arrogance and hatred create separation between a person and others. Separation is a defect, a deficiency in the soul. In their higher dimensions, souls are all interconnected and belong to a collective whole. Therefore, if one hates another, this feeling stems from one's own lack of the very soul component that exists within the other. In the spiritual sense, hatred and envy cripple a person.

For the same reason, an individual's concern for all Jews also has characteristics of concern for one's own self. For example, when we look after another, it is as if we are looking after ourselves. Rejecting or criticizing another person is a rejection of our own divine spark.

Hence, being nonjudgmental is a sound basis for loving others. Judgment and criticism push people away. According to the Tanya, a

---

10. Ibid., letter 69, 259.

person can't judge others, for two reasons. One is that we do not know how we would have behaved under similar conditions. In the physical world, we can't put ourselves in another position because we don't have the conditions the other faces. From one angle, things can look right, but from another angle, they may not appear the same. This is an aspect of true humility, to recognize our own worth while facing the truth that if someone else had the same skills and circumstances, that person could have had even greater success.

The second reason we can't judge others is that it's impossible to know the true virtue underlying the root of the other person's soul. Each soul has its own struggles and capacities. Every soul has a special role to play in the collective of souls, but we do not know what that role is.

Giving Criticism

Feedback is a tool for improvement and growth, but only when the person receiving the critique can accept it. Criticism is typically offensive, insulting, and humiliating. It creates seclusion and entrenchment. Sharp and piercing criticism is not a good way to influence someone to change behavior, improve, or make stronger efforts. Rather, kind words, attention, and space for self-improvement are much more effective.

The picture emerging from the Tanya indicates that the struggle to grow in personal holiness and refinement is not only an internal, personal process, but is also connected to relating with others. If others have a transcendent side and an animal side, then we have a choice of how to view them. Which side do we want to emphasize upon coming into contact with them? Everyone is multidimensional. The obligation, according to the Tanya's approach, is to seek out the potential in a person and not to place the spotlight on others' shortcomings and weaknesses. Contemplating one's weaknesses empowers those aspects, while focusing on their potential encourages the opposite trend.

A person who stops checking out others and focusing on their negatives testifies to being unthreatened. Seeing no evil in the other means apparently that the same evil is also not found in oneself, as the Baal Shem Tov teaches. Without having the need to challenge others, our real self-confidence is revealed. We find that our friends' successes do not endanger our own feelings of status. However, when we are critical, we often feel as if something has been stolen from us personally. Weaned off such an attitude, our perspective matures, and we become free.

The teachings of Chassidut emphasize that those who do not like having their own faults mentioned shouldn't criticize others. Those who give critique will be themselves criticized. It's better not to notice other people's flaws. Recognize the faults, problems, and mistakes, but don't make doing so a way of life. Being critical or addressing a negative word to someone is likened to taking his or her life.[11] And praising or saying a good word gives life to the person. A prosecutor's job is to be cruel, since he's trained in the despicable practice of seeing the weaknesses of others, not their virtues.

Other people are our mirrors. If you feel bad about yourself, your body, or your situation, then you will be impatient with your surround ings. Everything will feel like a nuisance. It's easier to see the flaws in others than to look for them in yourself. Thinking about our relationships with others will reveal some of the same barriers and negative traits that we ourselves evince, along with virtues and strengths.

The lesson noted above is highly relevant to the person who is doing the critique. One who feels a need to critique is likely to discover a similar defect within him- or herself. And when we love ourselves, we are quick to forgive ourselves, too. If we love ourselves, and love others as much as we love ourselves, then forgiving them and not seeing their faults is doable.

Unity is only possible with a change of perspective: recognize that there's a piece of the Creator inside everyone, as well as a lowly, earthly, physical side. In order to reach a state of unity, we have to connect with the sublime dimension that transcends the earthly part. The transcendence attests to spiritual growth and the discovery of the divine dimension in every detail of creation.

This message penetrated generation after generation of Rabbi Shneur Zalman's students and disciples, leading to quite a few prominent examples. One example comes from the activities of the Chabad center in Bangkok, since 1995 under the direction of Rabbi Nechemia Wilhelm, who regularly visits Jews imprisoned in local jails. Wilhelm makes

---

11. Talmud, *Bava Metzia* 58b.

sure to give these Jews kosher meals, tefillin, and as attentive an ear as possible. And all this is despite the fact that those prisoners were jailed for despicable crimes, including serious drug offenses. The reason for his willingness to help these prisoners lies in his recognition that every person has the potential of the godly soul as well as the animal soul. The godly soul may be hidden, but the spotlight has to be placed on it rather than emphasizing the animal soul. In his mind, the assistance he provides does not legitimize their actions. Rather, the help is part of the search for the unity among souls and the prevention of defects in the soul collective.

LEARNING TO GIVE

Of all the commandments in Judaism, there doesn't seem to be one that Rabbi Shneur Zalman encouraged or insisted on more than giving tzedakah (charity, literally "justice"). Over and over, in hundreds of his letters and conversations, he repeated the idea of giving, attributing great value to it. A common idea among Chassidim, influenced by Rabbi Shneur Zalman's letters on the subject of charity, was "In my bread is your portion."[12]

The main tzedakah he wanted his followers to give was "money for the Land of Israel." This was money collected by Rabbi Shneur Zalman in order to assist the Chassidim who immigrated to Israel in 1777. Led by Rabbi Menachem Mendel of Vitebsk, the mentor and friend of Rabbi Shneur Zalman, three hundred people left eastern Europe for the Land of Israel, of whom, only about one hundred were Chassidim from White Russia, and the other two hundred were immigrants who joined the caravan.[13]

The immigration, which was another link in a chain of traditional immigrations to Israel, was of great importance to Rabbi Shneur Zalman. The Land of Israel must be inhabited by Jews because of its unique spiritual value. The immigrants planned to devote all their time and energy to prayer and Torah study, and they needed constant financial support.

---

12. See Rabbi Yosef Yitzchak, *Sefer Hasichot 5705/1945*, 87.
13. See Etkes, *Rabbi Shneur Zalman of Liadi*, 122.

The primary support came from their former Jewish communities in White Russia.

The immigrants quickly found themselves in financial difficulties. One of the reasons for this was that the two hundred immigrants who joined them fell on the shoulders of the Chassidim. According to Rabbi Menachem Mendel of Vitebsk, they were poor "and they tended to rely on themselves and on miracles."[14]

When Rabbi Shneur Zalman became the leader of the Chassidim in White Russia in 1786, he viewed the oversight of collecting financial support for the Chassidim living in Israel as one of his primary tasks.[15] His mission was to encourage the Jews of eastern Europe, who in any case were in financial straits, to contribute from the little they did have in order to help support the Chassidim in the Holy Land.

In the years 1793–1794, the economic situation in Russia deteriorated, and many became impoverished. Nevertheless, Rabbi Shneur Zalman never stopped asking his followers to spare some of their money for the benefit of the Land of Israel. In one of his letters, he describes just how much he understands the state of the communities:

> My beloved, my brethren and friends, who are to me like my own soul. The hardships of these times are not hidden from me, in that the means for earning a livelihood have declined, especially among those known to me from your community, whose hands have faltered, so that they are without any providers at all, and they literally borrow in order to eat.[16]

In the continuation of his letter, he pleads with the impoverished who rely on loans to continue providing charity to the Chassidim in Israel. Tzedakah will illuminate their reality with light.

Another proof of the difficulty in giving charity is found in Rabbi Shneur Zalman's letter to Rabbi Avraham of Kalisk, who became the leader of the Chassidim in Israel after the death of Rabbi Menachem Mendel of Vitebsk. It was sent after the conflict between them broke

---

14. Ibid., 125.
15. Ibid., 132.
16. Tanya, *Iggeret Hakodesh*, siman 16.

out in 1797. A significant component of the dispute concerned the ways in which monies were collected and organized for the Land of Israel. Rabbi Shneur Zalman writes:

> For, if most of the members of the Chassidic brotherhood knew [Avraham of Kalisk] were against us, as it appears from the recent letters, they certainly would not have contributed with a full and wide hand. Rather, they would give the customary small amounts, and more would have switched to giving to the known charities operating outside of Israel.[17]

TZEDAKAH AND THE BATTLE OF THE SOUL

The difficulty in giving charity is also connected to the struggle between the souls. According to the structure of the soul, each person has aspects that are more difficult for him in life. One person finds it difficult to rejoice. He is not to blame. His natural inclination is sadness, and joy demands enormous capacity from him. Another cannot love those around her. She cannot help but envy and feel that she, with better talent, has less favorable circumstances.[18] Some are colder in nature and less attracted to certain things, while others are more attracted to the same things. Anyone who does not suffer from drinking will find it difficult to understand the alcoholic, who cannot spend a day without a drop.

A well-known rule formulated by Rabbi Shneur Zalman is that the place where we face the greatest resistance is the primary test we need to contend with.[19] Every person is a prisoner to a different difficulty. Each person's *yetzer hara* (inclination to do unholy things) is attracted to different things at different times. From the perspective of Chassidut, this analysis is correct regarding individuals, and it may be true for the Jewish people as a nation. In general, each generation and time period has its tests that the members of that generation have to face.[20] There

---

17. *Igrot Kodesh – Alter Rebbe*, 2nd ed., 123.
18. Tanya, *Iggeret Hakodesh*, siman 7; and see Talmud, *Shabbat* 118b.
19. For example, see Tanya, *Likkutei Amarim*, ch. 28.
20. See the discussion from the Lubavitcher Rebbe, 19 Kislev, 1969, *Maamarim Melukatim*, vol. 2, 74.

were periods in Jewish history when the main test was contending with the desire for idolatry.[21] In the modern era, if finances are the greatest societal challenge, one can assume that the most difficult mitzvah is giving charity.

The mitzvah of tzedakah has many facets. It can be expressed by giving attention, smiling, listening to another, or reaching out to a person in need. Giving is a trait that can do wonders in interpersonal relationships. Giving to others allows them to learn to receive, and it helps them believe in themselves. But perhaps the most difficult gift to give is money. Money is a primary concern for people. It's something we long for.[22] It's difficult to give away the money earned by the sweat of one's brow. Such giving is like giving of oneself.

Due to the battle between the souls, whenever we are asked to open our hands and give a tithe (Jewish law demands that a person give no less than one-tenth and no more than one-fifth of total income to tzedakah), a well-oiled rationalization kicks in to explain why it is preferable to close our hands. In these moments, the mind demonstrates its skill by presenting arguments to justify not giving.

This steadfast struggle is taking place all the time. For this reason, the act of tzedakah is the most important and perhaps the most difficult one to fulfill.[23] It requires overcoming our sense of "I." The "I" always needs more and asks for more, so it is hard for it to give of itself.

What are the great qualities of giving charity that elevate this mitzvah above all other commandments? In the writings and letters of Rabbi Shneur Zalman, we find several reasons:

Testimony to Faith

The struggle over giving is also a struggle for faith. We find it difficult to give because we lose faith in those very moments when we need to make a financial sacrifice. By giving, the giver testifies to the belief that

---

21. Such as the times of Menashe. See Talmud, *Sanhedrin* 102b, and in the commentary of Rashi there, "Hi'yot."
22. Given the thirst for money, seeking a level of awe of the Creator is compared to seeking money and treasure. "If you seek it like money or buried treasure..." Tanya, *Likkutei Amarim*, ch. 42.
23. "For tzedakah is greater than all of the mitzvot." Tanya, *Iggeret Hakodesh*, siman 3.

profits are not only the result of our work, but the result of the grace of the Creator, Who oversees every detail in reality.

The advice commonly given by Chassidic leaders to a person who complains of economic difficulties is to give a lot of tzedakah. Precisely when one's livelihood is shrinking, one must increase the scope of the charity one gives in order to escape economic crisis or speed up the success of business activities.

At first glance, this advice seems to express a strange paradox. It is not enough that the person is dealing with a shortage and great difficulty, but he or she is required to give from a small and constricted account to access the wheel of fortune. This expectation for tzedakah is even more puzzling when we're dealing with people drowning in debt and desperate for a lifeline to pull them from the murky waters into which they have sunk.

The contradiction can be reconciled in that the giving, the act of charity, is intended for the giver. "More than what the homeowner does for the poor man, the poor man does for the homeowner."[24] Rabbi Shneur Zalman so intensely impressed the idea that giving is a merit for the giver that a person was punished for poor behavior by not being allowed to give money to the Holy Land.[25]

Victory of the Spirit

The second reason is that the giving proclaims victory for the spirit in its struggle against the material, even for a few moments. The giver testifies to having been able to get free from physical bonds. Our daily routines, difficulties, careers, and worldly affairs are proportionate. The scramble to make a living is nothing more than a test, part of the way we fulfill our purpose of discovering the Creator's presence in the world. However, earning a living is not the purpose of life. The sense of satisfaction felt after giving is part of our sense of spiritual elevation, of success in overcoming difficulty. In this victory, material needs do not completely lose their importance, but they are understood as finite, limited, and unable to arouse us spiritually unless they are being put toward the good.

---

24. *Vayikra Rabbah*, ch. 34, 8, at the end. *Ruth Rabbah*, ch. 5, 9, at the beginning.
25. *Igrot Kodesh – Alter Rebbe*, letter 24, 13.

When giving from our own sustenance, we prove we are overcoming our anxieties. It is as if we have been freed from external forces, public opinion, what others think, pressure at work, and fears about meeting expectations, and then the chances of doing the right things is greater. Giving charity frees us from servitude to the external forces that hold on to us. According to this view, giving is a process of liberation that builds trust in the Creator.

In one of his letters, Rabbi Shneur Zalman teaches that the sages learn from the verse "And he will wear charity as an armor and a hat of salvation for his head." The giver of charity wears a spiritual chainmail. Chainmail is a leather garment to which are attached rows of metal plates, which are each attached to one another and together create a flexible protection for the body. The tzedakah we give adds to a "great account,"[26] which is like those scales that protect the body. How does charity protect the giver? When a person gives charity, he or she sacrifices part of the natural egocentric instinct, the tendency to only see oneself. The act of nullification prevents us from being arrogant and boastful. As mentioned, tzedakah envelops the person and prevents external forces from drawing away sustenance. The sense of "I" ceases to be the focus of everything, and our reality is no longer built around it. By increasing this awareness, which is expressed in the giving of charity, we are less troubled, anxious, and frightened. Our coping becomes more relaxed and more likely to succeed.

Increased charitable giving enables a greater flow of abundance. In addition to the armor, the giver wears a "hat of salvation on his head."[27] This hat is a drawing down of new light, which stretches down into our physical world through fulfilling the commandment. The tzedakah we give causes the Creator to turn His face toward us. Salvation is the Creator turning to us.

In Order to Receive

The mitzvah of charity does not only yield immediate fruits in the spiritual sense. It does so even in the physical sense. A third reason for the virtue of charity is that it is the only commandment in which the

26. Tanya, *Iggeret Hakodesh*, siman 3.
27. Yeshayahu 59:17.

Creator challenges us: "And, please, examine Me with this,"[28] says God, according to the sources which are quoted extensively in the writings of Chassidut. In Hebrew, "please" is related to the word for making a request. The Creator asks us to express our faith in Him via the act of charity, as the kindness we give to others returns to us, and more.

Nonjudgmental Perspective

A fourth reason for the importance of tzedakah is that it is evidence of a change in the giver's perspective toward others. As givers, we struggle to not judge others, not to think we deserve something special because of our actions while another doesn't for the exact same reason. We struggle to overcome fundamental jealousies and a sense of disharmony with where we are in life. When we give, we also accept that every person has unique life circumstances, and our role is to illuminate the environment, not to judge or to criticize. Our goal is to help and to spread warmth, not to be twisted. We can promote our outlook via our own personal practices and not by criticizing others.

By giving charity, the donor testifies to not living or acting out of a sense of disappointment, missing out, or frustration, but rather acting out of wholesomeness. Tzedakah helps us to adjust our relationships with others to be in accordance with reality, and thereby, to be in accordance with ourselves. The person who has the feeling of deserving more can never be satisfied with life.

Happiness

After the struggle to give is complete, giving leads to happiness. When we're concentrating on someone else, we forget ourselves. This is the beginning of the path to self-healing. According to this logic, a person who suffers from sickness should volunteer in a hospital. In light of the difficulties of others, our personal pain will likely diminish and may even be forgotten.

Justice

Another reason for the importance of charity is that it constitutes an act of justice and a means of spreading holiness in the world. It makes

---

28. Malachi 3:10.

equality between someone who has and someone who doesn't, and between those with the ability to influence and those who lack it. It makes the giver resemble the Creator and His actions in the world. Giving makes the world of selfish interests, in which human beings tend to care only for themselves, into a brighter world where others are not strangers, but part of the same existence. Charity is, therefore, one of the pillars required for the existence of a world of kindness.

By acting charitably, a person imitates the traits of the Creator and recognizes that the very existence of the spiritual and physical worlds is an act of supreme charity. When giving tzedakah, we serve as the "right arm of the Creator." In that moment, we become a vessel through which the Creator can do justice in the world and create a tool for His kindness.[29] The act of giving is the most important expression of the godly soul's victory over the animal soul. More than just refinement of our character traits produced by our readiness for self-nullification, tzedakah also illuminates even the lowest of levels. Our animalistic dimension, the physical inclination, becomes illuminated by the godly soul from within. Even if we give while in the midst of a deep inner struggle, and it's obvious that it's hard for us to give, the deed, which attests to our ability to overcome, becomes the main thing.

Based on all of the above reasons, it can be concluded that the performance of charitable acts helps a person discover the inner self, the spark of the Creator within. Thus, Rabbi Shneur Zalman writes the following in one of his letters that was intended to encourage the Chassidim to continue contributing tzedakah:

> For now, during the exile... there is also the commonly given advice for radiating some of God's light – the powerful dimension without the inner point of the heart – as it will be in future times. Namely, by arousing the spark of godliness within the soul, the aspect of great supernal mercies.[30]

And this, says Rabbi Shneur Zalman, can be accomplished by giving tzedakah.

29. Tanya, *Likkutei Amarim*, ch. 34.
30. *Igrot Kodesh – Alter Rebbe*, letter 57 (Elul 1798), 205.

The Majesty of the "Lowly Soul"

Most of the advice presented so far seems to have a distinct existential flavor. It can help anyone develop a full and happy life. Contemplation, the control of the mind over the heart or the intellect over the emotions, focus, removing thoughts about unreal things, positive thinking, dedicating time to soul-searching, acting with joy and energy, training to strengthen faith and trust in the existence of the Creator, making effort beyond habit, crushing our ego, diagnosing and releasing emotional blockages – all of these, and other tips that were woven in so far, can transform a person into a *pnimi*, an authentic person and not an external and superficial person subject to the unstable influence of public opinion or ephemeral forces and impulses.

Rabbi Shneur Zalman's advice, as was also the case with the unique structure of the psyche that he presented, is an inseparable part of his faith-based outlook. In his eyes, every creature has a role to play and a purpose to achieve in creation, and his advice helps us to achieve our role in the world.

THE LAST MONTHS

The two arrests that Rabbi Shneur Zalman experienced were not the only times in which a changing reality, unstable ground, and endangerment hovered over his head and those of his Chassidim. He spent his last months in this world in a wagon, on the run. For almost four months, Rabbi Shneur Zalman, his family, and dozens of his followers were on the road.

Napoleon's army managed to reach Moscow. Rabbi Shneur Zalman and his Chassidim fled from Liadi and were running from the French army. In the month of Kislev, which was December, the balance of power changed. The Russian winter overwhelmed Napoleon's army. At winter's coldest point, when mountains of snow blocked the roads and made travel difficult, Rabbi Shneur Zalman arrived at the head of a sixty-wagon caravan, escorted by a protective guard unit, in the village of Piana. At that time, Rabbi Shneur Zalman was sixty-seven years old. He was generally healthy, but he likely suffered from the severe cold he encountered in his last days. On Thursday it was clear that his illness was worsening. There were no Jews living in Piana, so Rabbi Shneur Zalman was set up in one of the local homes to recover and find shelter from the unceasing snow. When the Sabbath ended, he rose from his sickbed to do the Havdalah service that signals the end of the Sabbath. Instead of blessing on wine, however, he used a cup of black coffee.[1] Perhaps he did this because he felt weak, or because of the deep Kabbalistic meanings behind using coffee for Havdalah. Rabbi Shneur Zalman then asked for paper and a pen and sat down to write his last words minutes before his passing.

Rabbi Shneur Zalman knew that he was about to leave the world. He told his relatives that "the transfer from this world to the next world is easy and depends only on the one transferring. Some people take a while to pass. Their transfer, seemingly, is of the cruel harassment variety."[2] Despite his illness, he remained clear and aware until his last moments.

It stands to reason that the last words of a person on the level of Rabbi Shneur Zalman would be a summary of his life, a concentration of his thought and last will that he would leave behind for his Chassidim and the world. Rabbi Shneur Zalman wrote and taught a lot. Most of that work is characterized by an integration of the revealed and hidden dimensions of

---

1. See the analysis of Rabbi Yitzchak Ginsburg regarding the performance of Havdalah using coffee, 24 Tevet, 2000, http://www.malchuty.org/2011-01-20-01-37 -36/2011-01-20-02-08-55/288%20%E2%80%93%20q-q-html.
2. Rabbi Yosef Yitzchak, *Sefer Hasichot 5699/1939*, 338.

Torah, Jewish law and conduct, and deep contemplation and Kabbalah. To summarize his efforts in a few lines is not a simple task.

Indeed, his last sentences are full of meaning. However, they are somewhat obscure, lacking a beginning and a conclusion, and it takes effort to decipher his intention. The Lubavitcher Rebbe said that he once asked his father-in-law, Rabbi Yosef Yitzchak, about the last letter written by Rabbi Shneur Zalman and its strange nature. Rabbi Yosef Yitzchak smiled faintly but did not answer the question.[3]

The letter is meant to give meaning to life as well as to explain Rabbi Shneur Zalman's multidimensional efforts, his work in the world of Jewish law and in the world of Kabbalah and Chassidut, and his work assisting and guiding thousands of Chassidim.

As was his style, the letter combines the external, revealed physical reality along with the hidden, inner reality. On the revealed plane he sits, a respected Jewish leader, but also a war-tested veteran, in the hut of a Ukrainian gentile, in the middle of a winter storm that halted his caravan's movement. Outside the hut, dozens of families were waiting for his words. They saw him as an admired leader of unparalleled stature, a leader linked to the Creator and capable of bringing salvation to the world. These were families who used to consult with him about every question in every area of life.

Reports of the French army's defeat had long since arrived, but the concerns about the war were still great. What did he think in those very moments about the purpose of life, about the struggle of souls, about his role in the world?

TO REVEAL

Before creation, he wrote, the attribute of truth did not want the world to be created. It's a world of falsehood in which the evil grows stronger. A world of concealment and confusion, full of difficulties and suffering. But in the end, the attribute of kindness won over the attribute of truth. It decided that the world could be built, even if it was not a world of truth.

Now that the world had been created, a world of lies built with kindness that is not necessarily justified, the soul was sent down into it. It

---

3. "24 Tevet 5715," *Torat Menachem*, vol. 14, 1955, part 2, 185.

was lowered from the heights of its lofty level and sent down to the earth, into the structure of a physical body and a world of lust and passions. And the purpose? To discover, from the agony, hardships, persecutions, and anxieties, the truth beyond concealment, the truth beyond the lie.

Usually, when things are good for us, we don't ask why. At most, we are grateful for the kindnesses, but we are generally not aroused to ask questions about the attribute of *chesed* (kindness). But when things are bad and we experience grief or loss, and the meaning isn't clear to us, the questions start to flow. Why did the soul descend to this lower world? Why was it lowered from its high perch into a world of sorrow, hardship, disaster, war, jealousy, and competition, into a world of poverty, hunger, and conspiracy?

In Rabbi Shneur Zalman's view, the structure of the soul is such that our inner world is a battlefield, an endless battleground between the soul drives. These battles do not have knockout victories. The battles never stop. At most, there are slight breaks, but the overall war remains undecided.

The main function of the difficulties, evil, sickness, sadness, suffering, and profanity is to generate questions inside ourselves. The role of our good times is in fact similar, to place a mirror in front of us. If everything were always bad, we would never ask why it was bad. Thus, the external reality is the backdrop for our internal battles. In his final words, Rabbi Shneur Zalman asks his listeners to be alert to this struggle. The soul descends down into this world to discover the one and only truth. This takes determination and sacrifice.

VICTORY MARCH

In Rabbi Shneur Zalman's thinking, spiritual therapy and Jewish identity are intertwined. Each treatment requires the three stages he presents:

1. Diagnosing the situation.
2. Visualizing the ideal situation.
3. Actualizing the path to that ideal.

Rabbi Shneur Zalman identifies our spiritual struggle, our two souls, and the tendency toward ego as the source of human suffering. He outlines the image of the *beinoni*, the warrior who claims the right to choose his spiritual state and who wins battles at every moment, as a figure to aspire to and to imitate. Finally, he sets out a series of suggestions that can help us cope and overcome. All of those ideas are directed in one primary direction: rejecting our egocentric point of view, minimizing our involvement with the soul tendencies from which we suffer, and connecting to the essential point. In this way, a person elevates him- or herself and stops getting sucked into futile struggles. He avoids dealing with confusing questions and anxious thoughts that offer no benefit. The preoccupation with negative spiritual tendencies is, for Rabbi Shneur Zalman, an irrational and ineffective move. Those same tendencies disappear once a person becomes focused and connected to the purpose of the moment, and the external forces that try to pull him down are rejected. Why? Because he is ignoring them and discovering sacred alternatives that he can choose. Clearly, intellect and reason are the main means of inner change and transcendence.

Let's use an analogy that can help summarize this method of how the mind overcomes the emotions. A hungry person walking past a bakery will likely encounter his favorite kind of cake. Although he is diabetic and must abstain from the cake, there will be a struggle between opposing forces. The struggle would abruptly stop if he approached the window and saw that it was a plastic cake intended for decoration only. The lust would fade. This is true of anger, sadness, anxiety, and fear. If someone aimed a gun at you, you might be scared to death. But if you find out that it's only a toy and not a real gun, the fear will fade.

The purpose of contemplation is to make a person see reality differently and change vantage point, so that what seems threatening, paralyzing, and frightening from one angle is revealed as unrealistic or nonexistent from another. What seems to be an irritant is nothing more than a trivial thing: a test to assess our efforts at refining our character traits, nothing else. Once our ego and self-centered outlook departs, it turns out that the cake is merely plastic.

Formulating this perspective is the means to overcoming most spiritual problems. Through it, we control our emotions, desires, and instincts. We successfully distinguish between transient and meaningless desires and a true spiritual move of striving for transcendence.

This perspective change is not a simple process. It takes effort, perseverance, and training. Based on the writings of Rabbi Shneur Zalman, it can be said that to be a Jew is to be a warrior, constantly aware of the dangers that lie ahead, and overcoming them through his awareness and contemplation.

The revelation of the godly soul, the revelation of the Creator's power in the world does involve an endless war, but one in which victory depends to a large extent on the spiritual movements of those entering the battlefield. Chassidism adopted the idea that you go into battle with a march, with a song of victory.[4] Without the belief that we have the strength to win the race, and without the enjoyment of the tests, our chances of victory may be slimmer. We risk falling into bitterness, dissatisfaction, anger, and other negative reflections of the animal soul. However, the belief in success and our joy in preparation for battle are a first step toward attainment of spiritual health.

In one sentence from the Tanya, Rabbi Shneur Zalman encourages his readers toward the light constantly available to them during war.

> Therefore one should not feel depressed or very troubled at heart even if he be engaged all his days in this conflict. For perhaps this is what he was created for, and this is the service demanded of him – to subdue the Sitra Achra [other side] constantly.[5]

We will likely spend our entire lives in a state of internal fighting. However, this understanding is supposed to fill us with joy for waging the battles. If we were chosen to be warriors, we were also given the strength to win the battles. Perhaps for this purpose, for the sake of victories in war, we were created.

THE PURPOSE

The psychology of the Tanya has a purpose. It is supposed to bring us to identify our core, inner point, a point where there is no sin and no lack. The death of Rabbi Cordovero at an early age, as described in the Ari's eulogy, cannot conceal the inner, eternal point that most people are not *tzaddikim*, nor are they on the same level as Rabbi Shneur Zalman, the

---

4. Rabbi Yosef Yitzchak, *Sefer Hasichot 5705/1945*, 3, 59. *Sefer Hamitzvot 1950*, 104, 191.
5. Tanya, *Likkutei Amarim*, ch. 27.

Arizal, or Rabbi Cordovero. However, they too possess an eternal, inner point that they need to reveal in everyday life.

Rabbi Shneur Zalman brings down a goal that seems almost impossible to fulfill. He wants a community of people to give up worldly interests, honor, and dignity for one goal: to expose the inner truth and allow the godly soul to be revealed in the world. Foregoing personal interests encourages spiritual uplift. Fewer material interests mean less suffering, less jealousy, anger, and worry, as well as less loneliness and alienation. A person who practices self-nullification will less often fall prey to the advice of the natural inclination – advice that, if he had followed it, he would eventually have regretted adopting anyway. It is not that a person will become stripped of corporeality and live in a state of homelessness, without food and clothing. Rather, the less concerned one is with material needs, the freer one will be to grow, rise, and connect up with the truer reality. At any rate, one's needs will also be met. A person's livelihood is a good example: one must be active in the reality of physical life in order to earn a living. However, fears and worries do not need to be a part of that process. They only make it more difficult.

Rabbi Shneur Zalman is aware of the challenges of the mission. But, as he wrote in the Tanya, he was convinced that it is possible for people to succeed. On the title page of his book, he chose to lay down the principle upon which he says the entire book is based. "Because it is very close to you, in your mouth, and in your heart to do it."[6] The challenge is within reach and achievable – everyone can control the emotions of the heart.

Rabbi Shneur Zalman's optimistic approach is contagious. We *can* change. The path to it is not in the quest for spiritual heights, but in daily work. "Each and every day has its own required effort."[7] This idea is frequently repeated in the teachings of Chassidut. Every day has its own unique work requirement, new challenges, and along with it, forces and abilities provided to the person on that day. With those powers also come opposition and the tactics of the animal soul.[8] The renewal of these forces and the daily resistance we face up to ensure that life is never

6. Devarim 30:14.

7. Zohar 3:94b.

8. See an example from the Lubavitcher Rebbe, *Torat Menachem*, vol. 16, 1956, part 2, 110.

dull. The days are renewed, and along with them, so are we. That work is something we have to choose. Every day, we have to choose to fight and win. We have to choose to answer the question – "Where are you?" – that Rabbi Shneur Zalman asked the warden during his incarceration. The victories will ultimately be evident. Every day we have to change a little, win that day's struggle, and be a little less angry, nervous, anxious, stingy, irritable, or emotionally blocked.

SIN: THE TOUCH OF DEATH

In one of the letters he wrote before 1790, Rabbi Shneur Zalman presented, in perhaps the clearest outline of all of his writings, what he perceived to be the purpose of life.[9] The purpose is to reach true faith by abandoning all desires related to personal interests, livelihood, health, family, and more. The nullification of desires reflects a high level of recognition, knowledge that the world around us isn't real: there is nothing but the Creator, and a person should connect with Him. This awareness is the true faith to which a person should aspire. The Creator is creating the world in every moment anew; He creates something out of total nothingness.

This kind of faith eliminates all evil in the world and inspires a different attitude toward agony, worries, and anxieties. None of these experiences are real in the world of the true believer. It is not possible for a person to experience something in life that is not entirely good, if only for the fact it stems directly from the Creator.

"In all worldly affairs, yes and no are the same [for a person with an enlightened perspective] in total, real equality."[10] Good and bad and pleasure and suffering are all the same for a person with such an outlook on life, insists Rabbi Shneur Zalman.

Such a person will not hone in on what's lacking in life, but rather will focus on the perfection of it. External circumstances, however difficult they may be, do not present an excuse or opportunity to complain. If the believer experiences disaster, he or she will not feel that it is a disaster at all. In fact, the tests we undergo are intended to lead us to adopt this view.

9. Tanya, *Iggeret Hakodesh*, siman 11. And see *Igrot Kodesh – Alter Rebbe*, 51.
10. Ibid.

In his letter which discusses the proposed meaning of life, Rabbi Shneur Zalman does not encourage asceticism. But he does, however, want to fight against feelings of deprivation. This is a feeling that causes a person to be, among other things, troubled, resentful, and threatened. Constant spiritual maneuvering of the animal soul continually replaces one desire with another, thereby creating emotional blockage. This prevents authenticity, the discovery of the deep, inner dimension. A person who feels whole and is at peace with his or her life will not suffer from a sense of lack.

In Kabbalistic teachings, especially in the writings of the Arizal, the concept of sin receives comprehensive and profound explanations. It's understood in a light that is beyond its common understanding. Sin does not only mean doing actions that are forbidden according to Jewish law. In a deeper sense, and as explained by the Arizal, sin can be understood as a lack, as empty space.[11] That space has an aspect of death. It can be said that once a person fails to make sacred use of the moment, to be connected to the potential of the higher soul, a gap is created. Sin is the result of wanting what one mistakenly believes is missing, living with a feeling of imperfection. There is a yearning for an unattainable physical thing, and this pining can cut us off from the source of our being, thereby attaching us to death rather than to life.

According to an interpretation based on the teachings of the Arizal, the punishment of death was decreed on mankind because of that sense of lack. The first man, Adam, was surrounded in the Garden of Eden by every kind of good   he had abundant food and all that he needed. The original sin was the inability to be content with it. He was forbidden to take from the Tree of Knowledge, and that's why he wanted it. Life in the Garden of Eden wasn't worth it for him if he couldn't eat from that single tree. Our sages draw a parallel between Haman, the second-in-command to King Achashverosh (in Megillat Esther) and the question that God asks Adam in the Garden of Eden: "Was it from

---

11. See an example of this in Rabbi Chaim Vital's compilation of the Ari's teachings, *Etz Chaim*, Heichal Alef Heichal Eretz Yisrael, shaar 6, *Shaar Ha'akudim* 20, 3. It is explained there that when a person is in "the element of air," he won't sin as when he's in the *yetzer hara*.

[*hamin*] the tree I commanded you not to eat that you ate?"[12] In both cases, that of Haman, the enemy of the Jews, and that of Adam, who was tempted to eat from the Tree of Knowledge, the psychological attack is similar. In both instances, a perceived lack leads to sin and finally to death. Like Adam, even the wicked Haman could not be satisfied with all the good he had gotten. His wealth, well-being, and great scope of influence from India to Cush were not worth it as long as Mordecai the Jew refused to bow down to him.[13]

Rabbi Shneur Zalman's goal is to lead his readers to give up their natural, animalistic desires and instead direct their wanting toward the spiritual, to transform the sense of lack in the material world into an awareness of deficit requiring fulfillment in the spiritual world.

WORK ON YOURSELF

The purpose outlined by Rabbi Shneur Zalman is a practical one. As soon as he describes on the title page of the Tanya the key principle in his book, the principle that it is all possible and doable, he identifies the task he bears on his own shoulders: "to explain clearly how it is doable." The task is to show the way to achieving the goal. It is a path involving intensively working on oneself with alertness and awareness. There must be alertness to problematic traits in the soul such as rigidity, stinginess, a tendency toward sadness, and emotional blockage. The alertness is intended to encourage the appropriate treatment, based on the recognition that these attributes stem from the power-hungry animal soul, which must be balanced.

The change proposed by Rabbi Shneur Zalman begins with the garments of the soul: thoughts, words, and behaviors. Gradually, this change penetrates and influences a person's inner world. During the course of the change, the person will rise, but, being human, will not free himself completely from the struggles.

In one of his letters, Rabbi Shneur Zalman rebukes those who tend to run away from coping with difficulties in life. Asking for advice from him

---

12. Bereishit 3:11, cited in Talmud, *Chulin* 139b.
13. *Torah Ohr*, Megillat Esther, 236ff. And see "Parshiot v'Moadim," *Maamarei Admor Hazaken*, vol. 1, 388.

in physical matters, or asking any other rabbi, cannot serve as a replacement for taking responsibility nor can it rationalize covering your eyes. The advice seeker is like someone who is unable to cope with anguish and therefore stumbles around seeking advice from distant rabbis, as if it exempts the sufferer from deep contemplation and change.

> However, I will relate the truth to those who listen to me: "Love upsets the natural order of conduct."[14] For it is a covering of the eyes that prevents people from seeing the truth, because of their great love for the life of the body.... Thus, they are not able to bear [it] at all, to the point that it drives them out of their minds, causing them to tramp about from city to city to seek advice from afar. They do not turn to God by [penitently] returning to Him with humble spirit and submission of the body, to accept His chastisement with love.[15]

Rabbi Shneur Zalman compares people who rely solely on advice in physical matters to a child whose father, who is an exemplary figure, reproves him or her severely for inappropriate behavior. In such a case, a wise child does not run to find help or seek a defender against the father. The child knows that reproach is educational and serves as instruction to return to the straight path. This child does not even turn away from the father, but rather turns toward him, face to face, to absorb his reproach with love and learn from it. Hence, those who run to ask for material advice on every problem they encounter without doing any internal soul-searching are likened to a child who turns away from a father's rebuke and runs to the neighbors to ask for their protection. The escape from responsibility is like heresy due to the unwillingness to accept what has happened, yet the simultaneous lack of trust in his or her own abilities, intellect, and emotions, in coping with the current situation.[16]

Even though Rabbi Shneur Zalman urged his Chassidim to face things with their own faculties, he continued to advise them. His method can be likened to the attitude of two students toward their teacher. The

---

14. *Genesis Rabbah*, Vayeira 8.
15. Tanya, *Iggeret Hakodesh*, siman 22.
16. Ibid.

first student receives from the teacher the main course of study, the general idea, and asks questions about the homework only to request clarification of points that were not yet considered. In contrast, the second student refuses to exert any effort to absorb the material or do the homework. This student asks in order to be relieved of the effort, to be spared the need to fill in the answers. This student wants to lean on the teacher, and naturally does not fulfill the purpose of learning.

One of the main elements in the teaching present in the Tanya is that people hav e to stand on their own feet. They have to stand on their own merit. The more they concentrate on the negatives, the more they see the negative. If they change their vantage point and implement the tools and guidance they receive, they will be able to change their situation. Rabbi Shneur Zalman therefore asks those who turn to him not to think that he knows more about their physical future, but to concentrate on doing their own work:

> One more thing I will ask and seek to make clearly known – all those who long to talk privately in *yechidut* [one-on-one meetings], specifically those who are members of the Chassidic brotherhood, they are deceiving themselves to think I know more than they and can see it all clearly…[17]

For Rabbi Shneur Zalman, a true teacher and leader is one who places students on their own two feet, giving them the tools to cope and develop on their own. The underlying assumption of this approach to leadership is that no one can replace the personal work that lies at the doorstep of each person. The teacher, the rebbe, cannot spare the student from coping on his or her own. He can awaken a student and furnish the right tools, but the coping itself will have to be performed individually.

JEWISH IDENTITY AND REDEEMING THE SOUL

The ideal is that a person wins the soul battle independently. But this is only the ideal. At the end of his life, Rabbi Shneur Zalman acknowledged

---

17. A letter from the Rabbi Shneur Zalman relating to the Liozna regulations of 1793, *Sefer Hatoldot*, 69.

human weakness. In the moments before his passing, he actually admitted that this task was not simple for most of the public. Wickedness and selfish interests are on the rise in the world. "Awake and sing, you that dwell in the dust," says the prophet,[18] referring to emotionally blocked people as dust dwellers. People who dwell in the dirt are called so because they are close to dirt, to physicality, and it's not easy to elevate them. People in our time, recognized Rabbi Shneur Zalman, need help, a push, and the right advice as well. They need guidance. They find it difficult to stand alone in the face of hardship and agony. The power of the animal soul is too great. Therefore, even though he openly rejected the giving of material advice, he continued to grant it to the Chassidim.[19]

Helping people deal with their difficulties was singularly aimed at awakening in people the power of *daat*, so they would come to know the purpose of their lives. It was to inspire the broken and damaged to contemplate and seek. Ultimately, they should reach the point that their faculties of *daat*, of seeking and searching, would lead them to action.

Rabbi Shneur Zalman concluded his final words by saying that the pure, holy, humbled soul was lowered down into a world of concealment and *kelipah* so that each and every one of them would recognize the truth from among the false. Not a truth of two authorities, not the truth of evil and the truth of justice. Not the truth of business and the truth of giving, but that everything belongs to one truth, one authority, and the power of one Creator that is hidden within the reality that He creates. Into the reality of falsehood, the soul was cast. It was sent into a spiritual exile in order to transcend and discover its true potential.

The soul's struggle to emerge from the distortion of evil is the essence of our struggle in life, and the way to overcome spiritual and emotional problems is by foregoing our untrue desire. The Creator is indeed everywhere, but He is revealed everywhere to varying degrees. There are some places in the world that are so blanketed by evil that it can be difficult to identify Him, but He is indeed present there. The role of man, according to the Tanya, is to act to reveal the Creator, to make Him

---

18. Yeshayahu 26:19.
19. See the Lubavitcher Rebbe, "Sichah 20 Menachem Av, 5713," *Torat Menachem*, vol. 9, 1953, part 3, 127–28.

present by clinging to Him through inner work and developing. Hence, Jewish identity is characterized by the constant desire to discover the Creator in everything we see.

Shortly before his death, in his last hours, Rabbi Shneur Zalman called his grandson in to see him. He asked him if he could see the beam on the ceiling of the cabin. The grandson was surprised by the question. Rabbi Shneur Zalman continued, admitting that he himself did not see any beam. He only saw the Creator, the presence of the Creator, which was creating the beam.[20] Identifying the Creator's presence in the world is the highest level of consciousness. This is the redemption and freedom of the soul offered by Rabbi Shneur Zalman.

The word *geulah* (redemption) is mentioned only twice in the Tanya, in the context of charity.[21] Other terms related to redemption, such as the Messianic Era or the End of Days, are not common in the Tanya. However, contrary to some theories,[22] the inner drive of Rabbi Shneur Zalman was a drive for the coming of the Mashiach, the Jewish redeemer and harbinger of the *geulah*. The idea of the godly soul acting through the animal soul is part of the hope of redemption. The author of the Tanya suggests to his readers not only a goal to reveal the inner soul, but also the path to the redemption.[23] It is redemption from a reality of difficulty and suffering and the crises of the soul. *Yechidut* with Rabbi Shneur Zalman or sitting in the patient's chair is all a part of the journey to redemption.

---

20. Quoted in many sources; see an example in "Sichah 10 Shevat, 1966."
21. See Tanya, *Likkutei Amarim*, 37; *Igrot Kodesh*, 21.
22. See the words of Immanuel Etkes: "A few words on the concept of Mashiach: Despite the natural tendency of Chabad Chassidim to cast aside the Mashiach perspective and connect it to the founding leader – Rabbi Shneur Zalman of Liadi – there is no doubt he did not see himself as solely responsible for the promise of Mashiach's arrival. He didn't even fan the flames of desire for Mashiach among his Chassidim." "Biographia Chadashah," *Haaretz*, September 11, 2011.
23. Tanya, *Likkutei Amarim*, ch. 37

Print from a painting of Rabbi Shneur Zalman during his first incarceration in 1798. The print is owned by the Lubavitch Library in New York.

In Chabad literature, one can find testimonies that point to the accuracy of the picture and its precision in the details of Rabbi Shneur Zalman's appearance.

Rabbi Shneur Zalman's burial place, Haditch, Ukraine